The Facts on the Ground

The Facts on the Ground

—— A Wisdom Theology of Culture ——

William A. Dyrness

CASCADE *Books* • Eugene, Oregon

THE FACTS ON THE GROUND
A Wisdom Theology of Culture

Copyright © 2022 William A. Dyrness. All rights reserved. Except for brief quotations in critical publications or reviews, no part of this book may be reproduced in any manner without prior written permission from the publisher. Write: Permissions, Wipf and Stock Publishers, 199 W. 8th Ave., Suite 3, Eugene, OR 97401.

Cascade Books
An Imprint of Wipf and Stock Publishers
199 W. 8th Ave., Suite 3
Eugene, OR 97401

www.wipfandstock.com

PAPERBACK ISBN: 978-1-7252-9963-4
HARDCOVER ISBN: 978-1-7252-9964-1
EBOOK ISBN: 978-1-7252-9965-8

Cataloguing-in-Publication data:

Names: Dyrness, William A., author.

Title: The facts on the ground : a wisdom theology of culture / by William A. Dyrness.

Description: Eugene, OR: Cascade Books, 2022 | Includes bibliographical references and index.

Identifiers: ISBN 978-1-7252-9963-4 (paperback) | ISBN 978-1-7252-9964-1 (hardcover) | ISBN 978-1-7252-9965-8 (ebook)

Subjects: LCSH: Wisdom—Biblical teaching. | Wisdom—Religious aspects. | Theology and culture.

Classification: BS2545.W45 D35 2022 (print) | BS2545 (ebook)

12/10/21

Contents

Preface | ix

Introduction | 1

Part One: A Theology of Cultural Wisdom

1. Toward a Wisdom Theology of Culture | 11
    Our Cultural Indebtedness   13
    Common Grace and Creation   17
    Common Grace as Wisdom Theology   26

2. The Poetics and Practice of Wisdom | 33
    Poetics: Wisdom Begins in Wonder   33
        Poetics as Seeing   35
        Poetics and Art   38
        Wisdom, Patience, and Nonviolence   39
    Practice: Cultivating a New World   41
    God's Work and Ours   47

Part Two: Biblical Trajectories of Wisdom

3. Creation and Wisdom | 55
    A Wisdom Account of Creation   56
    Rereading Genesis 1 and 2   58
    Two Trajectories of Creation   66

4. The First Testament Trajectory of Life | 76
    Cultural Wisdom and Creation   77
    The Language of Wisdom   81
    Wisdom and the Cultures of the Ancient Near East   84

Lady Wisdom in Proverbs 8　88
　　　The First Testament and Violence　89
　　　The Humanism of Wisdom　91
　　　The Poetics of Wisdom　95
　　　The Limitations of Wisdom　98
　　　Conclusion　101

5. Christ and the Wisdom of New Creation | 105
　　　Christ the Wisdom of God　107
　　　A New Way of Seeing and Doing in Jesus' Teaching　109
　　　The Sermon on the Mount: A New Wisdom　112
　　　New Testament Development of Wisdom　115
　　　New Testament Wisdom in Its Greco-Roman Context　119
　　　The Cross and Resurrection as Wisdom Events　121
　　　　　The Wisdom of the Cross: Nonviolent Service　123
　　　　　The Wisdom of the New Creation: The Economics of Grace　127
　　　　　The Wisdom of the Resurrection: Regeneration of the Earth　130
　　　Conclusion　131

Part Three: Wisdom and Theology in Historical Perspective

6. From Wisdom to Theology in the Early Church | 135
　　　Christians in the Empire　137
　　　Early Christian Wisdom　138
　　　　　Patience and Nonviolence in the Early Church　140
　　　　　Irenaeus: *Against Heresies*　142
　　　　　Syriac Church: Odes of Solomon　145
　　　　　An Emerging Practical Theology of Patience　146
　　　　　War and Nonviolence　149
　　　Constantine and the Imperial Church　150
　　　　　Augustine: Greco-Roman Wisdom and Theology　152
　　　　　Augustine and Violence　158

7. The Poetics and Practice of Contemporary Wisdom | 162
    Modern Culture and the Gospel   164
    The Poetics and Practice of Our Contemporary World   166
        The Poetics of Fullness   168
        The Wisdom of Nonviolence   172
        Practices of Reform: Building a Better World   177
    The Multiple Forms of Contemporary Wisdom   178
    A Contemporary Rereading of Paul   186

8. Epilogue | 189

Bibliography | 195
Index | 205

Preface

THIS ATTEMPT TO EXPLORE the significance of wisdom for this cultural moment is a product of a lifetime of reflection on our Christian cultural calling in the light of the gospel. It might seem odd for a theologian of culture, who has written on visual art, and global theology and mission, to turn to wisdom as worthy of a book-length reflection. But after giving much thought to why certain visual forms work better than others, or how people hear and adapt the message of the gospel, I began to realize that the common element in these varied searches was best described as a quest for wisdom, both as a product and a process. I have been struck by the similar experience of Stephen Barton and his colleagues at the University of Durham during the 1990s, and by David Ford, David Kelsey, and Paul Fiddes more recently.[1]

The more I explored the topic with some (limited) historical and biblical lenses, as much for my own sake as for any plans to publish, the more the richness and potential of a theology of wisdom took shape. I realized that my earlier focus on "poetics" or "visual faith," while capturing one essential component of wise living, was leaving out an equally important emphasis on the performance of goodness and beauty. Similarly, in my extended reflection on contextualization and mission, I came to feel the activism reflected in my evangelical tradition often missed the patience and contemplation required for the ability to truly learn from cultural difference and grow together into the likeness of Christ.

More and more I realized that in our intramural quarreling we evangelicals have, by turns, demonized or ignored what goes on around us

1. Barton and his colleagues at the Durham center for theological research in the 1990s set out to explore the theological significance of family life and, in the course of conversation, realized that they really sought the nature and sources of wisdom. The result is the excellent collection of essays in Barton, ed. *Where Shall Wisdom be Found?* Something similar happened when the distinguished theologian David Ford, while seeking to sum up the Christian life, came to focus on what he called *Christian Wisdom: Desiring God and Learning to Love*. Cf. also David Kelsey, *Eccentric Existence: A Theological Anthropology* and Paul Fiddes, *Seeing the World and Knowing God: Hebrew Wisdom and Christian Doctrine in a Late-Modern Context*.

every day—what I'm calling the facts on the ground; we seldom deeply engage them. We seem constitutionally unable—as our spiritual directors would say—to "pay attention" to our lives. José Miquez Bonino once paid tribute to missionary statesman John Mackay for helping Latin Americans initiate a "dialogue of love" with their culture, in order to construct a new Latin American spiritual history.[2] I think Christians need to find a similar path in North America. Failure in this respect represents nothing less than the elimination of the ongoing work of the Holy Spirit in the various semantic and symbolic worlds in which we all live. Christ surely came to trouble and transform these worlds, but he did not come to do away with them. Though a focus on human effort and responsibility (by a Reformed theologian!) might be seen to threaten God's sovereignty, this book argues that divine and human freedom, when it is functioning properly, are complementary not competitive.

But the exploration, I confess, has led me into areas in which I have little expertise. The addition of "practice" to my ongoing treatment of "poetics" underlines the realization that a focus on poetics alone can lead to a mystical withdrawal. I wanted to learn: How can practices both extend and enrich life's poetics? Clearly my treatment of practice and ethics is less compelling than that of poetics—more an indication of a direction than a definitive statement. Similarly, my reading of history and Scripture is a decidedly nonspecialist one. Apart from critiques of my students, and long conversations with colleagues—especially my late and lamented colleague Glen Stassen—the results would have been even more meager than they are.

The events of 2020—indeed of the last few years—have offered striking examples of the inescapability of the facts on the ground, and, indeed, of their salience for theological reflection. All the more considering that evangelical Christians, while occupying such a visible—even dominant—presence in the public square, have provided little in the way of constructive theological reflection on these events. This weakness provided further impetus, if it were needed, to pursue the theological reflection advanced in these chapters.

Among my colleagues I want to express special gratitude to Robert Johnston and Zoltan Schwab, who have given generous attention to the project and to the chapter on biblical wisdom in particular. Thanks also to longtime conversation partners Justin Bailey, Nicholas Barrett, Joshua Beckett, Maria Fee, and Cory Willson—once students, now respected colleagues; and to insights from Professors Kutter Callaway, David Carlson,

---

2. Bonino, quoted in Sinclair, prologue to *Un esocés con alma Latina*, 15. I owe this reference to Cory Willson.

John Goldingay, Ben Lima, and Richard Mouw. Mentoring Mark Masucci, Christi Wells, Tamisha Tyler, and Andrea Roldan has provided as much learning for me as for them: their influence is evident in many ways in this offering. But the deepest gratitude is owed to my family, which provides the context in which reflection on wisdom has taken shape. From artist Michelle and paralegal Jonathan I have often learned much, and conversations with my three in-house anthropologists, daughter Andrea, son-in-law Enrique, and spouse Grace have stimulated much of what finally appears in these pages. But the greatest debt is to Grace, to whom I dedicate this book, best friend for fifty-two years, who has not only displayed the wisdom I write about, but worked to see it embodied in the world around her.

Escazu, Costa Rica
February, 2021

Introduction

AMIDST THE SWIRLING EVENTS of the year 2020—pandemic, protests, hurricanes and wildfires—it was often hard to make sense of things. This was true on a personal or family level as many struggled to negotiate life at home and the medical and economic challenges that have accompanied these events. And as people of faith, it has been hard to know what Christian and biblical sense to make of these events; the question presses on us, where is God at work? But despite these challenges—perhaps because of them—and even in the face of the suffering and pain that have resulted, I want to argue that something may be emerging that offers evidence of the hand of God. Consider the following three dimensions of our life together.

First, I sense, on the part of many, an almost visceral reaction against widespread practices that we have for many years simply taken for granted. Many of our neighbors have responded with horror at the growing practice of separating children and families at our borders, placing families and children in detention centers that are often worse than prisons simply because they have come to make a better life for themselves. Many more have recoiled when confronted with video evidence of the all-too-common cruelty imposed on Black bodies by law enforcement personnel—culminating in watching a white officer of the law place a knee on the neck of a dying George Floyd. Unprecedented numbers of the population have not simply supported Black Lives Matter, but have felt shame when confronted with the unmistakable and pervasive—but often subliminal—attitudes of discrimination, of racism and sexism, that infuse the rituals of daily life. People have taken to the streets in corporate expressions of protest against the growing soft and hard violence of our world, in numbers that have not been seen since the civil rights movement of the 1960s. Whatever the ultimate value of such demonstrations, it is clear that a growing number of people are interrogating their attitudes—they want to be better, more hospitable people.

This has led, secondly, to a visible and widespread appearance of concrete efforts to strengthen our communal bonds, to encourage us to take care of one another. Sometimes this encouragement is merely notional—as in the common signs on front lawns encouraging us to "Stay safe; Stay strong. We will get through this together." But frequently during the pandemic this concern resulted in concrete forms of mutual support. In large cities community food programs provided food for millions; even the protests were serviced by pop-up medical and social services. People have written letters of thanks to frontline medical workers who risk their lives caring for the sick. Around the world even the poorest communities found ways to organize themselves for mutual care—forming communities of mutual benefit. One can even manage to hope that our Western quest for individual liberty has been chastened by the deep challenges of these months, leading us to the sense that our very survival depends on the mutual support of all of us, together.

Thirdly, one can feel a sea change in attitudes toward taking care of our planet home. The increasingly destructive hurricanes and typhoons of recent years, the devastating wildfires in Australia and California, and the inexorably melting polar ice packs and rising sea levels have all put an exclamation point on the mounting scientific evidence of human-caused climate change. Polls show a majority of the population are sufficiently alarmed by these events to be determined to take the necessary action to attend to the processes of creation, and work together for a sustainable future.

Of course, one can always argue that making a positive case for the responses to these tragedies belittles the suffering that they have caused, and ignores the forces that would oppose these moves. But what I have sketched can be supported in multiple ways by many different kinds of evidence, and one can reasonably argue that such attitudes have come to represent the facts on the ground of our current situation. And I want to insist that they can usefully serve as the starting point of what I want to argue in this book. For better or worse, we always start with whatever wisdom surrounds us, and a clear-eyed understanding of this, and the historical factors that brought us to this point, is a necessary aspect of our Christian calling in this moment.

Assuming that current movements—toward more hospitable attitudes to both strangers and neighbors, the need for more vibrant and supportive communities, and an aggressive care for the earth—are growing, two problems present themselves for a person of faith. First, though Christians are certainly present—even visible—in the movements I have described, all of them are taking place emphatically outside the doors of the churches, in what we call the public sphere. In fact, we may put the situation even more starkly than this: the churches have more often been a center of opposition than a support for the impulses I have described. As Luke Bretherton has put this, many people observing the current cultural and political situation ask themselves:

> Can Christians imagine and narrate Christianity against itself when faced with the complicity of Christians, acting in the name of Christ, in generating forms of life that warrant such things as ecological devastation, patriarchy, white supremacy, and genocide? Or has the Holy Spirit moved beyond the historic churches? And is the Spirit better identified with nonconfessional social movements such as feminism or the environmental movement?[1]

Of course, as Bretherton would agree, the Holy Spirit has *always* worked outside the church, but it is remarkable that we even have to suggest such an alternative. Though I agree with the sentiment implied by Bretherton's indictment, my argument—like his—seeks to make a constructive contribution to Christian thinking and response.

There are several theological and historical reasons for this hesitance to work publicly for social transformation. A group of reasons lie in the mistaken notions of popular Christianity, some of which I will address in what follows. Among those we might name: an exclusive focus on personal salvation resulting from a misreading of the Reformation teaching of justification by faith alone—a justification that obscures the need for sanctification; an emphasis on personal sin that eliminates the social responsibility that Christian maturity entails; and an extreme (even deterministic) understanding of God's sovereignty. All these in various ways diminish the larger calling to work for the common good as a part of God's project of making all things new.

These brief theological references suggest a closely related problem believers face when confronted with the current situation: these movements have arisen without any particular theological fanfare or justification. Indeed, from all appearances we are observing the emergence of a kind of secular wisdom. And we are not at all sure how this is to be greeted: Should we celebrate these impulses? Lament the absence of a specifically Christian justification? Even oppose them in pursuit of a religious (and evangelistic) purity? Many Christians are not sure, and as a result there has been a dearth of Christian (or even religious) commentary on these events. A central premise of this book is that Christian theology at this point in its history lacks an adequate language and vocabulary with which to address processes I have described. To be sure, there are theological categories that come to mind when responding to movements like this: for example, providence, or general revelation. Providence, Peter Hodgson points out, has traditionally

---

1. Bretherton, *Christ and the Common Life*, 31. He goes on to makes clear his position: "I take the view that reformation and renewal are possible. This book should be read as a contribution to this task, a task that is perennially before the Church."

been understood as God's continuing work of creative preserving and sustaining of the created order. But, for various reasons, he thinks this has been challenged since the Reformation and stands in need of reformulation. He helpfully suggests it might be useful "to think of God's influence, persuasion, or inner directedness, in terms of 'shaping' specific patterns of transformative, emancipatory life."[2] Perhaps God is working in an indirect way in the present circumstances. Thinking of God's "shaping" work is helpful, but I argue the basic weakness of the category endures: the focus is primarily on what God is doing; the role (and responsibility) of human initiative is not helpfully explained. What about "general revelation"? Here the dilemma is similar. In William Abraham's definition of general revelation, "God is revealed in the natural world and in conscience" through "general and special acts undertaken by God."[3] Perhaps then the awakening of peoples' conscience through the movements we noted is a part of the general way God is revealed to people. This too is helpful, but it still places the focus on what God is up to; it does not help us understand how the human projects these people are engaged might be "theological": how precisely do they reflect God and to what end might God be working in them?

These traditional categories certainly provide guidance, but they are limited when it comes to fully engaging with human efforts and insights. The one theological initiative that offers more substantial help is the category in Reformed theology, developed by Abraham Kuyper, that he calls "common grace." This term, which seeks to account for the good things humans accomplish in history as part of God's creative purposes, will be the starting point of our journey in chapter 1. But there I will argue that its limitations reflect those of the previous two categories. Though ostensibly allowing for human agency, through what Kuyper calls God's "delegation," it too often, to my mind, overemphasizes divine action.

For reasons that we will explore in detail, I propose that the category of cultural wisdom is better suited to explain what we see happening around us. In the first and second chapters I will attempt to show that this notion, with its biblical moorings, offers a more helpful range of meanings for all that we can support and even celebrate in human history. And given the view of concurrence, restraint, and permission that I will develop, I believe it allows us to do this without diminishing or undermining God's sovereign purposes in creation and new creation. Hodgson's helpful description of God's influence, by the Spirit, of "'shaping' specific patterns

---

2. Hodgson, "Providence," in loc. He goes on to suggest that the metaphor of "wisdom" applied to the natural world might be helpful, something that we are suggesting in this book.

3. Abraham, "Revelation," 445–47.

of transformative, emancipatory life" moves in the direction that I will pursue in what follows.

The argument of the book then emerges in three stages. In the first two chapters, informed by the biblical tradition of wisdom, I describe the content of wisdom in practical and theological terms. In chapter 1, after an account of the privatized version of Christianity I have noted, I turn to a description of creation theology as this is developed in the tradition of common grace. As indicated, I will try to critically explore this tradition, interacting in particular with notions of "antithesis" and "sphere sovereignty" developed by Kuyper and his followers. This leads to the suggestion that the wisdom I will develop is the human delight in and learned appropriation of the order and fertility of God's good creation, especially as this, by the Spirit, can be taken up into the larger purposes of God in creation and recreation. In chapter 2, informed by biblical and theological reflections, I develop the notion of cultural wisdom in terms of human delight, that is the poetics that animate our life together, and the appropriation or practices that open up the potential of God's good creation. Finally, I develop there the notion of "concurrence" that describes human freedom as responses that are aligned with God's purposes in creation and recreation. Throughout these chapters I will seek to elaborate the significance of cultural wisdom as our human calling and responsibility to fashion lives and communities, and nurture a world that moves in the direction of God's final purposes.

After these introductory chapters, I turn in the middle three chapters to the biblical development of "wisdom," in the First and Second Testaments, especially as this comes to focus in the life and teaching of Christ. Chapter 3 reflects on the first chapters of Genesis and the creation stories there, especially the human creation in God's "image," as setting the stage for the dramatic response of the creature to its creator. This includes a development of the innovative potential inherent in the image as this is elaborated in the calling given to Adam and Eve, in Genesis 2, to care for, name, and nurture creation. The disobedience of the first couple in Genesis 3 upsets the order of creation and opens the possibility that wisdom can subvert, as well as support, God's created purposes—wisdom will develop trajectories tending to life, but also toward death. In chapter 4 these tendencies are reflected in the rich wisdom tradition that is so deeply influential on the First Testament story of God's purposes with Israel. Wisdom emerges in these writings as an international movement of what humans can discover from their careful observation of creation, learning and borrowing generously from the multiple wisdom traditions of the ancient Near East. Though wisdom is seen as a reflection of God's direction and the goodness of creation, in this Testament, its exact relation to the dominant accounts of the covenant purposes of God—that is God's saving work—seen in the deliverance from Egypt, the giving of the law, and the exile is unclear. Only later in the First Testament period, in the apocryphal books, is an integration suggested between these traditions—between human discovery and God's delivering work, one that anticipates what will be fully accomplished in Christ. In chapter 5 the appearance of Christ is described as wisdom incarnate, and the integration of God's saving purposes displayed in Israel with the original purposes of creation as this was seen in the First Testament wisdom literature. In Christ's life and work the perfect realization of God's human image appears, and the unified purposes of God for creation and the new creation are embodied—realized and extended. Further, in his teachings, the possibility of human participation in a new kind of wisdom is raised. At Pentecost the gift of the Spirit, poured out "on all flesh," raises the stakes of that participation, especially as this comes to focus on the community gathered in Jesus' name. This revelation of what we call the gospel, the good news of Christ, poses the question of what now will become of the wisdom of culture represented in the surrounding Greco-Roman civilization. That relationship is barely hinted at in the New Testament; the dominant influence on the first believers was the wisdom and prophetic writings of the First Testament.

These New Testament hints leave this fundamental question unanswered: What was the relation God intended between the good news of Christ and its new wisdom, and the wisdom of the surrounding cultures? The final two chapters seeks, in a very preliminary way, to map out the changing relationships of these wisdoms, as the human, dramatic response to God's program of renewal and recreation. In the first, chapter 6, the focus is on the early church up to Augustine. In the second, chapter 7, the focus is on the suggestion of what that relationship might be for contemporary believers, struggling with the challenges that we noted at the beginning of this Introduction. Chapter 6 traces briefly the development of the teaching of the gospel into what we today call "theology"—what James calls "wisdom from above" (Jas 3:15), and what David Ford has proposed as Christian Wisdom.[4] Augustine was among the first—and certainly the most influential—to develop this new wisdom in the categories of the surrounding Greco-Roman culture and thought—the reigning facts on the ground. And from the medieval, Reformation, and modern periods, the necessity and opportunity of formulating Christian wisdom as now part of the facts on the ground has constituted the ongoing challenge of the Christian church. In chapter 7 I suggest categories borrowed from Charles Taylor—benevolence and reform, influenced as they are by Christian wisdom—as a widely influential human

---

4. Ford, *Christian Wisdom*.

construal of God's purposes for creation and new creation in the modern world. More importantly, I argue that the evidence described earlier in this Introduction for movements in the direction of solidarity and nonviolence reflect in their way the long-term influence of the Christian gospel on the inherited facts on the ground. These facts, though they are powerless in themselves to save, can offer important pointers to the redemptive story of God's purposes, evident in Christ, for creation. These purposes, I argue, when understood as part of the movement toward the new creation, provide a potentially powerful witness to God's presence and purpose. The Epilogue makes clear that this vision is to motivate both our response to the current challenges, and our discernment and support of any emerging wisdom which the Spirit may be bringing about. For the promise of God's revelation to John in Revelation 21 and 22 is that all that is worthy in human culture and its wisdom will find a place in the heavenly kingdom.

Part One: A Theology of Cultural Wisdom

1. Toward a Wisdom Theology of Culture

IN THE INTRODUCTION I presented the dilemma of a (possible) widespread and secular movement offering glimpses of new forms of community and impulses toward welcoming the stranger and caring for the earth, on the one hand, and the equally common Christian (or at least evangelical) indifference or even suspicions toward such public movements, on the other. Though this book seeks to provide theological and biblical resources by which this dilemma might be approached, it will not address it directly. Stating things in such stark terms, however, does serve as a useful starting point, and it raises an interesting question: if this characterization is true, how does one account for the reticence and suspicions with which evangelical Christians view the current cultural challenges? Clearly all Christians believe God is somehow working in the dizzying array of economic, political, and cultural events swirling around us, and they would also agree that Christians are called to active engagement with the world they live in—that all of us are somehow responsible to it and for its future. But many Christians are not at all sure how these various assignments and responsibilities play out in real life. In the light of the multiple challenges of recent months, what does it mean to love God and my neighbor?

One narrative that is increasingly common in popular Christian circles goes something like this: there are basically two spheres in which we live our lives, a macro one and a micro one, call them public and private. Christian discipleship has primarily to do with the latter of these spheres, what some have called micro-ethics. According to this way of thinking, we need to follow Christ in our personal lives and seek faithfully to reflect his moral character in our family and social relationships. But when it comes to our responsibilities to the larger public realm—how to be a responsible voter, or consumer of cultural products and economic goods—from the standpoint of popular Christian teaching, we are pretty much on our own. That realm—call it politics, or culture—is a space where the fundamentals of Christian faith and practice play little or no role. This dichotomy is even reflected in how we interpret Jesus' teaching. He may have taught his disciples to "turn the other cheek" (Matt 5: 39), but, on this view, it is impossible to imagine this has anything to do with, say, military spending.

This division of public and private in turn reflects an implicit attitude toward theology. Theology—the developed understanding of God's presence and work as laid out in Scripture—on this view, is a self-contained set of ideas that reflect a spiritual world that has little or nothing to do with our secular lives in a sinful world. As a result, Christian congregations during the pandemic could flout the public guidelines on masking and social distancing because they were doing God's work, something that is necessarily more important than anything the epidemiologists might propose about human behavior. Calling people to Jesus trumps following the guidelines of the CDC.

But this division is not only unwise, it is impossible. The morality of Jesus' teaching was manifestly public; it always had to do with relationships and relationships are formed in community and formative of community. Consider this thought experiment. Suppose I feel strongly that loving my neighbor implies that everyone should have enough to eat. Suppose further I become aware of a large, underserved homeless population and begin a feeding program. I soon realize that I need additional support and so I go on social media to attract support. Suppose people begin responding to this appeal and the ministry expands to such an extent that it attracts the attention of city leaders. Loving my neighbor, and reminding others—family and friends—of the call to neighbor love, increases the reach of my own moral commitments, leading potentially to the pursuit of a larger social good. Though this might not have been my goal, this social good, and the support it attracts, even has political implications—that is, it calls attention to the way our community (our *polis*) is organized, and how it might be improved. As we will see, this works in the opposite direction as well: I can become suspicious of the presence of a strange—Black or brown—person in the neighborhood and be convinced he is up to no good. Further, I might also attract others to share my suspicion, which then gives my suspicions social power that, if multiplied, could even become a politically important movement. All moral impulses call for social embodiment; indeed, the very existence of community is dependent on such impulses. The impulses I traced in the Introduction all reflect a renewed collective sensitivity, a growing awareness that since our most intractable problems are communal, their solution must also be communal.

But separating the public and private is not simply a strategic or tactical mistake, it is ultimately a theological one—it misinterprets both God's presence and the nature of sin. For this dichotomy often implies that the public space, though deriving from God's creative work, because of the fall and sin represents such a deeply flawed order that any pursuit of the common good is impossible; and further, it implies that my private world and the new life made possible by the life and death of Christ provide an untouchable sanctuary against the evils of that larger world. In an extreme case, this has recently led to a proposal for a new monasticism in which Christians are called to withdraw from the (public) world and form their own (private) Christian communities.[1] But this would result in two failures: making the gospel resources of the church unavailable to the larger culture, and keeping the multiple gifts of that culture inaccessible to Christians.

So the argument of this book is that, in any responsible reading of Scripture, even if the precise relationship of these worlds has been problematic throughout history, they cannot be separated. The reason they belong together is that God's purposes for creation underlie both worlds. The story of God's creation and that of redemption in Christ are not two stories; they are a single story of creation and recreation. This story represented the center of Jesus' teaching and work—what he called the kingdom (or reign) of God that he sent his disciples to announce, and that would be only fully realized when he returned to make all things new. And this story is not only central to the church's mission, but it also gives meaning to the many cultural and political worlds outside the church—the multiple interconnections of human community.

These multiple human connections are the central focus of this book. I will argue that they all rely on a natural covenant that reflects the moral order of creation and God's presence and purposes there. These connections, I contend, represent the facts of the matter. The question I want to pursue is how to make sense of these various relationships; how we should see and manage them. The notion of wisdom that I want to develop involves centrally living out wisely and faithfully these multiple relationships. These relationships, which I am calling the facts on the ground, both precede and infuse all religious and political commitments and it is critical that we understand their importance.

Our Cultural Indebtedness

These facts on the ground are important in the first place because they are inescapable. What makes humans special is the particular reflexive relationship they sustain to their physical and social environments; their capacity to appreciate, explore, and develop their multiple inheritances—the connections that reflect what I have called a natural covenant. This accumulation

---

1. See Dreher, *The Benedict Option*.

of debts is embodied in the cultural wisdom (or, given the wide variety of cultures, wisdoms) that is the central theme of this book. I want to argue that Christian discipleship does not necessitate the formation of a new and exclusively biblical culture, but rather, always and inevitably, involves remaking and reorienting the received cultural situation. This process starts with layers of inheritance—from biological DNA to embodied cultural practices, artifacts and monuments, and even religious traditions—the synchronic relations that make up the human person. We always start the work of Christian discipleship with what is lying to hand. The gospel of course does not emerge from our culture; it must always be imported and received in some form or other—it is always *news* of God's creative and recreative work, revealed in Christ and made available by the Spirit. Christian conversion, the embrace of that gospel, is indeed a radical reorientation of the facts on the ground, but it is not a denial of those facts. The depth and extent of this makeover will vary with the context, but the necessity of cultural appropriation is constant. The response to culture is never simple acceptance or rejection, it is always a matter of discerning occupation; the differences are always internal to that culture, even to particular cultural forms. Our cultural projects may reflect the gospel, but they can also subvert this; our feeding programs, however important to community flourishing, do not constitute the renewing work of God that is available in Christ, but neither are they unrelated to that renewal. How our work—our wisdom—and God's saving work relate, is the central question of this book.

Contemporary Americans like to speak of the need for creativity and imagination in their lives. Advertisers have picked up on this desire in the presentation of their products; they offer experiences and products that promise to change our lives. There is certainly nothing wrong with the desire to be creative, as I will argue later, but it can obscure the way our efforts are always indebted to others. Only God makes things out of nothing—the Scriptures are emphatic on this point. This is why in the Christian tradition it was not until the modern period that humans were called "creators." Previously this would have been considered a kind of blasphemy for which there was no biblical or traditional precedent. Even the medieval Latin word *ars,* which is often translated as art, really meant making and shaping all kinds of things—from leatherwork to ship building. As a result, patristic and medieval Christians, and their Jewish forebears, had no illusions about their own "creativity." They understood that they started on their journey laden—and gifted—with the legacy of multiple cultures and innumerable ancestors. So today the cultural situation in which twenty-first century Americans find themselves is already filled with artifacts and practices, often, if one takes time to notice, things that carry a mixed heritage of good and evil. This surely fosters a sense of humility, and occasional puzzlement and dismay, toward what has been left for us. But in every case, it provides the terms and vocabulary of our American cultural calling. I want to explore this heritage in terms I will call cultural wisdom—the human project of developing the potential embedded in the created order, as this is sustained by God's renewing work in Christ by the Spirit. The central connection that I want to trace is that between the narrative of God's saving work in Israel and Christ and the layered narrative that constitutes our cultural inheritance—God's work and ours.

In recognizing these layers of inheritance, of course, we are already making an implicit theological claim that will be spelled out in multiple ways below. We are indebted creatures, because we are all rooted in God's good creation, and ultimately in God's creative love. Our creational embeddedness is the necessary condition for our constructive role in the development of cultural wisdom. People are often amazed by the beauty of a sunset and or the song of a bird. But beyond that, whatever their faith commitments, they are driven to make something of the world in which they are born—to make a good life for themselves and their family. But the materials for this making and building lie not only in the earth's potential, and behind this God's ongoing loving care, but in the achievement of mothers, fathers, and neighbors. For all that makes normal life possible is a gift of people with names and histories, and what they have left us is a communal not an individual possession.

We can speak casually at dinner about black holes, mirror imaging, or herd immunity, but we must remember that we appreciate these things because someone, or some team of people, somewhere, has taken the time to get to know about them and make them part of our common human heritage. All this speaks of our connections, but it also fosters our communal sense of responsibility. We vaccinate our children not just for their sakes, but for the sake of the community—so we can together reach the 60 to 75 percent vaccination rate that allows for the communal benefit of the vaccine. As we have seen in the 2020 pandemic, we cannot flatten the curve of infections unless the community works collectively and, together, follows public health guidelines. Even what we understand as rationality is communally built up and deployed—science itself is a social, shared commodity. Whatever pieces of these goods we enjoy—from the food we eat to the clothes we wear—we owe to the care and discipline of others.

Our earlier thought experiment emphasized that our connections with others can multiply the good we do, but they can also reproduce the evil that crouches at our door. We are embedded not only in a good creation of God, but within systems that have developed in ways that work against

God's purposes. The growing episodes of police shootings of young Black men and the resultant Black Lives Matter movement, or the #MeToo movement opposing sexual violence, has made many people rethink our common history. This has led many to realize that the centuries-long heritage of slavery has left a deep and lasting legacy in our culture; Jim Crow laws, the early twentieth century eugenics movement, even the development of the structures of capitalism reflecting this heritage have led to government policies and law enforcement practices that privilege certain groups while marginalizing others.[2] We are newly aware that this history has not only influenced our public spaces, it has subtly infiltrated our (private) feelings and attitudes toward other people. Even our assumptions about what constitutes true theology can imply that Euro-American wisdom is superior to other peoples' wisdom. Willie Jennings has proposed this assumption of superiority has resulted in a "diseased imagination," where our multiple connections (our natural covenant) with others has been obscured by suspicion and various forms of violence.[3] In some cases such attitudes have become so much a part of our thinking—our facts on the ground—that we fail to see their fundamental contradiction with the creation and recreation narrative of the Bible, and, in particular, the central teachings of Jesus and the early church fathers (something we explore in chapters 5 and 6 below). But notice the implications of what I am saying: this embeddedness in structures of evil applies not only to our unbelieving neighbors but to all of us sitting in church pews on Sunday. Whether we are aware of it or not, global processes influence not only public life, but they seep into conceptions of our private faith as well. The public and private cannot be separated. The humility and gratitude stimulated by recognizing our many connections—our indebtedness—to other people and other periods of history does not eliminate the need to read (and rethink) that history critically. Discernment is as central to an engagement with cultural wisdom as it is to our growing up into Christ in all things (Eph 4:15–16). All of this reminds us that discipleship and Christian reflection is both a private and a public project. The layers of our history, what passes as wisdom, as the place where God's good creation is developed or mishandled, provide the terms in which the gospel is heard, and our discipleship is exercised. But it works the other way as well: our personal, daily struggle to follow Jesus together gives us ever-new lenses by which to read and learn from that story of creation and recreation.

2. On this history, see Baptist, *The Half Has Never Been Told*.
3. See Jennings, *The Christian Imagination*. He frames this in terms of Euro-American narratives supplanting the narratives of others.

Common Grace and Creation

In what follows I will seek to explore this story in dialogue with the two centuries' long discussion of common grace, or, more recently, creation theology, as this is rooted in the Reformed theological tradition. I want to reframe this important conversation in terms that I call "wisdom theology," which draws on the biblical development of wisdom in the First and Second Testaments.[4] This theological heritage starts not with the work of Christ but with a robust theology of creation in terms of which Christ's work, and his teaching, must be understood. Taking its cues from the theology of John Calvin's *Institutes*, this tradition builds on the ample biblical references to creation as a theater for the glory of God, and to Jesus' appeal, which I will consider in detail, to "consider the lilies"—that is to pay loving attention to all the gifts that God has placed in this theater. This call is reflected in frequent admonitions, both in the First Testament and in Jesus and Paul, to celebrate and appropriate the gifts of creation with thanksgiving to God: "For everything created by God is good," Paul tells Timothy, "and nothing is to be rejected, provided it is received with thanksgiving" (1 Tim 4:4).

In the last two centuries the focus on God's sovereignty in creation and recreation has been developed by Dutch theologians Abraham Kuyper (1837–1920), Herman Bavinck (1854–1921), and Klaas Schilder (1890–1952), among others, into an important conversation that Kuyper called "common grace." These theologians developed the notion that culture reflects not only the fallenness resulting from Adam's sin, but also evidence of goodness and virtue—the human project of discovering and developing the good of creation and celebrating its boundless potential. The importance of this, according to these theologians, lies in the fact that creation was created not for humans, but for God, and it is preserved by the Spirit for the sake of Christ. Paul lays out the theological ground for this when he describes Christ as "the image of the invisible God, the firstborn of all creation; for in him all things in heaven and on earth were created . . . all things have been created through him and for him" (Col 1:15–16). For this reason, these theologians insist the cultural work that humans do is important to God: it is always carried out before the face of God, and, though it is human work, God is always and everywhere intimately present and working. While closely related to what systematic theologians call "general revelation," God's generalized presence in nature and history, and "providence,"

---

4. In this book I join other scholars in referring to the First Testament rather than the Old Testament. This helps us see continuity in the narrative of both testaments, and avoids the connotation that the Old Testament is now outdated. See Sanders, "First Testament and Second," and Goldingay, *Old Testament Theology*, 859–63.

God's preserving and upholding work, the common grace theologians want to focus attention on the particular calling (the responsibility) people have to serve God in and through the cultures they occupy and shape.[5] Kuyper's views have been taken in a slightly different, though influential, direction by Klaas Schilder, who stresses the human calling to develop the potencies that are inherent in the created order.[6] Schilder places the emphasis on the self-limitation of God who has given over to humanity the ability and privilege of opening up creation and its potential, whereas Kuyper places more stress on God's continuing presence in what he called "common grace." Kuyper intends to stress, following Calvin, that humans always discover the hidden potential of creation *in the presence of God*. We are able to pursue this project because God relaxes the curse placed on the world in Genesis 3. Kuyper believed this "curse" was directed not toward the world but toward what is sinful in it, enabling him to describe sin as an essential but not substantial category that does not inhibit people from making good things. One might describe the difference between these two views as a focus on what humans have been *already* able to do (Kuyper), and what they have *not yet* been able to do (Schilder).[7] Herman Bavinck emphasizes the fact that the grace administered by faith in Christ affirms and restores nature, a restoration that is anticipated by the resurrection of Christ.[8]

While I take this tradition as my starting point, I want to push the conversation in some fresh directions. My primary critical observation of the work of Kuyper and his followers has to do with the radical differences between the historical situation Kuyper faced and the very different challenges of our twenty-first century, and the theological implication of these differences.[9] Kuyper was convinced that the spirit of the age of his day represented an implacable unbelief, which he saw reflected in the radical biblical criticism of his day, what was called higher criticism. He believed this critical scholarship represented a refusal to be subject to God's voice as this comes to us in Scripture. This spirit, he thought, must be radically distinguished from

---

5. This was laid out in Kuyper's three-volume work *Common Grace* that is currently being translated into English. But his Stone Lectures, published as *Lectures on Calvinism*, summarize his views: "We must in every domain, discover the treasure and develop the potencies hidden by God in nature and in human life" (31).

6. See Schilder, *Christ and Culture*.

7. This is the way William Berends helpfully describes the difference in *The Evaluation of Culture*, 190.

8. See Bavinck, *Essays on Religion*.

9. Though I will focus here on Kuyper's notion of antithesis and sphere sovereignty, other issues could be mentioned. For example, Kuyper's idea that the nation-state is the "master planner" appears inadequate in the light of emerging indigenous and minority movements, and the resulting hybrid and transnational identities.

1. TOWARD A WISDOM THEOLOGY OF CULTURE

that of the believer's submission to Scripture, a situation he framed in terms of an *antithesis* between belief and unbelief. This dialectic of opposition was prominent for example in a very influential work by Kuyper's mentor Groen van Prinsterer, *Unbelief and Revolution* (1848), which argued that the French revolution marked a turn toward a distinctly anti-Christian cultural impulse that would be always at war with the Christian life world. As Kuyper describes this in his *Lectures on Calvinism*:

> Two *life systems* are wrestling with one another, in mortal combat. Modernism is bound to build a world of its own from the data of nature . . . while, on the other hand, all those who reverently bend the knee to Christ . . . are bent upon saving the "Christian Heritage."[10]

In his theology he even proposed this led to two kinds of people: "Both are human, but one is inwardly different from the other, and consequently feels a different content rising from his consciousness; thus they face the cosmos from different points of view, and are impelled by different impulses."[11]

To properly evaluate Kuyper's theology of culture at this point, it is necessary to keep in mind the context in which he was working. He lived his life in the shadow of what has been called the radical Enlightenment, a movement beginning in the seventeenth century and culminating in the French Revolution, which sought to challenge and indeed overthrow the structures of the church and all vestiges of authoritarian autocracy. Though having multiple sources, its seminal thinkers from Spinoza to Voltaire sought to make life in the world the basis of all politics and social thought, and this led some to a mechanistic view of the world.[12] It is not hard to see how Kuyper would make such a negative judgment of his time: all the developing world pictures that Kuyper confronted in his century—sourced in Darwin, Spengler, Nietzsche, and Marx—had severed all connections with their religious past, and indeed appeared openly hostile to Christianity, even when their views rested on long-term Judeo-Christian influences. It is not surprising then that Kuyper would assert that believing and unbelieving scholars cannot profitably work together. As he put it, we

---

10. Kuyper, *Lectures on Calvinism*, 11. Emphasis original. He goes on to say that this struggle is something that he had devoted his life to for "nearly forty years." Notice the stark dichotomy between "modernism" and the "Christian heritage."

11. Kuyper, *Principles of Sacred Theology*, 154. The following section even proposes this might lead to two different sciences.

12. See Israel, *Radical Enlightenment*. Israel's argument is that there is an overall unity to the radical Enlightenment which bears the indelible mark of Spinoza and his many Spinozist followers.

can make no covenant of neutrality with unbelievers: "We may not make a pact of neutrality with learning that proceeds from another principle, or sit at the same university table."[13]

Kuyper's cultural analysis has much to commend it and there is much profit in reading it today, but it is a historically situated reading of his cultural situation, and cannot be simply read as a generalized argument. We need to recognize how much has changed in the hundred years since his death. Rather than the threatening triumph of secularism and materialism, we live in a time when religions, and multiple forms of spirituality, are newly resurgent and even militant. As a result, I will argue that the struggle of our time is not between belief and unbelief, but between belief and what Charles Taylor has called "fragilized belief." That is, beliefs of all kinds have become fragile, threatened, not by totalitarian ideologies, but by the subtler influences of other religious traditions and the post-romantic sensitivities of contemporary people in the West. This means that our contemporaries are not only faced with a wider array of life stories, but they are charged with finding a "spiritual" place for themselves in these stories. As a result, Taylor notes, "the interesting story is not simply one of decline [of religious faith], but also of a new placement of the sacred or spiritual in relation to individual and social life. This new placement is now the occasion for recomposition of spiritual life in new forms, for new ways of existing both in and out of relation to God."[14] Modern people faced with a plethora of life choices face on ongoing call to rethink and revise their spiritual life.

Taylor calls attention to a further characteristic of our age that provides a background to the choices we face: the proposal that modern people live within an "immanent frame." As Taylor describes this, "We come to understand our lives as taking place within a self-sufficient immanent order, or better, a constellation of orders, cosmic, social and moral."[15] Taylor's argument is that people living in 1500 universally believed this order was created and sustained by God; today many people feel that the order of "nature" runs according to laws that modern science has been able to discover. Though for some—Taylor includes himself among these—this order is open to the transcendent, for others it is not. But the point is, all of us, believers or not, live our lives with many of the assumptions inherent in the immanent frame; the recourse to modern medicine and the contrivances of technology is reflexive and pervasive. It is, in part, this modern notion of the priority of

---

13. See Kuyper, *A Centennial Reader,* 481. Kuyper's idea that we can imagine two sciences resulting from these opposed positions has been developed further by Kuyperian scholars like Cornelius Van Til.

14. See Taylor, *A Secular Age,* 437. On fragilization of belief see 303–4.

15. Taylor, *A Secular Age,* 543.

the natural, and its associated habits of thought, that has led me to explore more thoroughly what Scriptures call "wisdom," our work in the light of God's work both in creation and recreation. This immanent order will be a persistent theme of this book, and, in the last chapter, the lens through which ideas of common grace, or cultural wisdom, will be read.

But I want to suggest an additional difference our age represents. Since we live in more subtly conflicted times, I believe we must develop more fine-tuned instruments to discern the signs of these times. This means first of all that we must acknowledge the gifts as well as the defects of our culture, and further, recognize the incalculable and varied influences of our time. Here one need only point to the consequential development of the social sciences over the course of the last century, something not yet envisioned when Kuyper did his work, to see how much has changed, and how our understanding of culture and its multiple institutions must also be adjusted. Cultural wisdom, or better cultural wisdoms, I argue, better reflect the amazing cultural variety that humans have brought about, and the hybrid and bi- and transnational identities that have emerged in our global world.

Seen with the lens provided by the social sciences, cultures and institutions can no longer be seen as fixed entities with fixed boundaries. They are better viewed as flexible and constantly changing processes, with porous boundaries where cultural goods and services are shared and exchanged. Therefore, separating the good from evil in culture—identifying the antithesis—becomes a difficult task. Kathryn Tanner, for example, has usefully traced the transition from a fixed notion of culture in the nineteenth century to a descriptive, contextual use in the twentieth century. A consensus emerged, she proposes, that culture was a human universal that highlights human diversity, and can be conceived as a total way of life associated with a social consensus that is constitutive of human nature.[16] As a result the institutions and practices formed in this globalized world have also taken on a dynamic and fluid character.

To insist on an antithesis between two opposing life worlds, as Kuyper does, implies that it is possible to actively separate ourselves from the reigning cultural assumptions. In fact, extracting ourselves from the spirit of the age is easier said than done; we are deeply embedded in this spirit for shared practices and resulting institutions, even for the language available to us. Here the developments of social science have helped us see how this is so. A century ago Emile Durkheim described the way cultures are formed and reproduced by a reigning social solidarity, which is also expressed in the

---

16. Tanner has described this emerging notion of culture in *Theories of Culture*, 25–29.

religion of those places. In the 1930s Ludwik Fleck further developed this idea in terms of the processes of scientific discoveries. These advances are possible because of what he called collective thought and the joint practices that facilitate this—seen for example in teams of people working in a scientific laboratory.[17] More recently these ideas have been developed in emergent terms, describing the emergence of group thinking, and social processes, that result from individual thinking, but that exercise a downward influence on individual thinking.[18] Christian Smith offers an important description of the human person existing in this web of relationships, but with ongoing and critical influence on the world around. But tellingly, he notes, this influence is constrained but not determined by the reigning social processes. Here is how Smith describes these relationships: "All social structures and institutions are *emergently* dependent upon the ongoing activity of human persons, whereas human persons are only *contextually* and *developmentally* dependent upon the social structures . . . that nurture and sustain them." Of course, Smith says, these structures can also exploit and exclude people has well as nurturing them, but in every case they offer a constant and ongoing constraint. Humans are inescapably embedded in these contextual constraints, but they are more than simply a node in the network. As created in God's image they are shapers of culture and not simply its products (something to be explored here in chapters 4 and 7).

As Fleck's proposal suggests, social constraints work for good as often as ill; the language and social potential of our cultural embeddedness has far-reaching ability to develop the goods of creation. And the use of this language and pursuit of these practices are essential tools we must use to shape compelling versions of the gospel story. A church without an appropriate respect—even love—for its culture, will not only lack influence, but its witness will give an uncertain sound. There is antithesis between faith and unbelief as a theological fact, surely, but the lived differences are often difficult to discern in the short term, and indeed Jesus seems to discourage such attempts, when, in his parable, he tells his listeners to let the wheat and weeds grow together, because "in gathering the weeds you would uproot the wheat along with them. Let them both grow together until the harvest" (Matt 13:29–30).

---

17. See Fleck, *Genesis and Development*.

18. This development is extensively described in Croasmun, *The Emergence of Sin*, 23–43, and in Smith, *To Flourish or Destruct*, 28–35. Smith's starting point with human personhood, I think, offers a more helpful view of human agency than Croasmun's description, which is overly dependent on the social solidarity Durkheim proposed. The quote that follows from Smith is at 30, emphasis in the original.

This does not mean of course that we do not make judgments about culture, or ignore the effects of sin. In stressing that wisdom expresses what humans make of God's good creation and indeed of God's presence there, we are also acknowledging the conflicted character of wisdom itself. As we will make clear, already in Genesis 3, and later in the major prophets and in Paul in 1 Corinthians 1, wisdom appears not only as a gift of creation, but also as a (very human) problem. Though wisdom is rooted in creation, God cannot be held responsible for everything humans do with that goodness. And wisdom, for its part, cannot save the world on its own. Joseph is portrayed in Genesis as one endowed with a special wisdom that protected God's people, but this wisdom couldn't deliver Israel from Egypt; God had to do that. Perhaps we might propose that the corollary of fragilized belief is ambivalence: everything that humans do before the face of God has traces of the original goodness, and, potentially, furthers God's creational purposes, though it also invariably expresses the brokenness of creation. As a result cultural products are always, in some degree, ambivalent, calling for discerning (and provisional) appropriation.

A second insight of Kuyper that needs critical updating in the light of our context is the notion of *sphere sovereignty*. Kuyper's ideas of sphere sovereignty builds on Calvin's early insight into the public sphere that the Reformer called the *forum externum*. This space, Calvin argued, is where humans are "educated for the duties of humanity and citizenship that must be maintained among men," where the concerns of this present life are expressed, having to do not only with "food and clothing but with laying down laws whereby a man may live his life among other men holily, honorably and temperately."[19] Significantly, in this shared social space Calvin believed people have the freedom to enjoy and explore God's created gifts. Kuyper followed up this notion by proposing that the human cultivation of creation results in the emergence of multiple spheres, each with their own practices, led by their own *virtuosi*. What is more, Kuyper taught, these developing structures have an authority that God endorses—in their own way they are continuing God's work of creation. Kuyper's proposal has proved highly suggestive and has been developed in various ways. It admirably captures the ordered and structural pluralism that Christians believe is a created good and it accounts for the many ways that human ingenuity has developed the potential of creation. These multiple possibilities—in for example science, art, politics, education, entertainment and media—represent the infinite potential built into creation. Of course, Kuyper recognized this diversity can

---

19. Calvin, *Institutes*, I.v.1. The activities filling this space, Calvin goes on to say, "are more important than is commonly believed" (III.xix.3).

be used for evil purposes as well as good. The creative impulses behind these spheres are invariably controlled by what theologians in Kuyper's tradition have called a religious ground motive that directs the process for either good or ill. In addition to the associational pluralism that God placed in creation, human efforts in a broken world result in what is called a directional pluralism—diachronic movements toward or away from God's purposes, what I will describe later as trajectories of life and of death.[20]

Kuyper's notion of sphere sovereignty has been taken up by others in this tradition and subjected to expansion and critique. Herman Dooyeweerd preferred to speak of the process as a process of differentiation; Craig Bartholomew has recently argued that Kuyper's ideas could be usefully extended to include what he calls "symbiosis," that is an appreciation of the mutual influences among spheres.[21] One might even propose that Alasdair MacIntyre's description of institutional "practices"—like architecture, or medicine—offer possible support and clarification of Kuyper's ideas.[22] Such suggestions recognize that cultural "spheres" as Kuyper explained them, however suggestive, were highly reified, leading to an essentialized and static notion of how culture works, something that social scientists have come to challenge, as we have seen. The dizzying transformation of communication and transportation options have changed drastically how we think about the sectors of society; the lines between, say, education and science, or politics and the church are increasingly difficult to draw. Holding to fixed notions of ethnicity and race, for example, can easily lead to unconscious expressions of prejudice; Kuyper seemed always to be uncomfortable with emerging notions of multiculturalism. These differences can no longer be ignored. The critique that Kuyper's ideas contributed to the rise of apartheid in South Africa, while often exaggerated, surely owes something to the reified notions of culture and the accompanying colonial assumptions of some of his followers.[23]

---

20. The religious ground motive has been most fully developed in the thought of Herman Dooyeweerd. A good exposition of associational and directional pluralisms is found in Mouw and Griffoen, *Pluralism and Horizons*.

21. Bartholomew, *Contours*, loc. 3059. This book is the best introduction to Kuyper's tradition and offers useful corrections to its teachings. I have been helped by his discussion of the strengths and weaknesses of the tradition.

22. See MacIntyre, *After Virtue*. MacIntyre does not himself make this suggestion.

23. The question is thoroughly discussed in Bartholomew's *Contours*. Raised in South Africa, Bartholomew knows well the difficulties associated with its theological history. See for example loc. 601 and 2972–96. Bartholomew's discussion can be usefully placed in relation to the critical light shed by Willie James Jennings's discussion of Bishop Colenso in South Africa—a person that Bartholomew also discusses in some detail. See Jennings, *The Christian Imagination*, chapter 3.

1. TOWARD A WISDOM THEOLOGY OF CULTURE

A more comprehensive way of thinking about the diverse dimensions of culture is suggested by another category proposed by Charles Taylor. All people live within a set of assumptions about life and the world that he calls a "social imaginary." This involves not only intellectual schemes or even sets of practices, but the many ways people "imagine their social existence, how they fit together with others, how things go on between them and their fellows, the expectations which are normally met and the deeper normative notions and images which under lie these expectations."[24] This describes what philosophers call the "background" of the lived worlds; it expresses feelings and expectations as well as concepts and beliefs and is carried in stories and songs as well as formal histories.

Taylor's social imaginary and what I am calling cultural wisdom calls to mind what we call "common sense." This notion has been widely discussed over the last century, especially in the light of violence that characterized that century. Is common sense something that can be trusted? What value does it have? These conversations have a direct bearing on my discussion of cultural wisdom. The political theorist Hannah Arendt and the Marxist Antonio Gramsci both developed ideas about "common sense" in their responses to the horrors of Nazi totalitarianism. The differences in their notions of common sense offer a window into what is at stake in this discussion.[25] Arendt was well known for wanting to build a political theory rooted in common sense. She believed this basic human facility—which she felt was overturned by totalitarian regimes—was the most important political quality because it comes closest to disclosing reality as it is generally experienced, revealing as it does our bodily presence in the world (49). Arendt was opposed to any system, however scientific or modern, that kept humans from freely expressing their basic human dignity. Antonio Gramsci, imprisoned by Mussolini in Italy, provides an alternative perspective in his Prison Notebooks, one that resonates with the biblical view of human wisdom. Common sense, Gramsci argued, is ambiguous; it reflects a variety of life worlds of people occupying various social and economic strata. Unlike anthropologists (and Arendt), Gramsci believed one cannot simply accept cultures as they are (51–52). The problem with common sense, Gramsci believed, is that it is a "product of a fractured world" (51). As a result, Gramsci argued, everyone has an obligation to "work out consciously and critically one's own conception of the world . . . [to] choose one's sphere of activity, [and] take an active part in the creation

---

24. Taylor, *A Secular Age*, 171.

25. See Crehan, *Gramsci's Common Sense*, 49–58. Pages in the text are to this source, and they include the references to Gramsci's Prison Notebooks (SPN).

of the history of the world" (53 SPN 323–24). Surprisingly, it is the Marxist here that articulates a view of culture that is closer to New Testament teaching. In Gramsci's proposal to become part of a new collectivity that will forge a new common sense and a new culture (53), one can almost hear the admonitions of the Apostle Paul—"work out your own salvation . . . for it is God who is at work in you" (Phil 2:12–13). Clearly Arendt's concern for human freedom is admirable, but Gramsci's realism is also relevant. Something like this widely shared sense of how things should go, both as a resource and as a problem, provides a good starting point for reflecting on cultural wisdom as this develops in Scripture.

Common Grace as Wisdom Theology

Though common grace will surely continue to provide a recognizable category for understanding the Christian's role in society, I want to suggest that a better way of framing this project is in terms of a theology of cultural wisdom. Cultural wisdom, I argue, avoids the weaknesses of common grace, and positively opens up more biblical ways of thinking about the human situation. I find, along with others, that the term "common grace" carries unnoticed connotations that make it potentially misleading. It is true we are debtors to a kind of natural grace that results from the goodness of creation—something many indigenous traditions call the "grace of the earth," what I have called a natural covenant—as this is underwritten by God's presence.[26] But the more particular theological meaning of "grace" in the biblical tradition is tied to God's saving activity in Israel and Christ, rather than to the more general presence of God in creation. Kuyper's use of the term *grace* was quite intentional as he wanted to underline the fact that God's presence grounds and supports human effort in opening up the riches of the creative order, and this presence was emphatically represented by Christ's lordship. In an appendix to *Common Grace*, volume 2, he defends the use of this term.[27] He notes that he intends it as a translation of the Latin *gratia communis*, which emphasizes the universal aspect of commonness (rather than meaning "common" in the sense of ordinary), as "something that is valid everywhere"; grace, he tells us, is used as "favor" despite its association with saving grace.

The problem here is that even this qualification contributes to the assumption that "common grace" is more about what God is up to, rather than

---

26. As in Tagalog (Pilipino): "Biyaya ng lupaw"—the grace of the earth. This is what Max Stackhouse calls "first grace." See his *Globalization and Grace*.

27. Kuyper, *Common Grace*, Vol. 2, 7c, d.

primarily stressing (and clarifying) human responsibility before God. To be fair, Kuyper in his development of sphere sovereignty wants to call attention to the human work of making and doing, even if this is done before the face of God. But his references to common grace sometimes appear to emphasize what God does almost to the exclusion of human effort. For example in a critical discussion of the relation to special and general revelation he writes: "All 'special' revelation . . . postulates *common grace,* i.e. that act of God by which *negatively* He curbs the operations of Satan, death and sin, and by which *positively* He creates an intermediate state for this cosmos, as well as for our human race, which is and continues to be deeply and radically sinful, but in which sin cannot work out its end."[28] Here common grace seems to be something God continues to make possible as an ongoing activity, rather than a delegated potential that is inherent in creation. Of course, God is always at work, in Christ and by the Spirit, upholding the order of things. But common grace, or as I prefer, the development of wisdom in its various forms, is *what humans make of this order*, work for which they are accountable to God. Kuyper's deep sense of antithesis caused by sin evident here (which I have sought to qualify) contributes to the impression that this is of necessity a divine work rather than a human one.

This imbalance is also reflected in Kuyper's successor at the Free University, Herman Bavinck (1854–1921). In an article on "Common Grace" written in 1894 Bavinck made clear that, in spite of the continuing *sensus divinitatis* (sense of God) resident in humans, common grace reflected God's determination that sin should not take its usual course: "God did not leave sin alone to do its destructive work. He had, and after the fall continued to have, a purpose for creation; he interposed a common grace between sin and the creation—a grace that while it does not inwardly renew, nevertheless restrains and compels."[29] Though this can result in a rich revelation of God among the heathens (41), and it helps us find a balance between worldliness and world flight (56), at the end of the day this is God's work: "The entirety of the rich life of nature and society exists thanks to God's common grace" (60). It rests on the order of creation that God preserves; "natural life in all of its forms has value in his eyes in spite of sin's corruption" (60). But science, art, and political life are "objects of divine good pleasure. He delights also in these works of *his* hands" (60, emphasis

28. Kuyper, *Principles*, 279. Italics original.

29. Bavinck, "Herman Bavinck's 'Common Grace,'" 51. Page numbers following in the text are to this source. James K. A. Smith's complaint that common grace too often is a kind of low octane grace that does not save but does some good, reflects Bavinck here and underlines the necessity of insisting that common grace, or, as I prefer, cultural wisdom, is primarily human work. See Smith, *Awaiting the King*, chapter 1.

added). As we will note, frequently this is true; God does delight in these works, indeed is eager, so to speak, to take credit for them, but they are still *primarily* the work of God's image, not of God. In spite of their sin, God holds humans responsible for this work—both in its positive and negative manifestations. Kuyper's notion of delegation, which we describe below, is not emphasized as strongly in Bavinck.

This holding back of sin is often described as the *restraint* that God continues to exercise, as a kind of leash that keeps the mad dog of evil in check.[30] But, with Richard Mouw, I want to ask: is restraint enough? In the section of Calvin's *Institutes* that is frequently cited in support of this notion (II.ii.3), though Calvin does say God "restrains"—puts a bridle over—evil, he goes into detail about many who live their lives honorably, in such a way that the better term seems to be "permission" rather than restraint. Calvin allows that "In every age there have been persons who, guided by nature, have striven toward virtue throughout life . . . These examples, accordingly, seem to warn us against adjudging man's nature wholly corrupted, because some men have by its prompting not only excelled in remarkable deeds, but conducted themselves honorably throughout life. But here it ought to occur to us that amid this corruption of nature there is some place for God's grace."[31]

Here is the problem: placing the emphasis solely on restraint—that God restrains sinners from doing all the evil they are capable of—opens God to charges of complicity when, as we have seen too often over the last century, the forces of evil appear *unrestrained*, doing all the evil they are capable of. Why can't we speak of "permission" reflecting God's self-limitation, rather than "restraint"? As with a radical insistence on antithesis, a focus on restraint alone results in two related mistakes: an overemphasis on the evil in culture and a corresponding naivete about the righteousness of believers.[32] The New Testament makes clear that we are all subject to what Paul calls (in Romans 5–8) the body of sin; the whole world lies under the influence of the evil one (1 John 5:19). But, as biblical wisdom makes clear, humans are still morally responsible; the evidence of their creation in the image of God, though impaired, still allows them to forge projects productive of the common good—things for which we can praise God. On the other hand, though Paul argues that by their baptism in Christ believers walk in newness of life so

---

30. This notion is described and the debate about it is laid out in Mouw, *All That God Cares About*, chapter 6, "Is Restraint Enough?"

31. Calvin, *Institutes*, II.iii.3.

32. I find this dual tendency infects James K. A. Smith's valuable "cultural liturgies" project. See *Desiring the Kingdom* and *Imagining the Kingdom*. Interestingly he seeks to correct this imbalance in his more recent work, *Awaiting the King*.

that sin no longer has dominion over them, empirically, as Romans 7 makes clear, believers are still subject to sin; as Luther famously put this, believers are simultaneously sinners and justified. As a result the space of the church offers no protection against the evils of the world; it can foster suspicion and prejudice as well as hope and forgiveness.

Though the precise nature of God's work—and the character of God's sovereignty—is often difficult to discern, Kuyper himself provides support for an emphasis on permission in what are probably his most often quoted words. In his inaugural address at the Free University he asserts: "No single piece of our mental world is to be hermetically sealed off from the rest, and there is not a square inch in the whole domain of our human existence over which Christ, who is sovereign over *all*, does not cry: 'Mine!'"[33] Kuyper's reference to Christ's sovereignty rests on Christ's own claim that "all authority in heaven and on earth" belongs to him (Matt 28:20). But interestingly, as Kuyper goes on to say, this is a delegated authority:

> If you believe in Him as Devisor and Creator and Director of all things, your soul must also proclaim the Triune God as the only Sovereign. Provided—and this I would emphasize—we acknowledge at the same time that this Supreme Sovereign once and still delegates his authority to human beings, so that on earth one never directly encounters God Himself in visible things but always sees authority exercised in human office.[34]

Kuyper's emphasis here on God's delegation of authority helps us understand how we can focus on human culture-making in ways that do not impugn God's ultimate sovereignty. I will consider the ground and character of this human culture making in chapter 2.

I would argue that a focus on wisdom does nothing to undermine, and much to promote, the basic thrust of common grace. In fact Kuyper himself had a great deal to say about wisdom. And, interestingly, he connected it, as we will do, not only with providence but also with the wisdom exhibited by the kingdom Christ proclaimed.[35] While expressed in creation, it is also inherent in the kingdom. Indeed he sees the latter reflected in ordinary life and in common grace, arguing that God's decrees reflect a

---

33. Kuyper, *A Centennial Reader*, 488. Emphasis in the original.

34. Kuyper, *A Centennial Reader*, 466. I have been helped here by Nicholas Barrett's unpublished article, "Reading Every Square Inch of Creation." This is not to say God is not free to work in special ways—in what we call miracles—but these still take place within the created order and, in the nature of the case, are exceptional.

35. Kuyper, *Common Grace: The Doctrinal Section*, vol 2, see chapter 47, 515–16 and 409–11. The discussion of the wisdom of God's decrees is at 675–76.

particular wisdom. In a recently published collection of his writings, *Common Grace in Science and Art (Gemeene Gratie en Wetenschap en Kunst)*,[36] Kuyper pays special tribute to the workings of wisdom in a way that offers support for my argument. Science belongs to creation, he writes, and would exist apart from the fall; in science we are discovering God's thinking in creation. There "God has revealed, embedded a rich fullness of his thoughts," and it is an expression of the corporate image of God that we only can discover this fullness together.

Cultural wisdom, as I will develop the term, draws on the emerging biblical picture of cultural practices and artifacts marking the human appropriation of God's good creation. This theme is especially developed in what is called the Wisdom literature of the First Testament (which we explore in chapter 4). From the very beginning of Scripture, in Genesis 1 and 2, special attention is called to the fact that God rested from the work of creation and gave (i.e., delegated) to Adam and Eve responsibility for caring for and naming the created order (something we will look at in chapter 3). God's rest after creation (Gen 2:2) is a dramatic posture of waiting to see what humans would make of creation's goodness, and it implies that what happens after this is now a human responsibility. Though God, by the Spirit, is everywhere and always at work in culture, ready to accept the credit and praise for the good that appears, and sovereignly working out the divine purposes for creation, one does not encounter God in visible things. The developing structures that exploit the goods of creation have an authority that God endorses—in a very literal sense they are continuing God's work of creation, though they are human work. Though Christ by the Spirit holds all things together and is personally present to all people, culture is still a space of freedom for the children of God to make something of themselves and their world. How these different "freedoms" work together is a critical question that will be addressed in the next chapter.

For these reasons I argue the insistence on "grace" in this universal context may well mislead rather than clarify, and I suggest the more appropriate term is "wisdom" (Heb. *hokma*, Gr. *sophia*) as this term—and its near relations—is developed throughout Scripture. With its more secure biblical grounding wisdom theology can help orient our thinking and frame appropriate assessments of contemporary cultural wisdom. The biblical treatment of wisdom, especially in the First Testament, offers valuable resources that can help us connect these materials both with God's creative work (as in Proverbs 8), and with Israel's life as God's covenant people. Though wisdom

---

36. The English translation by Nelson Kloosterman, interestingly, is entitled *Wisdom and Wonder*. See for what follows Kuyper, *Wisdom and Wonder*, 35–37, quote at 41.

always gestured toward its true home and context in Israel's calling to obedient life in the covenant (cf. Prov 1:7), for most of the FT period this relationship was unclear. Later in that period wisdom's place in God's saving work became clear, an integration that anticipated the teaching and work of Christ. Wisdom materials are further developed in the life and ministry of Christ, as this is embodied in what is called wisdom Christology, exemplified particularly in the Sermon on the Mount and his parables (something discussed in chapter 5 below). While wisdom terminology is integrated into the story of salvation Christ brings, it preserves the preparatory and adjunctive character of this aspect of God's continuing activity in creation.

Wisdom, as I will use the term, is *the human delight in and the learned appropriation of the order and fertility of God's good creation and, in and through this appropriation, the initial and ongoing dramatic human response to God's presence and activity in that order, as this points toward (or away from) the final (eschatological) purposes God has for that creation.* The terms "delight in" and "learned appropriation" underline the two aspects that I want to highlight: the poetics and the practice. On the one hand, it puts forward the delight in the boundless splendor that God has placed in creation, everything that allows human cultures a space to flourish and form bonds of loving relationships, what I will develop as the poetics of wisdom. This focus on desire and delight calls attention to the affective nature of cultural wisdom as a call directed to the heart, invariably involving practices and artifacts that express and spark love.

On the other hand, this definition points to the learned appropriation, the obedient response wisdom calls humans to make, to the fertility and potential of God's good creation, and ultimately to the trinitarian presence of God in that order. Based on the delight that creation has called forth, this ongoing response allows communities and culture exposed to the wisdom of the gospel to renew themselves, a regeneration based on the resurrection of Christ and prompted by the continuing presence of the Spirit. I argue that the New Testament development of wisdom embodied in Christ's life and teaching enhances First Testament wisdom theology by suggesting a pattern of life consistent with the new order begun with the resurrection: a pattern of life that I argue answers directly to the impulses that we noted in the Introduction. This wisdom, so I argue, offers the possibility not only of personal flourishing and renewal, but also—in places influenced by this gospel wisdom—of cultural regeneration. Personal and communal responses to God's work in Christ are not only productive of a community of faith, they (potentially) extend its reach, by the Spirit, to the possible renewal of societies themselves. A focus on obedient hearing and responding also underlines the dramatic character of the ongoing human response to creation and God's presence there, something that I summarize by the term *practice*. The larger framework of creation and recreation, as this is developed in Scripture, gives wisdom its directional (diachronic) quality, that allows movement toward the renewal of all things anticipated by the resurrection of Jesus. As I will argue, God's created purposes and creation's potential are bound up with the eschatological program of God laid out in Scripture. From this brief description, which will be elaborated in subsequent chapters, it is clear that wisdom, even as the work delegated to humans, has a profoundly theological character. It assumes the continuing presence and purposeful activity of the trinitarian God in that order, in terms of which human efforts of culture making must be understood and appreciated. It makes clear the human response to creation's potential always takes place in the active presence—before the *face*—of the loving and creative God. In the next chapter I develop this theology of culture wisdom, and describe in particular the two normative themes I will use as lenses for understanding cultural wisdom, its poetics and practice.

2. The Poetics and Practice of Wisdom

"If you indeed cry out for insight, and raise your voice for understanding; if you seek it like silver, and search for it as for hidden treasures—then you will understand the fear of the Lord and find the knowledge of God." —Proverbs 2:3–5.

IN THIS CHAPTER I want to describe in more detail the theology of wisdom that I introduced in the first chapter, what I propose as a constructive theology of culture. In the previous chapter I defined this wisdom as the human delight in and the learned appropriation of the order and fertility of God's good creation. This definition highlights the two aspects of cultural wisdom that I want to elaborate in this chapter, its poetics and its practice.

Poetics: Wisdom Begins in Wonder

To understand our human role in the large narrative of creation and recreation, I begin with an image that John Calvin uses in the first book of his *Institutes*. That book famously describes the splendor of the created order as a theater for the glory of God. But the starting point I want to highlight is Calvin's initial description of the human as a "spectator" of this dramatic theater.[1] The Reformer opens this section with the claim that some notion of God is inherent in human consciousness. It is, as he says, implanted in the human heart. But to make clear God's character, Calvin goes on, God appears "in the whole structure of the universe, and daily places himself in our view, [so] that we cannot open our eyes without being compelled to behold him."[2] For Calvin this initial experience is expressed in deeply aesthetic terms: "Wherever you cast your eyes, there is no spot in the universe wherein you cannot discern at least some sparks of his glory. You cannot

---

1. Theater, spectacle, spectator, player appear frequently in Calvin's work, highlighting the dramatic call to join creation's hymn of praise. See Dyrness, "God's Play."

2. Calvin, *Institutes*, I.v. 1. The quote that follows is from this section.

in one glance survey this most vast and beautiful system of the universe, in its wide expanse, without being completely overwhelmed by the boundless force of its brightness." But it is presented also in very dramatic terms. In his commentary on Genesis 1 Calvin invokes this special human role as spectator, as, in part, an invitation to join with God's celebration of creation's goodness. The animals, plants, stars and heavens described in the creation account, Calvin specifies, "serve as the garniture of that theater which [God] places before our eyes."[3] Moreover this splendor is an embodiment of wisdom, which, to be understood properly, stands in need of Christ's work. As Calvin puts this in the *Institutes*:

> This magnificent theatre of heaven and earth, crammed with innumerable miracles, Paul calls the "wisdom of God." Contemplating it, we ought in wisdom to have known God. But because we have profited so little by it, he calls us to the faith of Christ, which, because it appears foolish, the unbelievers despise.[4]

It soon becomes apparent that for Calvin the human response fails to recognize the source of this beauty and to properly praise the creator; as we noted in the last chapter, we cannot simply follow "common sense." Still, casting the human creation first as a spectator, called to observe, enjoy, and nurture the good creation in which they are immersed, is the dramatic starting point for God's program of recreation. Implicit in this beginning lies the continuing dramatic call of humans to respond to others, the earth, and, ultimately, to God. One way of thinking about this human assignment is to point out that the call to see and enjoy is also the call to praise. Humans are built to naturally celebrate what they enjoy—whether it is a lover, football team, or work accomplishment—by praising it. Whatever their religious affiliation (or lack of it) humans are natural worshipers. And the initial spark of this natural worship is the human setting in God's good creation, a setting common to people of all ethnicities and faiths.[5]

This central human assignment to praise I want to argue has special significance for twenty-first century North Americans. The human projects conceived by denizens of this cultural moment are often driven by what I want to call their poetic situation: the insistent calling to make something attractive of their lives. The human drive for meaning today is

---

3. Calvin, Genesis 1:6, *Commentary on Genesis*, in loc.

4. Calvin, *Institutes*, II.vi.1.

5. A consistent finding in my research in interfaith aesthetics was that people of all faiths, when asked where they most often experience beauty, respond by pointing to the beauties of creation. See Dyrness, *Senses of Devotion*, 80.

almost always aesthetically framed.[6] Earlier I expressed dissatisfaction with the received discussion of common grace because it was a theological response to a world that has changed in dramatic ways. Further I have noted, with Charles Taylor, that the cultural situation of the twenty-first century is characterized by what Taylor calls the post-romantic situation, what has been called the aesthetic turn in culture, where pursuit of a good or pleasant life—what Taylor calls "fullness"—has overtaken the quest for truth. Taylor believes this framework, which represents the continuing influence of the Romantic movement of the nineteenth century, defines our contemporary understanding of the human quest. It is characterized by the enlargement of spaces for the imagination to function and a persistent appeal not to what we know, but to what and who we love and are drawn to.[7] (I will return to Taylor's conception of fullness in chapter 7.)

The human role as spectator of creation calls attention to the fact that, no matter our race, nationality, or gender, we are all equally embedded in God's good creation. We are not separate from its teeming life and beauty, we are an integral part of it, both responsible and debtors to it. The special calling of humans as culture makers is rooted in the fact that we all live material and embodied lives—we literally live off of creation, not only in the air we breathe and water we drink, but in identities rooted in particular communities and geographic spaces. And, as we are seeing in the current refugee crises, for many people recovering their sense of place, returning to their home, or finding and making a new home, are matters of life and death. And, for these neighbors, the successful negotiation of that homemaking process is the primary arena in which cultural wisdom is accumulated and appropriated.

Poetics as Seeing

Poetics as I am using the term begins with our affective response as the spectator of creation—it privileges sight. Seeing, as I use the term, is an ongoing practice, always emotionally charged, that both reflects and structures our multiple bodily relationships. David Morgan refers to this practice as

6. I will use poetics to refer to what Aristotle called *poesis* (lit. a making by imitation), as the process of making sense of the creation by creative and constructive practices driven by the desire to live (and make) a good life. I have developed this notion of poetics at length in Dyrness, *Poetic Theology*.

7. See Taylor, *A Secular Age*. He acknowledges that this has "led great numbers into modes of free floating and not very exigent spirituality," but asks: "Doesn't every disposition have its own favored forms of deviation?" So that even if we had the choice, he thinks, we cannot go back to some previous era. See 513–14.

an embodied gaze: "As a way of seeing, a gaze is a practice, conscious or unconscious, which structures social relations, self concept, and experience of the sacred."[8] His recognition of the conscious and unconscious character of seeing, points to its passive and active sides. Seeing as a practice, he thinks, is "a proactive gesture, a means of looking for what one wants or needs." It is clear that we are working at the fundamental phenomenological level that is often thought to be pre-theoretical. But the seeing we have in mind is already an orientation toward the world that inclines the person to behave in certain ways rather than in others—a stance that is aesthetically charged and morally inflected. What we call beliefs grow out of such orientations. Morgan claims a "belief is a disposition to see, hear, feel or intuit a felt order to the world." The level of perception I am calling poetics, where wisdom calls us, is a recognition that, as Augustine put it, we grow not because of what we know, but because of the people and things we love.[9]

It turns out that our affective connection to the world, constituted by our perception, is the basis for all the development of knowledge. Philosophers since Heidegger have proposed that this engaged relationship with the world, that is experiencing the world as attractive or available for some desired purpose, is prior to a disengaged one. Further, our direct embodied experience of the world is always foundational for any subsequent disengaged exploration, as in science. Augustine recognized this when he proposed: "But whatever is possessed by the mind is had by knowing, and no good is completely known which is not completely loved."[10] In fact modern philosophers in the phenomenological tradition have proposed that the actual process of knowing begins with the immediate perception involving some attachment to the world, and moves on from there to more generalized knowledge. Children, for example, can learn about something new only in a context when the object in question sparks some emotional attachment. This is why children suffering from autism have difficulty making generalizations and develop this ability later than normal children. Nor do we outgrow our engaged and immediate embodied connection to the world.[11]

---

8. Morgan, *The Embodied Eye*, 68. Quotes which follows are from this page and pages 69–70 respectively.

9. See also James K. A. Smith's description of this in *You Are What You Love*. Augustine's discussion of these things is found in *On Christian Teaching*, bk. 1

10. Augustine, *Eighty Three Different Questions*, 66.

11. See on this Hubert Dreyfus and Charles Taylor, *Retrieving Realism*. On children and emotional connection, 36. They propose that the immediate connection to reality has been subverted by the representational mediation of knowledge proposed by Descartes and his intellectual descendants.

One might put matters this way: appropriate perception of creation and culture is the beginning of wisdom. In Glen Stassen and David Gushee's development of character ethics, they include "perception" as a central category.[12] According to Jesus' teaching, these authors point out, we see according to where we have placed our treasure (Matt 6:21–22). Seeing is central to an appropriate orientation to God's good creation. As Stassen and Gushee write: "Jesus emphasized *seeing* much more than most ethics does, and we believe that ethics needs to become much more self-aware and self-critical about how we perceive. Jesus often taught about how we see, or do not see, what God is doing." Here Jesus is continuing (and actually citing) a First Testament teaching: "Make the mind of this people dull, and stop their ears, and shut their eyes, so that they may not look with their eyes and listen with ears" (Isa 6:10, which Jesus cites in Matt 13:15).[13] Interestingly Jesus gives seeing (and not seeing) as a reason for his teaching in parables—the clearest example of Jesus' appropriation of wisdom materials. He tells his disciples: "The reason I speak to them in parables is that seeing they do not perceive, and hearing they do not listen, nor do they understand" (Matt 13:13). We will explore these teachings further, employing Stassen's method, in chapter 5 below.

Perception then is important because it naturally orients itself to the created order, and draws humans toward a connection with others, and if followed rightly, to God. The implications of this starting point are large. Recognizing and celebrating our connection with creation constitutes the condition not only for human flourishing but for any meaningful relation with God. On the Christian account of creation and recreation, God is not to be found somewhere outside of the created order, but within that order—our human habitation within Taylor's "immanent frame" offers no barrier to God's presence and activity. As Luther famously argued, we do not have to climb up to heaven to find God, but God has come to us in the manger.[14] In fact, it is precisely because God is creator and sustainer, who has entered personally into the creation in Jesus Christ, and in the Holy Spirit is poured out on *all flesh*, that God can be known intimately and personally. This personal presence within the goodness of creation, Christians believe, accounts for—and stimulates—the human desire for loving

---

12. Their ethical method also includes basic convictions and a passions/loyalty dimension. In my view passions *and* loyalty are expressed or sparked by perception and so cannot easily be divided. See Stassen and Gushee, *Kingdom Ethics*, 60–64. The quote that follows is at 64. Emphasis original.

13. All biblical references unless otherwise noted are from the New Revised Standard Version (NRSV).

14. Luther, "Sermon on the Nativity," 1530.

relations, for intimacy. As Miroslav Volf has argued, humans seek not only casual relationships, they seek to embrace the other.[15]

Poetics and Art

While poetics involves a broader sense of affective connection than that represented by poetry and art in a narrow sense, these activities still provide particular paradigms for the human desire for meaning. As we will explore in great detail in chapter 7, art for our contemporaries, as Taylor argues, can "serve to disclose very deep truths which in the nature of things can never be obvious to everyone, regardless of spiritual condition."[16] Roberto Goizueta goes even further by arguing that aesthetic experience is "the key category for interpreting human action."[17] The significance of the experience of art, he thinks, is its drive toward what he calls "empathic fusion." In the encounter with an art work or a musical composition we are drawn to become one with—to lose ourselves in—the object enjoyed. All interpersonal relationship aspires to be aesthetic in this sense: "The law of aesthetics is the law of love," Goizueta believes, and, as a result, there is a deep connection between enjoying beauty and the celebration of the liturgy. In both we seek to leave behind the trivia of life and enter a space of fullness and meaning. He writes: "Play, recreation, and celebration are the most authentic forms of life precisely because when we are playing, recreating, or celebrating we are immersed in, or 'fused' with the action itself, and those other persons with whom we are participating. Thus, we are involved in and enjoying the living itself."[18] To celebrate, as in participation in religious liturgy, one has to give oneself to the experience. Goizueta observes that "celebration implies relinquishment of control, implies a willingness to 'let go.'"

The fact that such practices spark affection speaks of the fact that what matters in life is rooted in the human heart, and is invariably motivated by passions of various kinds. Biblical wisdom consistently appeals to the human heart, the center of human consciousness that moves one to love and to act. And the aesthetic attraction of such drives is always kept

---

15. See Volf, *Exclusion and Embrace*.

16. Taylor, *A Secular Age*, 356.

17. Goizueta, *Caminemos con Jesus*, 89. Goizueta believes the theology of liberation, with which he identifies, was mistaken in making praxis (practice) rather than aesthetics (poesis) central to the quest for liberation.

18. Goizueta, *Caminemos con Jesus*, quotes at 92, 94. He attributes his aesthetic of fusion with the object enjoyed to the Mexican philosopher Jose Vasconcelos. Final quote at 110. This is why, he goes on to say, all human action is "at bottom, a liturgical celebration."

in view in the Wisdom literature. What we call poetry and other forms of art, in the modern sense, are important to this discussion, in addition to their drive toward unity, because of their role in calling our attention to what is worth seeing (or hearing) in the world. Artworks move us, call us to attention, they focus on the color and drama of the world, and underline our embodied connection with creation and its unfolding drama. As Jennifer Craft puts this: "art engenders self-consciousness about being-in-the-world and might help us reflect on how to dwell more fully in the places of our lives."[19] Artists provide important instances of the need to pay attention to the particularities of things—their surface and texture. This reminds us that learning wisdom in a more general sense centrally requires paying attention to the world around us—something that could be called the beginning not only of art but of science as well.

Art can help us live more wisely; it fosters skills that are highlighted in the Wisdom literature. In my nonspecialist, twenty-first century reading of the book of Proverbs I am struck with the insistent call to listen and look. After noting the Lord formed the earth by wisdom—the heavens, clouds and deeps of the earth, the preacher advises: "My child, do not let these escape from your sight, keep sound wisdom and prudence" (Prov. 3:21). Frequently we are called to listen—to parents, the instructions of the Lord, or advice of the righteous, issuing even in this synesthesia: "Don't let [these words] escape from your sight" (4:21). We are even called to notice the way ants organize their work together (6:6). Lady Wisdom encourages us to "be attentive to my words" (4:21), to "look forward" (4:25), because keeping your eyes open will ensure you have enough bread (20:13), and the light of the eyes will "rejoice the heart" (15:30).

Wisdom, Patience, and Nonviolence

As these verses show, wisdom embodies the virtue of prudence. Some would say learned discernment is wisdom's central virtue. But I see an equally important virtue that is central to wisdom (and to my argument): the virtue of patience. This virtue may be defined as the adaptation of persons to the exigencies of life, by connecting them to some particular transcendent narrative identity.[20] Patience is drawing increasing attention in the modern period from psychologists and even theologians. With the rise of positive psychology, and its focus on happiness, the virtue of patience was neglected,

---

19. Craft, *Placemaking*, 144.
20. For what follows see Schnitker et al., "The Virtue of Patience." Pages in the text are to this source.

but happily this is beginning to change. Patience, waiting "calmly in the face of frustration, suffering, or adversity" (265), involves a recognition that the self is immersed in a larger whole—the multiple connections we referred to earlier. Humans are born into a world and a narrative that they did not begin and that they will not complete. Adjusting their lives and expectations to this inherited set of relationships is a condition of maturity. As a result a growing number of studies have shown patience is consistently correlated with positive life outcomes. In the New Testament, patience (Gr. *makruthumia*) is so closely related to God's own patience, as displayed in the life of Christ, that it receives a whole new meaning (267). Indeed patience in the First Testament, and nonviolence to which it is related, prepares the way for the NT teaching that our forgiving is a response to God's forgiveness of us. In the competitive world shaped by a neoliberal regime of winners and losers, acquiring patience would seem a particularly necessary goal.

Proverbs emerges as a particularly modern book in the light of these considerations. It consistently recommends watchful waiting over headlong flight; a lowly (even cool) spirit over hotheaded vengeance (16:19; 22:24). If you move too hurriedly you will miss the way (18:12); but if you commit your work to the Lord, it will be established (16:5). Haste brings want (21:5); but one who is lowly in spirit obtains honor (29:23). So important is the virtue of waiting in humility that it often leads one to be a companion to the poor (16:19). Clearly the patience that wisdom describes is much more than a stiff upper lip or simple endurance. It is ultimately a productive virtue that leads to good words and good things (13:2). This wisdom fills in Calvin's description of the human spectator of God's glorious theater. But this perception, as we will see, growing from an awareness of membership in a larger community of meaning, leads also to a particular way of moving through life, a particular practice.

As all scholars of Wisdom literature note, and as we will explore in detail in chapter 4, wisdom is the art of paying attention to the way creation works. Wisdom is founded on the order God built into creation and that God's active presence continues to preserve. So paying attention to creation, carefully distilling its secrets, hearing its voice, is in a fundamental way, listening to God's own voice. The psalmist understood this: "The heavens are telling the glory of God; and the firmament proclaims his handiwork. Day to day pours forth speech and night to night declares knowledge" (Ps 19:1–2). Hearing, heeding this voice is the first movement in the conversation that we call prayer. Seeing and hearing involve experiences—of love, of beauty, even of divine presence—that are ends in themselves, but they are also the means to other ends that involve our multiple interactions with God's good creation. Seeing calls us to obedience.

Practice: Cultivating a New World

If poetics attracts our attention, and indeed calls us to account within the dramatic theater of creation, practice describes the embodied response to this call—the second half of the human job description. If paying attention is the beginning of wisdom, practice, as I will use it, is wisdom's performance. The primary metaphor used in Wisdom literature for this performative dimension are the multiple references to "walking" in particular ways. Described in the beginning of Proverbs as "learning about wisdom and instruction for understanding words of insight, for gaining instruction in wise dealing, righteousness, justice and equity" (Prov 1:3), so that the "discerning . . . acquire skill" (v. 5). This way of walking is laid out in the first Psalm—a wisdom psalm that represents a kind of First Testament mini-beatitudes. Blessed are those who do not "walk in the counsel of the ungodly" (Ps 1: 1, KJV; NRSV: "do not follow the advice of the wicked"). Consistent with our description of the human poetic motivation, those who walk in this way take "delight . . . in the law of the Lord, and on his law they meditate day and night" (v. 2)—indeed this delight fuels their walk. Those following this counsel, having their desires properly focused, are pronounced blessed in the sense of bearing fruit: "they are like trees planted by streams of water, which yield their fruit in season, and their leaves do not whither" (v.3).

This striking reference to ecological bounty, associated as it is with righteousness, justice, and equity, becomes standard in wisdom material and will be a subtheme of this book. This pastoral description, common in Wisdom literature, recalls not only the blessings of Eden ("Out of the ground the Lord God made to grow every tree that is pleasant to the sight and good for food," Gen 2:9), but also John's vision on Patmos of the new Jerusalem, where the angel showed the apostle the "river of the water of life, bright as crystal, flowing from the throne of God and of the Lamb through the middle of the street of the city. On either side of the river is the tree of life, with its twelve kinds of fruit, producing fruit each month, and the leaves of tree are for the healing of the nations" (Rev 22: 1–2). These blessings, this provision, are the natural accompaniment of wise walking, both its condition and its reward. So here is God's advice to the human spectator in God's good creation: enjoy and cultivate the goodness of the earth. Note the close relationship of this fundamental human assignment both with enjoying and taking care of creation. As Luke Bretherton notes, the basic biblical metaphor for human activity is not management but cultivation—caring for the things that grow.[21] As he puts this assignment: "Human activity understood as cultivation of a

---

21. Bretherton, *Christ and the Common Life,* 325. Interestingly he discusses this metaphor in his chapter on the "Economy." The quote that follows is from 312.

garden should seek to fructify creation, and so enable the wonder and goodness of what God has created to shine forth as part of fostering reciprocal relations of praise and thanksgiving with creation."

This central connection between wisdom and the cultivation of creation has a critical implication for practice. Human projects always, ultimately, work with the goods of creation, cooperating with (or impeding) the earth and its potential for development. Humans make something of this potential; they do not create things *ex nihilo*. Even the wonders of technology depend on and elaborate the bounty that God put in creation—as a distinguished professor told a friend who works on artificial intelligence, the final standard even for augmented reality is reality itself. As we are learning, we acknowledge this debt to what God made possible by humility and stewardship or we suffer consequences. The basis of wealth is creation itself.

The focus on cultivation, on caring for things that grow, calls special attention to the nurturing character of wisdom, the feminine characteristic of Lady Wisdom. Practicing our human spectator role, calls for a particular kind of non-dominating and supportive response that is the active equivalent of poetics' patience. I want to call this wisdom's nonviolent character. Let me continue here my nonspecialist reading of Proverbs—we will consult the experts later. Proverbs, as I read it, consistently urges followers of Lady Wisdom to a gracious form of speaking, to soft answers, a gentle tongue that dispenses knowledge (15: 1, 2, 4), to pleasant speech like a honeycomb (16:24); holding one's tongue from the "whispering" that fosters quarrels (25:20). Such an attitude consistently refrains from strife (20:3), since the love of strife and transgression are related (17:19). The opposite is the violent tempered person who will pay the penalty (18:19)—their violence will "sweep them away" (21:7). For it is the wicked, the fool, who devises violence (24:2), which is also the inevitable end of greed, scoffing, and strife (28:25). Most remarkable is the association of such attitudes with forgiveness: the one who forgives an affront fosters friendship (17:9), and one who confesses transgression "will find mercy" (28:13). Such wise persons will not rejoice even over the fall of their enemy (24:17). This summary of FT wisdom teaching, which we elaborate in what follows, already makes the case that these characteristics of wisdom—patience and nonviolence—together prepare the ground for a full development of the lifestyle of gratitude and mutual forgiveness developed in the NT.

A further First Testament example of this calling to nurturing practice is Jeremiah's advice to the exiles in Babylon found in Jeremiah 29:5–7. Though these sixth-century exiles were convinced their exile would be short, and, like refugees everywhere, were anxious to return to their homes and the lands they knew and loved, Jeremiah tells them God has other plans: "Thus says the

Lord of hosts . . . Build houses and live in them, plant gardens and eat what they produce" (29:5); they should marry, bear children, and even give their children in marriage. Because their calling—the perennial human calling—was to "seek the welfare of the city where I have sent you into exile, and pray for the Lord on its behalf, for in its welfare you will find your welfare" (v. 7); their welfare (Heb. *shalom*, holistic peace), and that of this city are bound up together. For the time being, God tells the exiles, this is your Jerusalem. You need to pray for eyes to see through this city to what God will one day do for the whole earth. In this trope of cultivation, I argue, lies the central human calling, one that is best described as living in and embodying the wisdom of God's good creation, while, funded by Christ's work and the Spirit's power, we wait and work with God to build the new creation.

Instructions about "walking" in the Wisdom literature are rich and many sided, but they all converge on forming people and communities in righteousness. This calls for special emphasis here. A superficial reading of Proverbs with modern eyes might lead one to see its instructions as primarily directed to individuals rather than communities. But a more careful reading gives the lie to such (modern) assumptions. The truth is these proverbs assume community and describe what is necessary to promote (or what destroys) these connections. Goodness and evil are both leveraged for (and against) this purpose in the proverbs. In an interesting anticipation of modern discoveries of mirror imaging, Proverbs 27:19 notes: "Just as water reflects the face, so one human heart reflects another," and as iron sharpens iron "one person sharpens the wits of another" (27:17). But evil also multiplies itself: "The leech has two daughters; 'Give, give,' they cry . . . the fire of evil never says, 'Enough'" (30:15–16).

If creation provides the raw materials for human projects, and ultimately the source of wealth, God's purposes for the human community provide the goal toward which the drama of creation moves. Israel in the FT and the church in the NT is made the special object of God's love and care not because of any special merit of theirs, but because God wanted to show in them the divine purposes for all human community. As God says through Hosea to eighth-century Israel: You were nobody [literally no-people], but you have become my people, 'children of the Living God'" (Hos 1:9–10). It is into this privileged community that wisdom is meant to draw our spectator of creation.

In Proverbs 8 wisdom is personified as Lady Wisdom calling out at the city gates "to all that live" (v. 4), instructing them in all that is "right" (v. 6), involving patience, the fear of the Lord rather than pride and arrogance (v. 13), leading to the insight by which kings rule well (v. 15), which Lady Wisdom summarizes: "I walk in the way of righteousness, along paths of justice, endowing with wealth those who love me" (v. 20). The significance of this introduction of Wisdom is made clear by the crucial verses that follow—on wisdom being with God at the creation, a personification we discuss in a later chapter, that situates wisdom in the closest possible relationship with the creator God. Walking in the way of goodness is walking justly (2:20), it assures success and brings pleasure (10:23), but it is also a sign of the presence and blessing of God, the final spectator of this theater: "The eyes of the Lord are in every place, keeping watch on the evil and the good" (15:3). And it is God who establishes the work of our hands (16:5).

As we will explore in a later chapter, this biblical wisdom was not the unique discovery of Israel; it was widely shared throughout the ancient Near East. In fact it resonates with indigenous wisdom everywhere. Keith Basso, for example, has noted the way the wisdom of the Western Apache in the United States is embedded in the names of places and the stories the elders tell of those places. These stories contain, Basso claims, "the preventive wisdom of moral norms. 'Don't make mistakes,' these places seem to say. 'Think sensibly and do what is right. For therein goodness lies, the goodness inherent in established patterns of social order, and therein lies survival.'"[22] The very landscape of the Apache is a repository of distilled wisdom. Dudley Patterson, one of the Apache elders Basso comes to know, describes the process of learning wisdom as following a trail. Here is how he describes this:

> How will you walk along this trail of wisdom? Well, you will go to many places. You must look at them closely. You must remember all of them ... Wisdom sits in places. It's like water that never dries up. You need to drink water to stay alive, don't you? Well, you do need to drink from places. You must remember everything about them. You must learn their names. You must think about it and keep on thinking about it. Then your mind will become smoother and smoother.

Patterson's description was offered in the cadence and poetic rhetoric of the Apache language—like the biblical proverbs, it was poetry. As Roberto Goizueta observes, aesthetics is not left behind in our practice, rather the ethical and political "mediates the aesthetic." As he writes: "The aesthetic is not a final stage beyond the ethical, but the fullest sense *of* the ethical."[23] For this reason, Goizueta insists, the aesthetic is only properly

---

22. Basso, *Wisdom Sits in Places*, 28, quote which follows at 126.

23. Goizueta, *Caminemos con Jesus*, 128. He is responding here to Vasconcelos's notion that aesthetics supersedes ethics. For what follows see 113 and 107. While aesthetics represents the fullness of the ethical, instrumental praxis, he thinks, depreciates affective

experienced within an ethical and political context. This context, in the first instance, is, for most people, the everyday experience of life in the home and family. As in Proverbs—and in all indigenous wisdom—this is where we learn to value human relationships as ends, and therefore as liberating and empowering. This relates to the idea of justice that Goizueta, and I would argue Proverbs itself, is promoting. Human relationships lived for their own sake, as ends in themselves, lead to works of justice. The latter is not a product, Goizueta insists, but a by-product of communal human life lived as an end. As we are asked to play along with the created order and tease out its secrets, so life shaped according to this dramatic play, though human work, will reflect divine action. Justice is meant to characterize wise walking; cultivating the goods of creation for the sake of building the righteous community. To this, wisdom calls us, as, mysteriously, God is also calling, so that we might become "like God."

But how do our actions mirror God's? These instructions make clear the multiple relationships and responsibilities inherent in wise walking. The wise person relates to the earth, their family, neighbors, even their enemies in ways that can reflect God's own care for all things. As we are seeing today, for many people "difference," as in culture, language, or religion, is threatening. Difference has become a problem, and indeed we can see the roots of the problem already in the Genesis account. On the one hand, as we will see in the following chapter, Genesis 1 makes clear that difference—temporal, geological, and biological—is not only built into the order of things, but is a source of delight both to God and the first couple. God called the teeming panorama of creation positively good, and gave it over to the human couple to care for and enjoy. But these multiple relationships had a negative potential as well. As we will see, this became evident in Genesis 3 when they came to be experienced by the first couple not simply as delightful difference, but sources of mastery and violence—when diversity reflected power differentials, and associational pluralism was twisted by directional pluralism. Because of human disobedience the creation story is not only one of ordering and naming of creation, representing the positive cultural vocation given over to humans—what I will call the trajectory of life, but the story also includes, with the events of Genesis 3, the impulse to disorder, disobedience, and eventually violence against other humans and the created order—what I will discuss as the trajectory of death. These trajectories, while clearly opposed, cannot always be untangled, and must often be discerned with prayer and patience. In fact they represent the necessary context for the

---

life (111). Basso cites stories in which, during times of severe drought, the medicine men kept singing, all night long, until the rain came. *Wisdom Sits in Places,* 137.

discernment of wisdom. For Proverbs describes not only the wise person but also the wicked and the fool. These unwise are also controlled by what they look for and what they see: The "eyes of the fool [look to] the ends of the earth," but they do not see wisdom (17:24). Their eyes are rather fixed on evil; they "throw off restraint" (14:16), are quick to do evil (4:14) and turn things upside down: they think it abominable not to do evil (13:20), bring strife not connection (18:6), tear down what the righteous have built (14:1). To top it off, they have the audacity to wear their folly like a garland (14:24).

Here, in this intersection of wisdom and folly, is where the tension between God's work and ours is poised. Surely God's purpose for creation revealed and embodied in Christ's life, will be finally realized. But ongoing experience with cultures (and reflection on their histories) has often prompted the sober realization that too many of these stories are drenched with darkness, and reveal tangled histories of suffering and oppression in which even religious people have sometimes been complicit—all the consequence of events in Genesis 3. These histories all reflect human response both to God and God's creation—they reflect human choices and practice, not God's purposes. Still, humans can choose life. And for this the wisdom tradition offers specific guidance. It makes clear that the wise person can choose a way that leads to life, or a way that leads just as surely to death. "The wise are cautious and turn away from evil, but the fool throws off restraint" (Prov 14:16). Christ, in one of his wisdom stories, similarly recounts the destruction that surely results from, foolishly, building one's house on sand and contrasts this with the wise man who built his house on a rock (Matt 7:24–27).

Here both the limitations and potential of the wisdom become clear. As we will discuss in more detail in a later chapter, there is a tension built into the wisdom tradition, representing, Roland Murphy says, an argument among the FT sages. In his discussion of these things Murphy notes that Proverbs 10–31 represents the original and ancient teaching on wisdom (chapters 1–9 were probably a postexilic introduction), which reflect an order of things that reflects God's purposes in creation.[24] Follow a just path, these sages teach, and things will turn out well for you; ignore them and your way leads to ruin—what Murphy calls the deeds-consequence pattern. But Israel's experience, especially after the destruction of Jerusalem (587 BCE), seemed to contradict such simplistic notions. So later sages put together the book of Job, where a righteous man suffers, and even later the book of Ecclesiastes, where the preacher endeavors to understand this complexity and comes away empty-handed. But in these two books the work

---

24. See Murphy, "Israel's Wisdom."

of God the creator stands as both a reproach and a prospect (Job 38; Eccl 11:5). As Murphy points out, though neither Job nor Ecclesiastes offer folly as an option,[25] they reveal not only the limitations of wisdom but also its conflicted character. Wise living is never easy or simple. God's ways are sometimes difficult to make out, but still we are called to embody our best sense of what I will call the trajectory of life; as Moses tells Israel, we are to choose life (Deut 30:19). Common grace and wisdom both represent the residue of such wise human choices.

But one might push this further and say that sometimes wisdom itself is not the solution but the problem. David Penchansky has argued that throughout the First Testament, there were sages who actively resisted the influence of wisdom as a temptation not to trust God. Their views appear already in Genesis 3, something we explore in the next chapter, but they can be glimpsed in Job's counselors, in Ecclesiastes, and in the prophets, who felt wise counselors sought alliances with Egypt rather than trusting God.[26] Wisdom is not simple and it does not save; but the pursuit of wisdom is still the fundamental human calling.

When the beginning of Genesis 2 says that God rested from God's work, it means that God waits and watches over the creation, and he especially watches to see what the image he has created will do with what has been made. In resting God is also delegating responsibility for human community and care of the creation to Adam and Eve. And just as God delights in seeing the world come into being in Genesis 1, so God will grieve over humans whose "thoughts of their hearts are only evil continually" (Gen 6:5–6). Later God watches with interest when Abraham believes God, and Israel takes shape, in such a manner that even the wisdom of Egypt is made a part of the sacred record. So important is this coworking characterizing Wisdom literature that hints of it are even found in the overwhelmingly divine work of salvation itself, where the creature is not suppressed, but released to be what God intended. Wisdom is human work, this is clear, but in some mysterious way, it is also God's work. Let us consider this paradox of noncompetitive coworking in more detail.

God's Work and Ours

Here the central paradox of wisdom material becomes both clear and inescapable. The goodness of God evident in creation is, for humans, a gift and the condition of their continuing survival. They are dependent upon it, indeed

25. Murphy, "Israel's Wisdom," 18.
26. Penchansky, *Understanding Wisdom Literature*, 15–16.

made a part of it. Humans are called to enjoy, live from, and take care of this goodness; their central calling involves nurturing, in all the multiple ways possible, creation's goodness. But they are in no sense its creators. Though this calling will eventuate in all the contrivances of technology that fill our lives, the fundamental responsibility is to preserve the goodness and fertility of the land itself. Indeed we will argue that this is in fact a deeply religious calling, for, in a way surpassing human imagination, the final vision of God's new creation is a garden city that will merge the splendor of a new Eden with all the preserved "glory" of human culture—its cultivation (see Rev 21:24, 26). This is entirely God's work—who can doubt it?—while at the same time it showcases human wisdom and celebrates human work.

How can we understand this mystery? To address this, let me return to the claim I made earlier: God's work in creation and redemption are not part of two (sometimes contested) stories. Instead, they make up one story—what Christ calls in his central teaching the "kingdom (or reign) of God." A wisdom lens allows us to see the ways Christ's life, death, and resurrection offer a new, enhanced kind of wisdom. The Apostle Paul stresses in 1 Corinthians 1 that the coming of Christ represents an invasion of power and of wisdom that comes from God and that works for the renewal of creation. As Paul writes there, "[God] is the source of your life in Christ Jesus, who became for us wisdom from God, and righteousness and sanctification and redemption" (1 Cor 1:30). The substance of Christ's wisdom is laid out in Matthew 5–7, which we explore later, but the medium of Christ's becoming wisdom was his death and resurrection—through the cross, in which Paul says "God chose what is weak in the world to shame the strong," God reveals a wisdom from above (v. 27). In this respect it is critical to remember that the resurrection was something that happened in and for creation, and not, as is sometimes assumed, something that has relevance only in and for the church (or worse, only for one's own personal salvation). This means that creation now, as Paul explains in Romans 8, by the working of the Spirit, has taken on a resurrection impulse. It is groaning and waiting for its final renewal (8:21), a renewal that is anticipated by Christ's own resurrection and the gift of the Spirit described in Acts 2. If Paul is right in what he writes to the Corinthians and Romans, it is now possible to argue that, because of the work of Christ, wisdom embraces a new cultural category: not merely its power of personal forgiveness and renewal, but its capacity for social and environmental regeneration. And it is within this enhanced capacity that the human cultural vocation is now located.

But how does this new wisdom that Christ offers enhance human freedom while embracing all that is good in the human story? Clearly this new wisdom opens such vistas that it even puts received legal and liturgical practices in the shade, as Paul concludes abruptly in Galatians 6:15: "For neither circumcision nor uncircumcision is anything; but a new creation is everything." Nevertheless, the climax of the story in Revelation 21 implies that none of the good made from the original creation will be lost or wasted when the "kings of the earth will bring their glory into" the new Jerusalem (21:24).

But how are God's new creation and our cultural wisdom related? To help answer this, consider a similar paradox expressed in Paul's appeal to believers in Philippians 2:12–13. After his encouragement to the quarreling Philippians to "be of the same mind, having the same love" (2:2), which he goes on to describe so movingly, in poetic form, as having the mind of Christ: an obedience and humility that led to suffering, death, and exaltation (vv. 5–11), he specifies that their obedience involves working "out your own salvation (Gr. *sotarian*) with fear and trembling, for it is God who is at work in you, enabling you both to will and to work for his good pleasure" (vv. 12–13). But what does it mean to work out our salvation? Since these verses articulate a fundamental assumption that drives this book, it is important to understand what Paul is teaching us here. Isn't salvation an unmerited gift of God, received by faith? Of faith and not of works? Of course. This is clearly Paul's teaching in Romans. But the competing demands of these practices—faith and works—had been troublesome from the beginning, as the book of James makes clear. The context of these verses is Paul's appeal throughout this letter to the Philippian Christians to "live [their] life in a manner worthy of the gospel" (1:27). We are to look not to our own interests but to those of others, by having the mind of Christ, a way of doing demonstrated by his life of obedience and submission to God's will. It is having this mind—embodying this new wisdom—that, Paul implies, allows these believers to "work out your own salvation with fear and trembling."

Salvation is clearly the work of God, based on Christ's death and resurrection. But Paul implies in this passage (and this letter) that if, enabled by this grace, the lives of Philippian believers do not take on the character of Christ, Paul will have labored in vain, and they will have lived in vain (2:16). And Paul later in the book goes even further. In chapter 3, reflecting on his life and ministry, Paul can admit: "Not that I have already obtained this or have already reached this goal, but I press on to make it my own, because Christ Jesus has made me his own" (3:12). Careful reflection on passages like this reveal the working of a particular—I would argue biblical—contour of divine sovereignty. God's working is such that the creature, who responds in obedience and submission, is nurtured into becoming, freely and joyously, what God purposes for her, so that in the sense Paul means here, salvation becomes the creature's work as well.

Notice what this implies. While salvation is God's work, the process of becoming like Christ is, at the same time, a human responsibility. Indeed this implies that growth to maturity itself rests on the fact that Christ is the perfect expression of God's human image, whose faithful obedience accomplished our salvation (2: 8–9). Christ then becomes the model human life that believers, by the Spirit, are meant to appropriate. But this biblical truth has been mostly lost in popular Christianity—as noted in the Introduction, justification has too often supplanted sanctification. In too much teaching and preaching Christ's work has been reduced to a sacrificial death for our personal salvation that is simply accepted by faith. This oversimplification is compounded by a fear of a works righteousness (that we can "earn" our salvation). These distortions have kept Christians from seeing their own responsibility to work out their salvation.

I believe that one can make a similar claim, mutatis mutandis, for the relation between the human work of walking in wisdom and God's active renewal of creation. Wisdom, I have claimed, results from God's delegation of care for the created order to the human family—a claim that will be argued more fully in following chapters. God has certain purposes for the creation that will infallibly come to pass—the new creation is God's work, but God has shaped the order of things in such a way that the human creature, the express image of the creator God, has been elevated to the position of steward in this process to such an extent that it becomes, at the same time, their work as well. Here we recall the amazing proposal Kuyper made in his Free University inaugural: God has delegated his authority to human beings "so that on earth one never directly encounters God Himself in visible things but always sees authority exercised in human office."[27] John Winthrop delivered a similar message to the settlers in his famous sermon on board the Arbella when arriving in Massachusetts in 1630. Winthrop meant in his sermon to suggest foundational values for a new kind of society that they hoped to build in the new world. Winthrop starts with the common recognition that there are rich and poor, a situation which offers a particular challenge. Here is what he proposes: "As it is the glory of princes to have many officers, so this great king has many stewards, counting himself more honored in dispensing his gifts to man by man, than if he did it by his own immediate hand."[28] So that, as we will show in multiple ways, God can actually take delight in the work of human wisdom, even taking credit for it, as though it was something God had done directly, by God's own hand—even

---

27. Kuyper, *Centennial Reader*, 466. I have been helped here by Nicholas Barrett's unpublished article, "Reading Every Square Inch of Creation".

28. Winthrop, "Model of Christian Charity." I owe this suggestion to the article by Marilynne Robinson, "Which Way to the City on a Hill?"

if one never directly encounters God in visible things. This way of working, I would argue, is God's ordinary way of working; God is free of course to work in exceptional ways—in miracles and theophanies—but these by their very nature are unusual (and I would prefer to call them enhancements rather than interruptions of the created order).

This biblical construal of human and divine concurrence stands in stark contrast to views of God's sovereignty evident in popular religious culture. These can range from a functional Deism in which God exercises a kind of distant control but leaves much of the ordinary processes to run on their own, to a deterministic view that God controls everything down to the smallest detail. In either case the precise character of human accountability is obscured, either by neglecting God's active presence or by reducing human responsibility to simple faith in God. But if God's presence is of such a character as to liberate the creature to fulfill its created potential, then creation's impulse to order and our human calling to wise walking are together both the fulfillment of God's commands and, *at the same time*, an expression of human freedom. And this means further that the human development of wisdom, both in its poetics and its practices, is also a theological site where God is always mysteriously present and active. That this perspective represents a consistent biblical teaching will be argued in the following three chapters of this book. Indeed we will see it is evident from the very first verses of Scripture, and it is to these verses we turn now.

Part Two: Biblical Trajectories of Wisdom

3. Creation and Wisdom

"This is the God who as Creator is free for man [sic.], and the corresponding being is the man who as a creature is free for God." —Karl Barth.[1]

THE CLAIM ADVANCED IN the first chapter is that the story of creation and that of Christ is a single story, not two separate stories. Further, our focus on wisdom as the domain in which the multiple human relationships are played out, rests on the assumption that creation and Israel, and Christ's life and work, along with the recreation represented by the new Jerusalem of Revelation 21–22, reflect the biblical framework in which wisdom, that is wise human living, is to be understood. The next three chapters attempt to support and fill in this assumption. This chapter and the next focus on the original creation and its significance and development in First Testament notions of wisdom. Chapter 5 introduces the new wisdom that lies at the center of Christ's teaching and work, as these reflect, embody, and anticipate the new creation—the new heaven and new earth.

Our shorthand for the story we are telling is creation (Israel), recreation (Christ), and new creation (new heaven and earth). Now this version of the story has had stiff competition from another version that goes like this: creation, fall, redemption, and escape to heaven. Both views take sin seriously, but the second, in my view, gives sin (and the fall) a much more central role than these are meant to play in Scripture. It tends to paint Christ's work as kind of rescue mission for a fallen order, rather than seeing God's intention for creation *fulfilled* in Christ. Another way of putting this is to say that redemption is for the sake of creation, not creation for the sake of redemption. This is critical for our understanding of wisdom as part of God's creational purposes because, as Terrence Fretheim puts this, "redemption makes ordinary human life possible once again . . . redemption is in the service of creational ends."[2] Thus we can say that God's

---

1. Barth, *Church Dogmatics* (hereafter *CD*) III/1, 196.
2. Fretheim, *God and World*, 125–26.

purposes for his people Israel and for the church, as for all people, is to have them live in tune with God's creational purposes. And these purposes, Christians believe, are best seen in the life and teaching of Christ. Further, I will argue, sin does not intrude from some other (supernatural) order, but emerges from within creation; it is a result of the autonomy and contingency that God extended to creation, challenging, though not overthrowing, God's purposes for that good creation.

A Wisdom Account of Creation

To support these claims we turn to a rereading of the Genesis accounts of creation. This creation story, shared by Jews, Christians, and Muslims, marks the beginning of God's creation project, and the origin of our human journey. For these texts claim not only that God created and set the world on its journey, but made the man and woman in the divine image to be stewards of the goods of the garden. Creation is both a developing ecological system and the first act of the divine drama that we call the reign or project of God, and it provides the continuing structure—the limits and possibilities—of human culture and its wisdom. As will be clear from our rereading, the narrative of these three chapters offers fundamental insights into the calling to care for the planet and to shape the human community that calls that planet home. I want to frame this account as a wisdom story, because creation and its microcosm Eden, as the human homeland, is a place of poetics and practice, that is, it evokes delight and calls for discerning response.

The two creation accounts offer evidence for wisdom's dual character—its attraction and its challenge—as a call to see and respond to God's good creation. Further, in their answer to the call of creation, humans register their initial response to God's presence and call rooted in that order. The poetic structure of the initial creation story (Gen 1) suggests humans are invited to share in God's own delight and enjoyment of the goodness of creation. And this invitation is an important reminder that both accounts appeal first to the imagination; they spark wonder as well as insight. Ellen Davis has called the creation accounts Israel's "poem of creation" that asks Israel, and by extension everyone, to share in God's own riposte to what is seen, repeated on each of creation's six days: "It is good . . . it is good . . . it is very good." It is "good" (Heb. *tavod; kalon* in LXX Gr.), here meaning both morally good and aesthetically pleasing. God's exclamation, Davis thinks, underlines the "immediacy of [God's] response."[3] This instinctive reaction follows from the fact that God speaks creation into existence in Genesis

---

3. Davis, *Scripture, Culture, and Agriculture*, 45.

1 as an expression of his love, and then, in chapter 2, becomes potter and gardener, forming Adam from dust and planting a garden for him (vv. 7–8). Speaking, shaping, and planting are intimate activities that speak of God's familiar relationship with creation.

The beauty and goodness of creation then reflects the beauty and goodness of the creator God. With each day of the Genesis 1 account the creation emanates more light and life, with each day it reflects more of God, until on the sixth day, the very image of God appears. Each day embodies more of God's generosity. As Walter Brueggemann writes, "Yahweh has authorized in the world the inscrutable force of generosity, so that the earth can maintain all its members, and so that the earth has within itself the capacity for sustenance, for nurture, and regeneration."[4] This means, he thinks, that wisdom is the "critical, reflective, discerning reception of Yahweh's generosity." In terms we are using, wisdom is paying attention and promoting—enjoying and cultivating—the connections that keep the world generative.

The text invites readers, as spectators of this theater, to look with wonder at what is displayed before their eyes, as it lays out creation's dramatic origins. But such looking implies something more. Enjoyment is an end in itself, embodying the praise of God—its "wow" and "thank you"—but it is also the necessary first step in discerning both God's presence there, and the purpose for which all this was created. And in fact humans invariably experience the particular fruits of creation as a call to make something of its potential. The nature of the created order is such that its splendor carries an intrinsic appeal to practice. Holding its fruit, collecting its flowers, we are faced with an inevitable summons: we will either explore, nurture, and share the bounty, or it will spoil and wilt. Both God's instructions to Adam and the nature of the order itself suggest what I called earlier a natural covenant, an arrangement that God will use as the context and template for God's redemptive covenant. This natural covenant says to us: take care of this cornucopia and it will take care of you. Later when Israel is called to "follow the path that the Lord your God has commanded, so that you may live" (Deut 5:33), it is not, Fretheim notes, "reward talk," but instead such "benefits are intrinsically related to the deed."[5] Human practice, then, responds necessarily and naturally to the structures of creation and God's gracious presence there. And this structure and the presence it bears will be consistently developed in the Torah, God's world-forming instructions.

---

4. Brueggemann, *Theology of the Old Testament*, 529. For what follows see 532.
5. Fretheim, *God and World*, 150.

Rereading Genesis 1 and 2

Let us turn then in more detail to the two accounts of creation in Genesis. The first (Gen 1:1–2:4), described in 2:4 as a "genealogy" of the heavens and the earth, portrays God's creative work in the form of a liturgical litany. Each day's work unfolds in an orderly way as a kind of call and response: "And God said . . . and it was so. The first day . . . the second day . . ." It climaxes with the creation of the man and woman as the pinnacle of God's creation, all of which together God pronounces very good (1:31). We are invited to play along with the developing spectacle before our eyes, as Ellen Davis puts it, to catch its rhythm. Clearly God enjoys watching what is made—God is also amazed: watch how the waters bring forth leviathan and sea creatures! And see the way the earth brings forth radishes and roses—a response that anticipates Jesus, who enjoyed watching the lilies grow (Matt 6:28). God loved what was happening in creation, and the more God worked on it the more it came to resemble its creator, pleasing God even more: "my, this is good."

Creation by the word emphasizes God's transcendence, but the language of Genesis 1 also stresses immanence: beginning with the spirit (or wind) from God sweeping "over the face of the waters" (v. 2) to the repetition of God's permission, "let the waters be gathered together/ let the earth/the sea bring forth abundantly . . ." The biblical account does not suggest any conflict in these relationships. David Fergusson has argued that Charles Darwin is actually to be thanked for helping us see God as immanent in the process of creation—present and active throughout, taking personal delight in each detail. "The model here," Fergusson writes, "is of God's 'letting the world become itself,' not in such a way as to abandon it but in the interest of a patient accompanying that seeks to work within and alongside creative processes."[6] Letting the world become itself fits well with the image of God's noncompetitive sovereignty that we developed in the last chapter. Moreover, it finds confirmation in the discovery of contemporary cellular biology of "self-organizing processes."[7] And, throughout, God takes delight in all that is going on, repeating: "this is good." Neighboring ancient Near Eastern creation accounts are frequently stories of the gods' struggle to form human society. But the Genesis account is different. Here God works directly, by a word—anticipating the centurion's request

---

6. Fergusson, "Interpreting the story of creation," 170.

7. James W. Haag et al., in "The Emergence of the Self," argue that biological life at all levels acts according to purpose, so that the human "self" can be understood as "the synergistic relationship between numerous self-organizing processes" that allows the human self flexibility to do multiple and diverse forms of work (322–32, quote at 329).

of Jesus in Luke 7, "just say the word and my servant will be healed" (v. 7, CEB).[8] Indeed these chapters in Genesis are centrally about God, what God has done and continues to do by speaking and calling out to the creature; the spoken word, the most intimate initiator of relationship, recalls the luminous words of John: "In the beginning was the word . . . and the word became flesh and dwelt among us and we have seen his glory" (John 1:1, 14). God's word creates an unbreakable bond between creator and creature. Terrence Fretheim helpfully describes the close-knit nature of the relationship: "To see nature so closely bound to God indicates that God is internally related rather than externally related to it; nature does bear Yahweh." He thinks the many theophanies (that is appearances of God) in the FT function as forms of revelation because a "theophany is only an intensification of what is true in nature otherwise."[9] And all this prepares the way for that climactic appearance of God in human form.

This appearance of God in creation is anticipated not only by God's speaking creation into existence, but by the unexpected appearance of God's own likeness in Genesis 1:26. The litany continues, so that "And God said . . ." is repeated with an addition of personal intention: "Let us make human kind in our image, according to our likeness." Let me reflect a bit on this peculiar formulation, because it is important to what I want to argue. The precise meaning of this strange use of cohortative, first-person plural of making (Heb. *na-aseh*): "Let us make the man in our image" (1:26) has been the subject of much debate. The verb forms of "let us make"[10] and " let them rule," are both imperfect, the plural of uncompleted, future action. Of all the suggested explanations of this phrase, the most convincing to me is to call this the plural of self-deliberation, stressing God's reflexivity.[11] As Karl Barth expresses this central conception: "In the 'Let us make man' we have to do with a concert of mind and act and action in the divine being itself."[12] I believe this holistic self-determination provides a critical clue to the meaning of the *imago Dei*. Surely it is the whole person, embodied and breathed on by God, that images God, but at the center of this stands this reflexive ability to both know and transcend oneself, and to imagine a possible future and work toward it—it is this ability that makes humans like God. Adam

8. CEB is the Common English Bible.
9. Fretheim, *God and World*, 261.
10. The Heb. *bara* "to create" in v. 27 is used only of God.
11. Jürgen Moltmann, Hans Walter Wolff, and Umberto Cassuto have all suggested something similar to this. For an excellent recent summary of the discussion see Pascal Bazzell, "Toward a Creational Perspective on Poverty," 233–34. Though as Barth notes all this is best understood against the backdrop of God's triunity (*CD* III/1, 192).
12. Barth, *CD* III/1, 192.

and Eve, unlike the animal creation, are defined by a reflexive awareness of themselves, an awareness that reflects the ability to imagine a future that does not yet exist and to propose a movement toward that future. But the reflexive ability does something more fundamental that makes this movement possible. The "let us," Barth argues, expresses a fundamental relational sense, an "I-thou" character that expresses something fundamental about God—who also exists in relationship. Barth writes: "This is the God who as Creator is free for man [sic.], and the corresponding being is the man who as a creature is free for God."[13] So the image expresses the relational nature of the human—the connection to each other, the creation, and ultimately to God. This latter relationship of course is central to all the others; this will become clear in Genesis 3 when God continues to seek out the human, despite the folly that had already reared its head. Barth notes in support of this "let us" character Wilhelm Vischer's claim that in the human, God has a real counterpart, to whom God could be revealed, and who could become the "eye of the body" of creation, able to see and celebrate God's presence in the glorious bounty of creation—even turn to this God in worship and praise.

Clearly the human ability to "have dominion over the fish . . . birds . . . cattle and all wild animals" expresses this central human relational capacity. I will return to the discussion of the "rule" or "dominion" given to humans presently, but here notice the detail the passage employs to describe the blessing that God pronounces: "Be fruitful and multiply, and fill the earth and subdue it . . ." (v. 28). First consider that God now addresses Adam and Eve directly, acknowledging the personal bond with the creature. Rather than "let the earth bring forth," God turns to Adam and Eve and says: "[You, plural] be fruitful and multiply . . . [you] have dominion," an assignment that God's special endowment makes possible. Then notice how this bounty of the earth is spelled out in a long paragraph too often passed over:

> See, I have given you every plant yielding seed that is upon the face of all the earth, and every tree with seed in its fruit; you shall have them for food. And to every beast of the earth, and to every bird of the air and to everything that creeps on the earth, everything that has the breath of life, I have given every green plant for food (vv. 28–30).

Sounding a theme that will reverberate through Scripture, the abundance of creation is a gift God offers for the man and the woman, but also provides for the animals and birds, indeed for "everything that has the

---

13. Barth, *CD* III/1, 196. This is not to say this is direct reference to the Trinity, though Barth thinks it is not entirely mistaken to understand it in this way, as the early Christian Fathers have done. Reference to Vischer that follows is at 194.

breath of life." Later God will offer manna in the wilderness, and Christ will urge people not to worry about what they will eat or wear—because the Father provides for the birds and flowers (Matt 6:30)—but to ask the Father to "give us today the bread we need" (Matt 6: 11). Christ will go on to demonstrate this provision by feeding the multitude beside the sea. God the creator provides the most basic of the creature's needs, its food, in abundance. Here, Norman Wirzba says, is glimpsed "God's love, made delectable."[14] No wonder God looked one final time at all that was made and saw, "indeed, it was very good" (v. 31).

On the seventh day when "the heavens and the earth were finished, and all their multitude" (2:1), God rested, and blessed and hallowed it because "on it [i.e., that day] God rested from all the work he had done in creation" (2:2). Thus the Sabbath (from Heb. *hashabbat* "to stop, close down") became the weekly day of rest, of fullness, of completion, but also of anticipation. Significantly the text emphasizes that God had "finished" creation (repeated twice), indicating that now the dramatic focus is not on God's creative work, but on the creature's response. Notice there is here a clear delegation of responsibility to the human couple. But this delegation does not entail God's withdrawal. To the contrary, in this rest, Karl Barth insists, "God associates himself with [creation] in the fullest possible way," in a way that speaks of the end for which creation is made. Barth writes: "It is by the divine blessing and sanctification of the Sabbath that the week, and time, is concretely and teleologically constituted and ordered."[15]

Much has been written about God's image, and its responsibility to care for what God has made. Humans have been called the vicegerent of God's rule, reflecting democratically God's reign wherever this image will go, unlike national and civic images of leaders posted to remind the people who really is in charge. This responsibility has always been closely connected with the idea of "stewardship," the delegation of responsibility that belongs to the image of God. We need to recall that a steward takes care of things in the absence of the owner, a delegation featured in Jesus' parables. Throughout Scripture, God is portrayed as the owner of creation; humans exercise their stewardship on God's behalf. "The earth is the Lord's," the psalmist says, "and all that is in it, the world, and those who live in it" (Ps 24:1). Still, what Barth calls God's association with creation is evident on every hand: the earth is full of God's glory (Isa 6:3), and of God's "steadfast love" (Ps 33:5—Heb. *hesed,* "mercy"). But this presence

---

14. Wirzba, *From Nature to Creation*, 124.
15. Barth, *CD* III/1, quotes at 216 and 226 respectively.

supports human initiative and creativity, it does not undermine it. God's freedom is noncompetitive with ours.

Though obviously an important, even climactic, strand in the creation narrative, strangely, not much is made of the *imago Dei* in the rest of the FT. The term appears again only in a single reference in Genesis 9:6 in the blessing to Noah, where God reminds him that since humankind is created in God's image, their blood should not be shed. (Though Psalm 8:5 "You have made [human beings] a little lower than God [or angels] and crowned them with glory and honor," is surely an indirect reference.) Not until the New Testament does the image come into its own, but now it is focused on the person of Christ, who appears as the perfected image and likeness of God (Col 1: 15). Clearly the idea has deep theological significance, but, Ellen Davis argues, its meaning is open-ended, so that "one must keep reading and living in biblical faith, in order to know what our creation in the image of God might mean."[16]

When we move to Genesis 2 and 3, the perspective changes from global to local, from a wide-angle (even cosmic) lens, to an intimate close-up. If the first account resembles a litany sung in temple worship, the second recalls stories the elders tell around campfires. God bends down and forms Adam out of the soil, according to this account, before the plants spring up, and intimately breathes into Adam "the breath of life." And, only after this, God plants a garden—for Adam and Eve—with every tree that "is pleasant to the sight and good for food" (2:9), strategically placed among four rivers, which are carefully named and described (vv. 10–14). Consistent with its local focus, the text pauses to describe this landscape and the treasures it contains: Pishon the first named river flows around the land Havilah where there is gold—and, by the way, the text says, it's good gold—and bdellium (a fragrant resin like myrrh) and onyx stones are there too. Creation's goodness includes precious stones and spices as well as good fruit, items both pleasant and tasty, and all common and readily available. As we have seen, such images of the earth's fertility and its riches appear at critical points in the biblical narrative. They speak of the natural covenant, that community of mutual benefit, which is meant to enliven every human project. They season the FT instructions; they animate Christ's parables, and they will play a central role on John's vision on Patmos in Revelation 21–22, where references to gold and precious stones recall Eden. But, like the democratic abundance of Eden, on John's account, they will no longer be confiscated by the elite of Babylon or Rome (see Rev 17:4), but will be made into the very foundation and streets of the new Jerusalem for everyone to enjoy (Rev

---

16. Davis, *Scripture, Culture, and Agriculture*, 56.

21:19-21). Such widely shared delight in creation's splendor was God's intention from the beginning, and it will be fulfilled at the end.

God, the gardener host, makes sure Adam understands this bounty is his to savor—within limits. God encourages Adam: "You may freely eat of every tree of the garden; but of the tree of the knowledge of good and evil you shall not eat." For the day you eat of it, God says, you will die (vv. 16-17). Here in the very center of the garden God prepared for the first couple appears not the limitation but the contour of their freedom. As Dietrich Bonhoeffer notes, the limits placed on the first couple are the condition of their freedom; the reminder stands in the middle of the garden, not at the edges. The limits are built into creation's nature, something, sadly, Adam and Eve will have to learn by experience. Meanwhile, Bonhoeffer notes, Adam has knowledge in ignorance, which for him was a kind of grace.[17] Seeing and embracing the inherent limits of human life sets one on the road to wisdom. Creativity is constituted by constraints.

And a major part of that permission within limits was the work God gives Adam to do, a good and important work, the work of wisdom. God put Adam in the garden "to till it and keep it" (2:15). Adam is caretaker of the garden—its cultivator, as we noted, not its manager. On the face of it, the contrast between this version of the human assignment and that of Genesis 1:28 is striking and calls for comment. Earlier God tells the first couple: "Be fruitful and multiply, and fill the earth and subdue it; and have dominion . . ." (1:28). Subdue (Heb. *yirdu*) sounds like a different job description than tilling and keeping (2:15). These differences have led scholars to suggest these accounts leave us with pictures seriously at odds with one another. Ellen Davis denies this discrepancy and argues for their fundamental unity; both accounts present the same drama of God's placement of humans in the closest possible intimacy with creation, in a drama of soil (Wirzba's phrase). Davis argues along with other scholars that the call is not to rule in the absolute sense but literally to watch over, as a shepherd (which is one meaning of the Hebrew). One key to this is the image of the just ruler in Psalm 72—which uses the word *yirda* in v. 8: "May he have dominion from sea to sea." Here is a king who rules in righteousness, defending the cause of the poor, bringing about peace not war (v. 7), whose rule issues in abundance of grain (v. 16), summarized in a striking pastoral reference: his rule is "like rain that falls on mown grass, like showers that water the earth" (v. 6). Here the image emerges of dominion as nurture and not control. And here too appears the integration of private and public virtues in the person of the wise ruler.

17. Bonhoeffer, *Creation and Fall*, 52-53.

This softer picture of "rule" comes into clearer focus in God's instructions to Adam in chapter 2, v. 15, when God "put [Adam] in the garden to till it and keep it." Ellen Davis argues that the agrarian context illumines the meaning of these verbs. "To till" (Heb. *labadah*), means to work for someone, as a servant, or even to serve as a worshiper. It implies work done with and for the soil, serving its needs. The "to keep" (Heb. *lasmerah*) has the fundamental meaning to keep as in "observe," and is used for keeping (observing) the Torah. "Observe" is perhaps its most salient meaning for our purposes, as in "acquir[ing] wisdom by observation of the workings of the world" (cf. Ps 107:43).[18] So observing the way nature works, sensitive to its needs and potential, amounts to a kind of sacred calling. Davis writes: "So it may be the human is charged to 'keep' the garden and at the same to 'observe' it, to learn from it and respect the limits that pertain to it." Observing and caring for the earth are a fundamental human vocation, as Davis notes: "the land itself is the medium or even the agent through which we may experience life as divinely blessed or cursed." We need to recover, Davis thinks, this sense of human responsibility *among* the creatures, an exercising of communal power, rather than having dominion over it; living as part of the landscape itself.

Both Davis and Wirzba lament the fact not only that human activity has reduced the productivity of the land (by 40 percent or more), but, even worse, that modern people live their lives largely disconnected from any immediate contact with the earth and its processes. Since the goods of creation are mediated to us by huge impersonal agrobusinesses and supermarket supply chains, we are no longer struck by the earth's irrepressible fertility. Its goods are commodities, bought and sold, not gifts of God's delectable love.[19] The natural covenant may seem broken, but alas it remains in effect: since we do not take care of its bounty, we are increasingly aware the earth may not continue taking care of us.

Still God continues to watch over creation and, in the text, notices that Adam is alone, observing: "it is not good that the man should be alone; I will make him a helper as his partner" (v. 18). But surprisingly God does not immediately create Eve, but first forms the animals and parades them before Adam, "to see what he would call them" (v. 19). And thus begins the taxonomic calling of science; whatever the man called the animal, and the plants and trees, the fish and birds—giraffes, rosemary, white ash, perch and robins—that was its name, and God continues to watch the world become itself.

---

18. Davis, *Scripture, Culture, and Agriculture*, 29; quotes which follow from 30, 104, and 55 respectively.

19. One of the blessings of the 2020 coronavirus was the recovery of family gardening and the cultivation of flowers and vegetables.

But it turns out none of the animals alleviated Adam's isolation, as the text points out, "there was not found a helper as his partner" (v. 20). So God made a woman from a rib of Adam and brought her to the man, and they were both naked and unashamed. And Adam celebrates the connection: "This at last is bone of my bones and flesh of my flesh" (v. 23). The other, Bonhoeffer points out, is made out of my life—we are connected.[20]

So the man is created in a dynamic set of relationships, each reflective in their own way of God's triunity. As modern science is showing us, we become who we are within networks of biological and environmental structures. Even our thinking reflects our deep connections to the surrounding physical world, where geography and other people help form our language and moral sensitivities. As Andy Clark and David Chalmers point out, our environment drives cognitive processes; my desires for food extend to the waiter bringing my favorite dish, my beliefs are connected to my lawyers and accountants, so that our minds extend themselves out into the world.[21] But to leave things there might suggest humans are bound by this network of relations. But as the image of the creator God, human self-reflexivity offers the ability to respond appropriately, and to transcend, each relationship—to make something of the responsibilities that each entails. While the earth exercises its agency, displays its colors and scents, the man and woman are called to look, enjoy, but also to take responsibility. They are placed in a force field of desires and longings, in social structures they shape and that shape them. Their relationships are ecological; they can tend toward nurture (or later disruption), they can reflect (or betray) creation's natural covenant. The attractions are both aesthetic and moral, but together they constitute a calling to make a world out of God's gifts.

But there was already a potential problem. The attractions were not the same in all direction—the pushes and pulls exerted cross-pressures that were neither possible to resist nor easy to manage. And notice further that there were already limits and structure built into the working of things, not only between day and night, earth and sea, but between the human and the creatures; and centrally, while there was plenty to see and enjoy there was one place in the garden that was off limits. Adam and Eve were instructed not to eat of the tree of knowledge, as God says, "For in the day that you eat of it, you shall die" (2: 17). Clearly, God intended both permission and constraint. Flannery O'Connor described this in relation to the creative process. "Possibility and limit mean about the same thing. It is the business of the writer to

---

20. Bonhoeffer, *Creation and Fall*, 61. We are connected in love, Bonhoeffer notes: "Sexuality is nothing but the ultimate realization of our belonging to one another" (62).

21. Clark and Chalmers, "The Extended Mind."

push his talent to the outermost limit, but this means to the outermost limit of the talent he has."[22] So stepping back from the scene in chapter 2, while tragedy did not strike until chapter 3, we observe already there are frictions built into the account. As John Goldingay describes this:

> There was a tension built into the creation story. It issued from thought and it generated laughter, and it reflected a systematic week's work that was especially pleasing when completed. But it gave its key players a demanding task of managing a world that had a mind of its own.[23]

Consider the elements of this tension, this field of forces in which Adam and Eve were made. They were made to reflect God, specifically in their ability to imagine and work toward a future that did not yet exist—"Why don't I go back to school and get an MBA?"; "Why don't we build a house on that plot?"; "Why don't I draw the image in this way with these colors?"—but always in the context of the goods of creation as expressions of the goodness of the creator, which they were responsible to tend and manage. Imagining finds its way in the materials; the artist thinks and feels in the act of drawing; she thinks in lines and colors. But the materials themselves carried limits, and trespassing these would lead to death. The pushes and pulls were exhilarating, but perilous. There was always the chance that the human reflexive imagination could go wrong: the suggestion "you shall be as gods" provided the spark.

The Two Trajectories of Creation

As I have hinted, though God continued to watch the world becoming itself, there were already pressures at work. One wonders: how could a good creation go wrong? The key I think is to recognize that the accounts offers two trajectories that exist in tension with each other—a tension that can be either creative or alienating, and that continues to inform human cultural projects. Let me suggest how this might be. First, creation appears, in Genesis 1, fundamentally as the good work of God with no inherent sense of challenge—let us call this the trajectory of life. One comes away from reading these verses with a sense of delight and joy in all that was made and that Adam and Eve were created to enjoy. Let's call this the "original good" of creation. Now Christians, especially Protestants, have not been good at appreciating this, for it

---

22. O'Connor, *Mystery and Manners*, 170.
23. Goldingay, *Old Testament Theology*, 131. Cf. Barth, "From the very first this place is not without serious problems" (*CD* III/1, 250).

often appears their theology only begins at Genesis 3. In Eastern Orthodoxy by contrast, Adam did not fall from a state of perfection to one of misery, but from a "state of undeveloped simplicity." As Timothy Ware describes this, quoting from an Orthodox hymn sung at funerals:

> "I am the image of Thine inexpressible glory, even though I bear the wounds of sin." And because he still retains the image of God, man still retains free will, although sin restricts its scope. Even after the fall, God, "takes not away from man the power to will—to will to obey or not to obey."[24]

Our Orthodox friends have their hands on the trajectory of original good and its continuing influence, and this offers a perspective that we need to keep in mind.

They are on to something. Eden, after all, means "delight," and God's first command is an invitation: to "freely eat of every tree in the garden." The tone is one of permission, of fertility, of life and growth. Unlike the neighboring religions, the stars and sun are neighbors not gods; the waters and animals are friends not alien powers. Notice especially two dominant characteristics of all this wondrous creation: separation and difference. God takes care to separate the night from the day, and the dry land from the seas. And God also creates abundance and difference: "the birds multiply on the earth" (1:23), the earth brings forth "living creatures of every kind" (v. 24). But the separation and difference are not problems to be solved as they are in Greek thought, they are gifts to be savored—in the same way that the multiple gifts of the body of Christ are to be celebrated (1 Cor 12)—all are necessary to bring things to maturity, to fullness. It is impossible for us to know what it was like to live in such a world, but we might imagine it was like having the freedom and opportunity, as John Goldingay puts it, "to learn obedience and grow to moral maturity."[25] The contemplation this trajectory calls forth leads to gratitude for these blessings on the one hand (the poetics), but also to a keen sense of responsibility to and for its order (the practice). Norman Wirzba calls this learning "to understand and live within the order that governs your life."[26] This call to "practice" is learning to experience all things as part of God's ongoing dramatic project, as humans come to see, by painful experience, how to say their lines and play their part. Still, it already could be said: "When pride comes, then comes disgrace; but wisdom is with the humble" (Prov 11:2).

---

24. Ware, *The Orthodox Church*, 228–29. The second quote Ware takes from Dositheus's *Confession*, Decree iii.

25. Goldingay, *Old Testament Theology*, 146.

26. Wirzba, *From Nature to Creation*, 34. And see 67 on God's drama.

To grow into obedience and maturity, but also to grasp the opportunity to exercise genius and creativity, as when the man wonders: What if we could find a way to ride those horses? Or let that dog come and lie by our fire? Or what if we crossed this daisy with that one, what would that be like? Notice how this reflexive spark lies behind all creativity—all culture making. Paul Fiddes argues that this moral sense and this creative imagination are responses to God. "The reaching of the imagination towards a new world," he says, "is the result of God's reaching toward us."[27] God wanted to see what Adam would call these creatures, and in giving over this role, God allowed humans to make culture—to learn wisdom—watching all the while with intense interest. But you can see the danger here: this imagination can always head out on its own, flying out beyond all supposed limits.

And this is what happened in the second trajectory—let's call this the trajectory of death. Genesis 3 records this tragic string of events where permission is squandered and the reflexive imagination is unleashed. But first note the serpent that appears is identified as "more crafty than any other wild animal that the Lord God had made" (3:1). The use of wisdom language ("crafty"; "subtle" KJV) for one of God's creatures, and indeed the appearance of the serpent itself, implies that this temptation, and the evil it entailed, comes from within the goodness of creation, which must have contained this possibility as a condition of its goodness. Satan does not appear in this account; indeed he does not show up until the end of the FT period, and really doesn't play a central role until John Milton retells this story. We must resist the notion that this evil came from somewhere outside of creation, as this has developed in the common notion that the serpent here is a form of Satan, a fallen angel as this has been developed in Christian traditions.[28] Better to say that evil is not some separate force or being that opposes God, thus implying an impossible dualism, but as something that happened, and, in taking on various social forms, has infected the good creation. Ideas of Satan and the demonology evident in the NT developed during the intertestamental period and were employed there primarily to show Christ's superiority and the finality of his work on the cross and resurrection. This Genesis account offers no indication of the source of evil.

Let me emphasize the two elements of significance in these verses: first the temptation arises from within creation (not from outside it), and secondly the general agreement that wisdom language is used in describing

---

27. Fiddes, *Freedom and Limit*, 30.

28. Goldingay points out that the name "Devil" (as in Matt 4:1) comes from the Greek *diabolos* meaning literally "slanderer," which is the equivalent to the FT "Satan" denoting an "adversary" in a legal setting who accuses Job or Joshua, implying the core of evil is opposition or distortion of God's purposes. *Old Testament Theology*, 796.

this strange figure. The serpent is emphatically described as a creature, specifically "a wild animal that the Lord God had made" (3:1), but here he speaks—"crafty" captures nicely the Hebrew (*'arum*), sneaky but also wise. Notice that in this passage that what I am calling the trajectory of death is associated with wisdom, making clear at the earliest stage of human progress that the creative imagination is both gift and problem. As we noted, the wisdom tradition would make its contribution to the story of God's liberation, but it could also oppose and complicate that story; wisdom could not bring in the kingdom.[29]

The serpent's insistence that "you will not die, for God knows that when you eat of [the fruit] your eyes will be opened, and you will be like God" (3: 4) is clearly meant to spark a response. In fact what the serpent claims turns out to be true: they did *not* die, and their eyes *were* opened to good and evil. The serpent then anticipates later "wise" counselors who urged Job, or people in the time of the prophets, to trust their traditional wisdom rather than God. But this is the significant point: the serpent's wisdom appeals precisely to that imaginative capacity wherein the man and woman reflect God. Though Satan may not appear, we can be sure that something went tragically wrong, and that it involved centrally imagining some other goodness than that God provided in the ordered bounty of creation, and doubting God's promises—all the main tools that would later appear in the Great Adversary's arsenal.

The serpent knew what buttons to push. It asks Eve to wonder: What if you took the fruit from that tree? What if you really did become "like God knowing good and evil" (3:5)? The Serpent presses the point: What would that be like? The account anticipates the devil's question to Christ: "All the kingdoms of the world . . . I will give you" (Matt 4:9). After all, the fruit of the forbidden tree was "good for food, . . . and a delight to the eyes"—a description originally given of all the trees, now perversely employed to characterize the one forbidden tree. T. S. Eliot has captured this moment:

> Between the idea
> > and the reality
> Between the motion
> > and the act
> Falls the shadow: For Thine is the kingdom

---

29. This leads David Penchansky to propose that the wisdom language in the Genesis account derives from a source that was hostile to wisdom: "The Garden of Eden story that the Israelites told reflected their ambiguous relationship with the wisdom tradition and to the sages." *Understanding Wisdom Literature*, 15–16.

> Between the conception
>
>   and the creation
>
> Between the emotion
>
>   and the response: Life is very long.[30]

The idea "you shall be as gods" proved the father of the act. Eve took the fruit, ate it, and gave to Adam, and he ate, and the text notes ominously, "and the eyes of both were opened" (3:7). Immediately they become ashamed of their nakedness and they hide from God—needing, in their weakness, a special intervention. Separation and difference are no longer friends; they have become enemies. Still God watches and pursues them, asking: "Where are you?" "Who told you that you were naked?" "What is this that you have done?" Notice that God is still letting the world reveal itself, and despite this tragic turn, still pursues its flourishing. Because the man and the woman failed to see that only in seeking the welfare (the shalom) of that place would they find their own welfare (cf. Jer 29: 7), God had to send Adam out of the garden, "to till the ground from which he was taken" (3:23). Still, even in their shame God continued to care for them, seeking them out, even preparing clothes for them: "the Lord God made garments of skin for the man and for his wife, and clothed them" (3:20). In this God anticipates that later and greater intervention when, similarly, "we were weak, at the right time, Christ died for the ungodly" (Rom 5:6).[31] Like the loving father waiting for the prodigal to return, God waits and pursues the good of the creature, even when it has dissipated its goods in some far country.

The origin of this sad turn of events was the misdirection of desire. Desire is the natural response to the goodness and attraction of creation, it reflects the appetite that God had placed in Adam and Eve, providing the motivation to reach out to creation, to each other, and ultimately to God. Desire, says the medieval theologian Bonaventure, is the movement of the soul toward God. But now this desire, this movement of the soul, has been turned away—a misdirection that is the root of sin.[32] But what or who is at fault here? Were the multiple attractions necessarily leading to this end? And who was responsible? Was the serpent responsible? Adam? Eve? Even God? There is a strange reticence in the text. The truth is the account leaves these questions open; and keeping them open enriches our understanding

---

30. Eliot, "The Hollow Men," 81–82.

31. Goldingay notes, "God's knowledge of us comes about through having a relationship with us." *Old Testament Theology*, 137.

32. This is the convincing argument of Sarah Coakley in "Sin and Desire." She suggests the contradictions about responsibility should be held together.

of these verses. The Bible gives no information on the origin of evil, Bonhoeffer reflects, but it does "witness to its character as guilt and as the infinite burden of man [sic]."[33] These verses are not meant to answer the question of where evil comes from or why it exists, because the human challenge is not to answer those questions, but to live responsibly in the world that resulted.

And the bad news is that now God—and all of us—must reckon with the fatal rupture that has occurred—what theologians, since Augustine, call "original sin." However we understand this passage, clearly something happened in the course of the history of creation that has disrupted the good order of things.[34] The temptation to take the fruit of the knowledge of good and evil proved irresistible for Eve and then Adam. The tension among the pressures of creation and the imagination of the man and woman was too great. They ate of the fruit of the knowledge of good and evil. Perhaps Adam and Eve would have grown into that knowledge in time,[35] but rather than trusting God to give what they needed, like Prometheus they reached out and stole what did not belong to them.

The result might be described as ecological disorder. Now the natural covenant in which humans and the creation care for one another has been marred. God describes the result: pain in childbirth, unequal relationships, work entailing toil and trouble. The disorder, Norman Wirzba observes, involves utilizing the creature in a way that leads to domination rather than cultivation, making our lives into a drama of rebelling against our own creatureliness.[36]

Adam and Eve's disobedience involved a transgressing of limits and a despoiling of creation. The relationships in which they had been created were disordered, and they were set on the path that led to death. Remember, God had promised that in the day they ate of the tree of knowledge they would surely die. Sure enough, death did enter, following disobedience like a shadow, as Paul notes in Romans (5:12). Rather than the peace and friendship that existed with the animals, there is enmity (Gen. 3:15); rather than mutual caring between the man and the woman, there is distorted desire and domination (v. 16); the natural covenant is disrupted, so that we struggle to nurture the earth's goodness and by the sweat of our brow we eat

---

33. Bonhoeffer, *Creation and Fall*, 65. To ask "why," Bonhoeffer says, is to evade responsibility for the "that" (76).

34. Cf. Marguerite Shuster, "Something intruded, in space and time, upon what God had made." *The Fall and Sin*, 5.

35. This is the suggestion of Goldingay, reflecting an Orthodox theme. *Old Testament Theology*, 146.

36. Wirzba, *From Nature to Creation*, 34, 67.

our bread (v. 19). And this disruption, Scripture insists, is universal. It affects everyone, in all places and times. It has become, as Paul Fiddes notes, a universal fact and not an occasional problem.[37] Though it is a problem for each of us, it is also a fact for all of us together. There is solidarity in sin that inflicts our missteps on our children, even on our neighbors. Worse, there is an inevitability to sin, that, try as we might, we cannot contain; indeed, we sense in ourselves and the world around us a moral gravity, a historical momentum toward evil.[38] Sin is part and parcel of the trajectory of death. All of this is graphically illustrated in the subsequent chapters of Genesis: a growing corruption, the loss of even the ability to imagine goodness. God is still part of this story, and he watches this process with horror, grieving in his heart that "every inclination of the thoughts of [human] hearts was only evil continually" (Gen 6:5), and determines to intervene in the flood narrative. But after the flood, though "the inclination of the human heart is [still] evil from youth" (Gen 8:21), God will not destroy the earth but will bless it and the descendants of Noah, and of Abraham. And in Israel God will hold out to the world a chance, as Moses tells his people, to choose life (Deut 30:19). Israel, and the nations, could still pursue the original trajectory of life, that impulse that resided in what the Eastern Church has called the original good. Even here the focus on "original" as in "original sin" risks paying too much attention to that event, and too little on our ongoing call to live responsibly in this broken world.

The biblical account captures precisely this situation of being poised on the intersection of the two trajectories I have sketched: between the original good, and the original evil, between life and death. We cannot escape either, but neither can we find a way to reconcile them. Paul Fiddes concludes that "God has put us in a situation where it appears easier to resolve our anxieties in some other way than trust in God."[39] Another way of putting this is to say it is easier to be like God than to live out, in Jesus Christ, the (renewed) image of God. This situation Bonhoeffer describes as the impulse to live as God (*sicut Dei*), rather than as the image of God: without limits, alone, living out of oneself, rather than being free for the other.[40]

But I want to stress that, despite the upheaval, the human responsibility for the earth and its processes endured, just as the potential of creation survived. In fact, its goodness was never a completed goodness. It required

---

37. Fiddes, *Freedom and Limit*, 60.

38. On this see the excellent pages in Cornelius Plantinga, *Not the Way*, 29–33. The historical momentum of sin is his term.

39. Fiddes, *Freedom and Limit*, 81.

40. Bonhoeffer, *Creation and Fall*, 69–70.

3. CREATION AND WISDOM

careful and extended tending, and its gifts could only emerge over time. Adam's disobedience grew from the tensions inherent in creation, imperfections that made the subsequent disorder possible, though not inevitable. But this is what makes the disruption of Genesis 3 so critical and so tragic. As Douglas Farrow notes, Adam's sin introduced a whole new imperfection. In his discussion of Irenaeus's view of the fall, Farrow describes this:

> The "imperfection" is this: The love for God which is the life of man cannot emerge *ex nihilo* in full bloom; it requires to grow with experience. But that in turn is what makes the fall, however unsurprising, such a devastating affair. In the fall, man is "turned backwards." He does not grow up in the love of God as he is intended to. The course of his time, his so-called progress, is set in the wrong direction.[41]

Because now, Farrow notes, creation's disorder reflects not just the weakness of finitude, but "the recalcitrance of sin."

Despite this recalcitrance, God's loving commitment to the creation continues. Recall that God's continuing presence is internal to the created order. As we will see in the development of wisdom, this presence takes on the form of a call from within creation itself to see, hear, follow, and learn. However evident and painful the cumulative defects of Adam's disobedience, this call is persistent and inescapable. Karl Barth in a section on the "Patience of God and Wisdom" points out that the nature of mercy and grace bear unmistakable marks of patience, because God, for the sake of this mercy and grace allows space for another: "Space and time for the development of its own existence, thus conceding to this existence a reality side by side with his own, and fulfilling his will towards this other in such a way that he does not suspend and destroy it as this other, but accompanies and sustains it and allows it to develop in freedom."[42] As Colin Gunton puts this: "It is part of [God's] wisdom in action that it allows, or, better, enables things to take their course."[43] That the creature lives and develops in space and time is not a defect, it is part of creation's goodness. Note that both Barth and Gunton describe this "enabling" as an expression of God's patience. God created the world with an end in view that would fulfill its created potential. But such fulfillment takes time—maturity and fertility require cultivation over time; the world did not appear in a perfect state but in one ordered toward perfection.

---

41. Farrow, "St Irenaeus of Lyons," 348.
42. Barth, *CD*, II/1.1, 409–10.
43. Gunton, "Christ the wisdom of God," 256. For what follows see 258.

As Gunton notes, such patience implies that creation needed to be "fabricated"; fabrication, cultivation, as we noted, are both the essence of wisdom, they involve the process of making something out of the goods of creation. This call—to obedience and patience—did not change with the coming of Christ. The earliest Christians understood the messianic age involved the healing of the earth, and that Christ's resurrection was a down payment on this promise. But already in the New Testament there were signs of impatience. Everything seemed to be going on as before. Believers were asking: where is the promise of his coming? Peter responds to these concerns by calling attention to God's patience and mercy. For God, Peter points out, one day is like a thousand years: "The Lord is not slow, as some think of slowness," Peter writes, "but is patient with you, not wanting any to perish, but all to come to repentance" (2 Pet 3:8–9). The delay expresses God's patience, which James says, in a book deeply influenced by wisdom traditions, should characterize our behavior. Addressing the economic inequality that characterized the Roman empire ("Your gold and silver have rusted, and, their rust will be evidence against you"—5:3), James illustrates our posture of waiting with a typically agrarian reference:

> Be patient, therefore, beloved, until the coming of the Lord. The farmer waits for the precious crop from the earth, being patient with it until it receives the early and late rains. You also must be patient. Strengthen your hearts, for the coming of the Lord is near. (Jas 5:7–8)

For James this patience is an expression of the particular wisdom from above that is peaceable, gentle, full of mercy and good fruit (3:17), for which James says at the beginning of the letter we should ask God: "If any of you is lacking in wisdom, ask God, who gives to all generously and ungrudgingly, and it will be given you" (1:5). For James this wisdom, clearly embodied in the life and teaching of Christ, is meant to be extended—cultivated, and lived out in the life of the believer.

Our claim is that the key that unlocks the mystery of wisdom lies in the life and teaching of Christ, and we will need to explore this in a later chapter. Since we are claiming the biblical narrative represents one continuous story, it will become clear that Christ's wisdom must itself be placed in the context of this creation narrative, as both sequel and climax, and placed in the context of the development of FT wisdom. As John's prologue describes this: "[Christ] was in the world, and the world came into being through him; yet the world did not know him . . . But to all who received him, who believed in his name, he gave power to become children of God" (John 1:10, 12). But before turning to that part of the story, we first need to explore the ways

Israel found to live wisely in the new situation that God created for them in the exodus—portrayed in the text as a kind of creation event, and how they learned to live wisely in ways that borrowed from their neighbors and, with the covenant promises, glimpsed a possible new world. How did these various—divine and human—assignments play out in the First Testament? Exploring that question is the work of the next chapter.

4. The First Testament Trajectory of Life

"The sages regarded the world of nature as a sacred text upon which Yahweh has written important insights about life."—David Penchansky[1]

IN PREVIOUS CHAPTERS I argued that the many projects of human culture—from growing strawberries to exploring the genetic codes of viruses—reflect the good creation of God and the potential that resides there. These projects, I argue, are animated by the human capacity to know themselves in relationship and imagine a possible future. This human dynamic, I claim, was a fundamental aspect—the driver as it were—of the human creation in the image of God. In the next chapter we will see how that image is best seen, as Paul says, in "light of the gospel of the glory of Christ, who is the image of God" (2 Cor 4:4). In this chapter I want to back up and consider further the capacity God gave over to the man and woman: the ability to name and frame the good order of creation, as this developed in Israel and her neighbors.

The tensions inherent in this order, we recall, tempted Adam and Eve to transgress the limits imposed on their calling—to trust their own view of the future rather than God's, and the order and resulting wisdom, was disrupted. But God continued to intervene and create new possibilities for faithful response. In an important sense God's creative work continues in the creation of Israel.[2] And the human capacity to explore and discover the goodness of creation continued to develop. Both the divine interventions and the dramatic human response, and the relationship between these as they anticipate the coming of Christ, are the subject of this chapter.

Humans and the land were created together, and were meant to make a single whole in what I have called a natural covenant. But alongside, and responding to this work of divine creation, indeed in many ways integrating

---

1. Penchansky, *Understanding Wisdom Literature*, 2.
2. Richard J. Clifford points out that the First Testament often conflates the creation of Israel with the original creation. Cf. "The Hebrew Scriptures," 514. Cf. Pss 135, 136.

and interpreting it, was the human work of building homes and cities—the reflexive project of making a life in community that reflects, and sometimes subverts, the work of God. This project would need to be recalibrated and reoriented by the coming of Christ, but even this re-creation makes good out of the large cultural inheritance represented by Israel, and, to a lesser extent, the patterns of life inherited from the ancient Near East.

In this chapter I want to explore further this creative drive to build a world in the First Testament (FT) period, and the cultural inheritance that made this possible, as both a theological and a human project. The human calling, both its potential and its tensions, came to be expressed in the various traditions of wisdom in the FT. Starting with the home and family and moving out into the care and ordering of the goods of the earth and even the structure of public life, this cultural process was at times a faithful response to God, at other times an attempt to create a tower that reaches to heaven, but it was a consistent presence. In what follows I want to describe how the project of making a life is tied in the closest possible way to the stuff and processes of creation and the responsibility and delight these evoke—its poetics—and at the same time, constitutes the necessary context of peoples' response to God—its practice. Let me reflect on these aspects.

Cultural Wisdom and Creation

The First Testament, what is also called the Hebrew Scriptures, is fundamentally a religious book. But the relevant point for my argument is that this religion of Yahweh was built upon a way of life whose parts reflect the physical order and structure of creation on the one hand, and the cultural heritage borrowed from this or that neighbor, on the other. Notions of family and economic life, even of sacrifice, and priesthood, things often regulated by the law God revealed to Moses, were all shared with neighboring cultures of the Near East.[3]

This accumulation of traditional knowledge, what I am calling the wisdom of culture, is collected in the Wisdom literature of the FT—Job, Proverbs, Ecclesiastes, Song of Solomon, and in many Psalms—but its presence is frequently evident outside of these books, from the story of Joseph, through Samson's riddles, to the poetry of the Psalms and the aphorisms and oracles of the prophets. Wisdom (Heb. *hokmah*) represents what we call common sense, the kind of insights most people use without thinking to live their lives: that honesty is best in the long run, bribery is wrong, moderation and

---

3. Terence Fretheim argues that even the notion of "sin" had a prehistory outside of Scriptural revelation. *God and World*, 72.

restraint are good things, and so on. This common knowledge, characteristic of the book of Proverbs in particular, proposes what has been called a deeds-consequence wisdom, a structure that rests on the fact that creation itself has a moral structure—honesty and foolishness generally have natural (good and bad) consequences. But the sages from the earliest period knew things do not always work out the way we expect—wise people are not always successful, and fools often prosper. So reflection on life in these traditions came also to include more speculative musings about why innocent people suffer (Job), or whether human effort has any final meaning (Ecclesiastes). But overall wisdom comprised a body of knowledge that made life comprehensible, even enjoyable, and represented the roots of what we today call philosophy and science. And later in the FT period it was responsible for forming patterns of instruction that would prove influential even on the New Testament. But for the people of Israel there was no question that wisdom, at its best, reflected the way God put the world together—it reflected the patterns and purposes of creation.

Is it possible to be more precise about the content of FT wisdom? Scholars are not sure. Some, like Stuart Weeks, believe the idea of a wisdom tradition "is essentially a modern construct to which no reference is made in the Old Testament."[4] He points to the existence of general advice literature in many cultures that do not necessarily indicate some particular movement. The Hebrew word *hokmah*, Weeks points out, can mean skill, intelligence, or even simply education, even if its deployment is always highly literary, displaying a concern for style and form. Some scholars, following Weeks's lead, have gone so far as to suggest the whole category of "Wisdom literature" needs to be challenged. Not only does its study only date to the nineteenth century, but references to creation appear in a wide variety of contexts, and the supposed wisdom vocabulary is fluid and influential on a wide variety of FT writings.[5]

Ronald Clements acknowledges its marginal character, something that is evident not only by the ambiguous connection with the covenant and election, but by its foreign provenance.[6] Walter Brueggemann demurs, and points out that the very closeness of the sages to Israel's everyday life "gave to Israel a sense that Yahweh is present in, with, and under daily, lived

---

4. Weeks, "Wisdom in the Old Testament," 21.

5. The best summary of the current conversation is Kynes, *An Obituary for "Wisdom Literature."* I owe this reference and insight into the scholarly discussion to Zoltan Schwab.

6. Clements, *Wisdom in Theology*, 20. He notes that even wisdom's importance in later writings is undermined by their absence from the biblical canon (14).

experience."[7] This quotidian focus allowed the tradition to develop later into an important factor in Jewish life, providing leverage, Brueggemann argues, for people to "talk back" to Yahweh in prayer and lament.

From the beginning of the Hebrew Scriptures, wisdom played a role in God's purposes for Israel. Wisdom moved them to explore carefully God's world—to see it clearly, and it gave them a language that oriented them to this world. Raymond Van Leeuwen summarizes its role: "Biblical Israel conceived of wisdom as a divine or human capacity rooted and revealed in creation, and implicitly inseparable from the covenant as its theological presupposition."[8]

But in the earlier stages, the connection with the saving work of God was unclear. As James Crenshaw has argued: In the main wisdom writings (Proverbs, Job, and Ecclesiastes) "one looks in vain for the dominant themes of Yahwistic thought: the exodus from Egypt, the election of Israel, the Davidic covenant, the Mosaic legislation, the patriarchal narratives, the divine control of history and the movement toward a glorious moment when right will triumph."[9] Though wisdom taught a trust in God's creation that found its secret in the fear of the Lord, and though it connected God and wisdom with the work of creation (in Proverbs 8), some scholars believe wisdom represents a different thought world from what we think of as "the mighty acts of God." Gerhard von Rad describes the separate discourses that resulted: "In the one case, it was a question of stating what was universally valid, of noting general, human experiences; in the other of occurrences which established unique political and cultic facts."[10] Scholars puzzle over the separation between advice on living well in God's world, and the narrative and interpretation of God's saving work.[11] As we will see this would put the sages and the prophets at times in conflict with one another. But given the increasing use of wisdom language and parables (even in the prophets), it is clear the separation was not absolute. And even the sages would surely have endorsed the constant FT testimony: "The Lord is my light and my salvation, whom shall

7. Brueggemann, *Theology of the Old Testament*, 688.

8. Van Leeuwen, "Theology: Creation, Wisdom and Covenant," 1, unpublished paper, 2018 (available at Academic.edu). He notes that it is "creation that makes both wisdom and covenant possible."

9. Crenshaw, *Old Testament Wisdom*, 29. As we have seen, Crenshaw's view is contested.

10. Von Rad, *Wisdom in Israel*, 289. See also Crenshaw, *Old Testament Wisdom*, 29.

11. Penchansky argues that the absence of reference to God's saving acts in Wisdom literature is a silence that needs explanation. But after exploring the various options—that sages didn't know of it, or knew about it but ignored it, even knew and approved from a distance—he concludes, rather unsatisfyingly, that they had other interests and did not feel the covenant was that important. *Understanding Wisdom Literature*, 83.

I fear?" (Ps 27:1). Though the sages' wisdom could not deliver Israel from Egypt, neither was it unrelated to that deliverance, even if the relationship between these was not always clear.

Later, during the Second Temple period (c. 500–100 BCE), wisdom began to be intentionally integrated into the mighty works of God. Peter Schafer points to this integration to argue for wisdom's centrality to Jewish identity. During that period, Schafer points out, Torah went from being instructions to being a book, and Torah scrolls (together with their ongoing interpretation in the Midrash) came to define post-biblical Judaism. Sirach and the Wisdom of Solomon integrate both Israel's sacred history and its sacrificial system into the discourse of wisdom. For Sirach, to fear the Lord also means to honor the priest: "give him his portion, as you have been commanded: the first fruits, the guilt offering . . . the sacrifice of sanctification and the first fruits of the holy things" (Sir 7:31). During this period, Schafer notes, wisdom was even conceived as the literal building plan for creation (one possible construal of the Hebrew in Genesis 1:1 is "by means of wisdom"). Since Israel alone had wisdom and only Israel was given the Torah, she alone could restore a creation disturbed by sin.[12] The later Wisdom of Solomon (mid-first-century BCE) connects God's work, and the presence of the Spirit, even more firmly to wisdom by understanding this as "a breath of the power of God, a pure emanation of the glory of the almighty" (Wis 7:25). The final chapters (Wis 10–19) are an extended commentary on God's deliverance of Israel from Egypt. And in this book one sees the first evidence of Greek wisdom, when learning from wisdom is made to play a parallel role to the curriculum of the contemporaneous Greek gymnasium: discerning the structure of the world, the solstices and seasons, the constellation of stars and nature of animals, but now taught by "wisdom the fashioner of all things" (Wis 17:22).[13] This incorporation of wisdom into the work of God at the end of the FT period prepared the way for Jesus' definitive integration of God's salvation with the wisdom of creation.

However we define the nature of Wisdom literature, Will Kynes suggests we explore the biographies of these texts, discovering how they "live" through their various readers—reading them intertextually with other FT and even NT material.[14] In our discussion we will seek to follow Kynes's advice. What is constant throughout wisdom's history is its connection with the order of creation and its availability for human observation, and

---

12. Schafer, "Wisdom Finds a Home," 38–40. One cannot find a clearer anticipation of Christ's saving work than this intuition.

13 Crenshaw, *Old Testament Wisdom*, 149, 177–78. It is significant, however, that both of these books are deuterocanonical (not usually considered part of the FT canon).

14. Kynes, *An Obituary for "Wisdom Literature,"* 7 and passim.

appropriation. Ben Witherington offers a helpful summary of this consensus. Jewish wisdom, he thinks, is creation theology that teaches that life is good and that creation has a moral structure.[15] Wisdom reflects the deep structure of the created order—the way God made things to work, both at the natural and the social level. As Gerhard von Rad has famously argued, "God makes creation bear witness to himself . . . creation itself has something to say which man [sic.] can hear."[16] This word of God Proverbs portrays as Lady Wisdom calling out (8:22–36). Still, this call had to be worked out; it had to be discovered and explored by the human ability to pay attention to what is there and make something out of this—wisdom throughout was a human project. But whether they realized it or not, it was also a response to the voice of God. This speaking and hearing is expressed clearly in Psalm 19: "The heavens are telling the glory of God and the firmament proclaims his handiwork. Day to day pours forth speech, and night to night declares knowledge. There is no speech, nor are there words where their voice is not heard" (Ps 19:1–3). And as we will see, this calling out, personified by Lady Wisdom in Proverbs 8, in the fullness of time would appear in human form in Jesus Christ.

The Language of Wisdom

Creation speaks to people, but it also speaks through people. On the most basic level linguists have pointed out that language is necessarily grounded in a physical and temporal environment. We speak of getting on top of things, or going over something or feeling beaten down by things—these terms, Mark Johnson has argued, are not simply dead metaphors but expressions of the physical grounding apart from which we could not communicate with each other.[17] It follows that every setting, with its special geography and social network, will give rise to a particular "language"—both literal and figurative, that carries with it the marks of its settings. Here it is relevant to note that, contrary to what is sometimes assumed, there is no culturally neutral metalanguage—Latin, and later French, were not such languages in the past,

---

15. Witherington, *Jesus the Sage*, 112. This has been a consensus of scholars since Walter Zimmerli wrote his influential article over fifty years ago. See "The Place and Limit." "Wisdom thinks resolutely within the framework of a theology of creation" (148).

16. Von Rad, *Wisdom in Israel*, 225. Referring to God's answer to Job in chapter 38 he notes that this is something "factual that happens every day." In preparing this chapter I have been helped by the excellent survey of this literature by Craig Bartholomew and Ryan O'Dowd, *Old Testament Wisdom Literature*.

17. Johnson, *The Body in the Mind*.

nor is English today. Every attempt to understand each other is an exercise in translating meaning from one setting to another. It follows that behind every language is a (unique and different) cognitive network that reflects the special historical and cultural setting in which it arose. And, positively, every language has its own resources, its special cognitive capital, that express its kinship and values, and by which it can bless or curse others.[18]

But language reflects something deeper about the created order, what Rowan Williams has described as its communicative character.[19] From a purely empirical point of view, he notes, scientists have come to see the way the biomass itself is textured in a symbolic network of communicative meaning in which even trees can communicate with each other.[20] Our ordering and orienting ourselves would be impossible apart from this diffused intelligence operative in the world. Language itself would be impossible apart from "the communication of ordered interrelation[ship] and operating as part of a global or rather cosmic system of interacting signals."[21]

This situated, embodied character of human life is important not only at the level of human language and communication, but equally fundamental, at the level of human identity. The human sense of self and its flourishing is invariably related to the place (or places) in which one was born and raised and what one remembers and loves about those places—those multiple connections we described in the first chapter. And, as the First Testament (and, subsequently, modern colonial history) makes clear, when a people is displaced, their sense of identity is threatened; the exile was both a political and existential tragedy for Israel.

Wisdom reminds us that neither religion nor morality carries any human meaning apart from the shape it takes in particular spaces and times, apart that is from the actual practices of loving one's neighbor within a particular geographic narrative. As Willie Jennings notes, moral sensitivities are "space textured."[22] And it is in their particular geographic and cultural space of Palestine that Israel had to learn obedience—their religion was textured by that place. Though their wisdom ultimately had to be understood in the light of God's covenant purposes for Israel, that covenant only made sense in the land where they lived—something they painfully discovered during the exile. Proverbs makes clear that the "fear of the Lord is the

---

18. I owe these observations to Professor David Carlson, a linguist at Africa International University, Nairobi, Kenya (conversation, August 2012). See also Margaret Archer, *Being Human*.

19. Williams, *On the Edge of Words*.

20. See Peter Wohlleben, *The Hidden Life of Trees*.

21. Williams, *On the Edge of Words*, 115–16.

22. Jennings, *The Christian Imagination*, 54.

beginning of knowledge" (1:7); it is "the Lord that gives wisdom" (2:6). But it works the other way too: the one who seeks and finds wisdom, like hidden treasure, will "understand the fear of the Lord, and find the knowledge of God" (2:5). So following the way of wisdom is part of living faithfully in the covenant God made with Israel. As a result it was understandable that Israel should come to feel that they alone possessed wisdom, though the sages in the oldest period knew differently. They recognized that wisdom was also a part of the natural order of things that Israel's neighbors also comprehended—creation was calling out to them too. For example, when Proverbs 5 urges husbands to "rejoice in the wife of your youth" (v. 18), the reason given is that "human ways are under the eyes of the Lord and he examines all their paths" (v. 21). So, husbands, remember your creator and the promises you have made to God. Yet in the very next verse, it is "the iniquities of the wicked [that] ensnare them, and they are caught in the toils of their sin" (v. 22). The results are not only a judgment from God, but they are also the natural consequences of foolish behavior. Israel's neighbors observed and commented on these connections too. Wisdom, wherever it was found, was secular but it was also religious. Wisdom, though a human project, is directional. Not only is "the fear of the Lord the beginning of wisdom," but "fools despise wisdom and instruction" (Prov 1:7). And, as we will see, wisdom can be mistaken: "Sometimes there is a way that seems to be right, but in the end it is the way of death" (Prov 16:25). And "the mouth of fools are their ruin" (Prov 13:7). Wisdom or its lack plays into the trajectories of life or of death that began in Genesis 2 and 3.

Wisdom invariably reflects these trajectories; it is powerless to escape them. This limitation of wisdom calls for special emphasis. Cultural wisdom can tend toward life or death, but only God's redemptive interventions—in bringing Israel out of Egypt and into the land, in the life and work of Christ and the giving of the Spirit—are truly liberative. Only these will bring creation to its intended end and bring about the full redemption of humans and the earth. The sages reflected a deep concern for the poor, but they could not imagine a deliverance that would produce true social justice. From watching the way creation worked, they understood retributive justice, but they knew nothing of distributive justice.[23] But this liberative work, we recall, is tied in the closest possible way to God's original purposes in creation and its trajectories; it enhances true wisdom, it does not overturn it. Because in an important sense the wise person, in paying attention to creation, is listening for the voice of God.

---

23. On this distinction see Bruce C. Birch, *Let Justice Roll Down*, especially chapter 9, "Wisdom and Morality."

Wisdom and the Cultures of the Ancient Near East: Egypt and Babylon

Israel's sages paid close attention to the "voice," the communicative structure of creation, but so did the sages in neighboring societies. Just as God watches and delights in creation becoming itself, so the careful observer of the world finds joy in discovering the way things work. But note that Israel, like every people group, did not know creation in its pristine form—Adam and Eve, remember, had been expelled from the garden. Though Israel spent time in the wilderness—in both testaments a liminal space, a place of testing—the land they finally settled in already possessed layers of culture and civilization. And this exposed them to the wide-ranging traditions of wisdom that were common across the ancient Near East and that were to have profound influence on the shape of the FT and on the people of Israel. This international wisdom was a cultural commodity, von Rad notes, "with respect to which Israel was a recipient and not a donor."[24]

Israel was subject to the influence from two major centers of cultural influence, Babylonia to the east and north and Egypt to the south. This is not surprising. Palestine for most of its history was a minor crossroads that was poor and politically unstable; Babylonia and Egypt during long centuries were the opposite: sophisticated and wealthy—the object of envy and targets of immigration. Egypt was the first state to have a centralized government and its scribes, during the Old Kingdom as early as 2500 BCE, were probably the first in history to create manuals of successful behavior and ethical insights. (Israel's Wisdom literature by contrast dates from the sixth to the second c. BCE, though it surely circulated in earlier centuries in oral form.[25]) Such a manual can be seen in its fullest form in the Wisdom of Ptahhotep, dating from the Old Kingdom, though copied in many subsequent versions. Much of its advice is familiar to readers of the book of Proverbs:

> Do not be proud of your knowledge,
>
> Consult the ignorant as well as the wise;
>
> The limits of art are not reached,
>
> No artist's skills are perfect;
>
> Perfect speech is more hidden than the greenstone,
>
> Yet it is found among maids at the grindstones.[26]

---

24. Von Rad, *Wisdom in Israel*, 9.

25. Gordis, *Poets, Prophets, and Sages*, 161, 162.

26. See J. D. Ray, "Egyptian Wisdom Literature," 17, quote at 19. My comments on Egypt are indebted to Ray's discussion. Following quotes at 19 and 21 consecutively.

4. THE FIRST TESTAMENT TRAJECTORY OF LIFE

Though we don't know much about the fall of the Old Kingdom, it was surely a traumatic experience for Egyptians and led to texts which focused on retribution, as in this Instruction for "Marikare": "To every action there is a response; while generation succeeds generation, the god who knows character is hidden." As the Middle Kingdom gave way to the more expansive New Kingdom, older texts were reedited and new instructions were written. The most famous of these and the most influential on the FT is the Wisdom of Amenemope, an ancient classic (dating probably from 1250–1100 BCE). This wisdom is preoccupied with fate and the possibility of moral responsibility, and its imagery is often compared to Proverbs. The "heated man" is contrasted to the "silent," recalling the fool and wise person, and wisdom's focus on patience; the call to modesty and trust in God resonates with the call of Proverbs to fear the Lord:[27]

> Do not lie down in fear of tomorrow . . .
> Man knows not how tomorrow will be;
> God is ever in his perfection,
> Man is ever in his failure.

What is particularly striking however is the way that a single large section from this work has been adapted and taken over into Proverbs 22:17–23:11—labeled "Sayings of the wise" by modern editors.[28]

The Sayings begin with the typical call of wisdom: "Incline your ear and hear my words, and apply your mind to my teaching" (v. 17). They go on to warn against robbing from the poor (because the Lord pleads their case), associating with hotheads, and removing ancient landmarks, but also contain advice about eating with rulers. But from the outset the Hebrew sages place this advice within their Yahwistic faith:

---

27. Ray notes these references to God appear strange in the light of the fact that Egypt was not, strictly speaking, monotheistic. He thinks they refer to the local god or gods, which could be referred to in monotheistic terms. "Egyptian Wisdom Literature," 24, quote that follows at 25.

28. Modern scholars had long puzzled over Proverbs 22:20 "Have I not written for you thirty sayings," until in 1922 a researcher in the British Museum, while translating the Wisdom of Amenemope, came upon this expression and became aware of the similarities, which were too close to be accidental. Robert Johnston tells this fascinating story in *God's Wider Presence*, 75–76.

Amenemope:	**Prov 22:17–19**
Give thine ears, hear what is said.	Incline you ear . . . for it will be
Thou wilt find it a success.	pleasant if you keep them . . . if all
Thou wilt find my words a treasury of life;	of them are ready on your lips.
Thy body will prosper upon earth.[29]	That your trust may be in the Lord I have made them known to you.

Note the wisdom is taken over wholesale, but, despite its foreign provenance, it is framed, not as a means to earthly success, but as encouragement to trust Israel's God, becoming a part of Israel's (and now Christians') sacred text. God continues to watch and celebrate the human creation becoming itself, not only in Israel but even within neighboring countries.

A similar influence was exerted by the culture of Babylon, the other major power, placed to the east and north of Palestine. Babylonian terms for "wise" and "wisdom," as in the FT, can refer to any kind of skill whether the manual skill of a cabinetmaker or the intellectual skill of scribes and duties to the gods.[30] In fact as W. G. Lambert notes, as in the FT, from this dual base of commonsense observations and religiously derived principles, their "wisdom" developed into a philosophy of life (31). But, as in the FT, when performance of religious duties went unrewarded issues of cosmic justice arose, and theodicy and the futility of human efforts became a common theme of Babylonian wisdom literature—suggesting an influence on both Job and Ecclesiastes. Already in 1700 BC the theme of futility is expressed by Gilgamesh: "As for mankind, their days are numbered,/Whatever they do is wind" (37). This recalls the use of vanity (Heb. *hebel,* wind) in Ecclesiastes, but its usage in Ecclesiastes has this difference: while Babylonian literature suggests sacrifices were probably futile and suicide may be an option, worshipers of Yahweh could not draw such conclusions (37–39). Still the Emar edition of a Sumerian fragment (a thirteenth-century version of an older text) can raise questions that resonate with the Preacher of Ecclesiastes.

---

29. D. Winton Thomas, *Documents,* 176.

30. See W. G. Lambert, "Some new Babylonian wisdom literature," 2. Subsequent pages in the text are to this source.

4. THE FIRST TESTAMENT TRAJECTORY OF LIFE

... The whole of life is but the twinkling of an eye.

The life of mankind does not last forever ...

How is life without joy superior to death?

Overthrow and drive out grief! Despise gloom!

As a substitute for a single day's happiness can one pass

36,000 years in days of silence? (40)

Particularly striking is the appearance of "Siduri," a goddess of wisdom in the Gilgamesh epic who discourages Gilgamesh from his travels in quest of eternal life. Her advice recalls, and almost exactly parallels, Ecclesiastes 9:7–9 (which scholars believe was not written until much later):

	Ecclesiastes 9:7–9
As for you Gilgamesh, let your belly be full,	
Day and night ever rejoice,	Go, eat your bread with enjoyment
Every day have pleasure,	and drink your wine with a merry
Day and night dance and make merry,	heart, for God has long ago
Let your garments be clean,	approved what you do. Let your
Wash your head, bathe in water,	garment always be white; do not let
Look at the little one who holds your hand,	oil be lacking on your head. Enjoy life with
Let your spouse have constant pleasure in	the wife whom you love all the
your bosom.	days of your vain life ...
This is the task (?) [of mankind] (31).	because that is your portion in life and in your toil.

Notice that the Preacher, like the compiler of Proverbs in using Egyptian literature, takes over the full teaching of Gilgamesh, even embracing its paradoxes. As Walter Zimmerli notes, international wisdom is not altered when it is taken into Israelite wisdom—"wisdom has to do with man (*adam*) not with Israel as the people of God."[31] But it is clearly reframed. Notice first the insertion of the claim that "God has long ago approved what you do" (Eccl 9:7)—a clear reference to Genesis 1 and God's invitation to enjoy the good creation. In fact, references to Genesis and creation abound in Ecclesiastes, and it ends with a clear invitation to "Fear God, and keep his commandments . . . For God will bring every deed into judgment" (Eccl 12:13–14).[32]

Lady Wisdom in Proverbs 8

Aside from indicating some relationship with the Preacher, Siduri as the personification of wisdom anticipates Lady Wisdom in Proverbs 8:22–36. Like the woman in Proverbs, Siduri calls Gilgamesh to enjoy the common life he has been given. In neither account is it possible to say whether this is an actual person, a personification, or a hypostasis, but these voices speak with special authority. The verses in Proverbs, however, go further and make the astounding claim that this Lady Wisdom is born of God (v. 25), as Roland Murphy has it, "in a timeless beginning."[33] She is with God as a "craftswoman," verse 30 says, a delight, playing before God all the time: "I was daily his delight," she says, "rejoicing in the inhabited world and delighting in the human race" (8:30–31). As in the Gilgamesh text, the emphasis is on the delight and joy humankind is to know—indeed this characteristic is stressed in Dame Wisdom (expressed four times in these two verses). This delight is spontaneous, and recalls God's judgment at creation: "This is very good!" Moreover, though related to God, and with God in the beginning, the directional focus of Dame Wisdom is toward humans and their activities—"delighting in the human race." What is this play of wisdom to which this "person" calls attention? Murphy argues that this must refer to the whole of the admonitions of Proverbs—that, he thinks, is the only possible connection.[34] The play of wisdom and its delight is the experience of someone who hears and follows the call of wisdom detailed in the chapters of Proverbs. Notice the delight, the poetics, fuels and motivates the hearer to respond with alacrity—it is a call to the heart. But note too the implication of this connection between Babylonian and Israeli wisdom: When Christ took on the role of Lady Wisdom calling

---

31. Zimmerli, "The Place and Limit," 147.

32. Though scholars have suggested that this conclusion, making the connection with the law, was added by a later editor. Robert Johnston, in private conversation.

33. Murphy, "The Personification of Wisdom," 225.

34. Murphy, "The Personification of Wisdom," 225.

out in the market to hear his voice, he was replaying the call of wisdom not only of Israel but also of this gentile neighbor!

Still there is this difference. Though the idea of wisdom calling out, and giving advice has been found earlier in this Babylonian epic, which may have been influential, the call of wisdom in Proverbs does more than urge humility, or simply personify the "world order" (as von Rad puts it).[35] Wisdom in Proverbs 8 is framed as God's personal emissary making explicit the intimate relationship between wisdom and the ordinary life of Israel. And though this intimacy is to be expressed by the joy and delight God desires all humans to know, it was to be visibly displayed in the special calling of Israel. As Roland Murphy summarizes this aspect of wisdom: "She has assumed the burden of the covenant, fidelity to the Lord, in language reflecting the old struggle so mercilessly bared in the book of Hosea."[36] It is as though this intimacy reflects what modern people might call a profound spirituality. But it also reflects the centrality that is given to Israel's human life in God's good world. Lady Wisdom is described here as "rejoicing in [God's] inhabited world, and delighting in the human race" (8:31). As Terence Fretheim summarizes these verses: "Pleasure and playfulness are built into the very structure of things."[37] And their presence is central to the call of wisdom.

The First Testament and Violence

There is a further implication of this incipient spirituality that I want to underline. One of the most troubling characteristics of the FT narrative is the widespread and inescapable presence of violence and incessant warfare—much of it specifically directed by Yahweh during the settlement in Canaan. As one of the most frequently mentioned stumbling blocks of modern people to the biblical narrative as a whole, this must be faced and engaged. There are ways that this has been traditionally understood, either as a justifiable response to the evil practices of the people resident in Palestine, or as an anticipation of God's purposes to bring about justice in the last days (where God causes desolation as a means of "making wars cease to the end of the earth"—Ps 46:9).[38] But for my purpose I would rather point to two significant places where this inclination to violence is challenged: In the Psalms that speak of the righteous king, and in the Prophets' picture of

---

35. Von Rad, *Wisdom in Israel*, 151.
36. Murphy, "The Personification of Wisdom", 226.
37. Fretheim, *God and World*, 217.
38. One good discussion of such responses is Meredith Kline, *Images of the Spirit*.

the new Jerusalem God promises. Both of these are important for their own centrality in FT teaching, but also for the vital connections they sustain to the life and ministry of Jesus.

Among the Psalms speaking of the righteous king, Psalm 72 stands out, as we observed in the last chapter. Though framed as a prayer for guidance of Israel's king, Psalm 72 is understood as an ideal picture of the coming messianic reign that will bring prosperity and peace to God's people (72:3). This is a universal reign (v. 8–11; see also Ps 2:8–12); it is centrally concerned with righteousness (vv. 2–3; see Ps 45: 4, 6–7); and, notably, its concern for the poor is a condition of its prosperity (vv. 2–4; 12–15). But in the center of these characteristics is an agrarian reference not only to abundance but to peace:

> May [the king] be like rain that falls on the mown grass,
>
> like showers that water the earth.
>
> In his days may righteousness flourish,
>
> and peace abound until the moon is no more. (Vv. 6–7)

It is not hard to hear echoes of Jesus' teaching in these verses, both in his parables and his teachings on the abundance of God's provision and the associated nonviolent and forgiving way of living in the world.

But the glimpses offered by the prophets of a time when violence will no longer be accepted as the usual way of settling human difference are equally telling. There are the more familiar passages that speak of the day when, Isaiah writes, people will go up to the mountain of the Lord, who will "judge between nations" so that

> they shall beat their swords into plowshares,
>
> and their spears into pruning hooks;
>
> nation shall not lift up sword against nation,
>
> neither shall they learn war any more. (Isa 2:4)

This promise is reiterated in Hosea 2, where God promises through Hosea that God will "make for you a covenant on that day with the wild animals, the birds of the air and the creeping things of the ground; and I will abolish the bow, the sword, and war from the land; and I will make you lie down in safety" (Hos 2:18). Note the covenant that assures peace and safety is with the earth and the animals, which are also part of God's concern and provision. But later in Hosea there is an image of the heart of God in relation to Israel that offers an even more significant (and poignant) picture of nonviolence. For in chapter 11 one sees the response of God to Israel's ingratitude, one that is willing to suffer pain rather than inflict it. In an image that recalls Isaiah's Servant Song in chapter 53, God speaks through Hosea. Though Israel insists on turning away from God, despite God's tender care and protection, God cannot give up on them. God is bound to them with "bands of love" (Hos 11:4). Though they will suffer at the hands of others, God will not judge them: "How can I hand you over . . . My heart recoils within me; my compassion grows warm and tender. I will not execute my fierce anger; I will not destroy Ephraim. For I am God and no mortal . . . and I will not come in wrath" (Hos 11:8–9). What this revelation of God's heart would eventually mean for human life, Israel could not have known; and the fact they continued to suffer at the hands of their enemies was their doing, not God's. Only with the teaching of the one who came not be served but to serve, not to incite violence but undergo it, would these intimations come to full illumination. The letter of John offers the most trenchant commentary on these verses: "In this is love," John writes, "not that we loved God but that he loved us and sent his son to be the atoning sacrifice for our sins" (1 John 4:10). The result of this love would be a liberation from traditional expectations, and the new possibility of a servant people willing to forgive rather than incite violence, a people who would display a higher order of wisdom that is from above. Though the vision of the prophets was illumined by Jesus' teaching, it was not of course wholly fulfilled; we still wait and pray for full unveiling of that peaceable kingdom.

The Humanism of Wisdom

Throughout this history the human calling to explore and cultivate the earth prevails. Humans remain responsible for their actions, as the prophets consistently taught. God's saving interventions do not relieve humans of the responsibility to care for each other and for the earth. Though God's saving acts do give wisdom a new context and open up new possibilities for its realization, they do not offer escape from the results of folly. Remember, the discovery of wisdom is primarily human work. Though God takes note of it, approves of it, even integrates it into his redemptive actions, responsibility for it has been delegated. The goal of wisdom is life, a full embodied human life. Proverbs 10:17 says: "Whoever heeds instruction is on the path to life, but one who rejects a rebuke goes astray."

Finding wisdom then is, at the same time, finding the life that humans were meant to live. Remember: God, in the first instance, gave over to humans the responsibility of finding this path. A generation ago Walter Brueggemann argued that this was a key element not simply of Wisdom literature but of biblical faith in general. Humans have the primary responsibility for their destiny; they are able to decide responsibly.[39] This is seen throughout the FT, as when God seems to give David a blank check, apparently not bound, Brueggemann thinks, by normal ideas of holiness; and God holds on to the covenant promises when Israel had gone astray, however painful this proved to be for God (cf. Hosea).

This trust in what humans will do, as we saw in the discussion of creation, was present from the very beginning. We noted that God brought the animals to Adam to see what he would call them, and whatever Adam called them, that was their name; God was satisfied. But God also brought the animals to see if they could fill the emptiness of Adam's loneliness that God had noticed. But none of the animals filled this role; Adam was not satisfied. And note that when Eve was brought to him, it was up to Adam to finally declare in a poetic outburst: "This at last is bone of my bone and flesh of my flesh" (Gen 2:23). As Terence Fretheim notes: "The human being, not God, deems what is 'fit for him.' The future of the human race in some basic respect lies in human hands."[40]

Notice the character of mutuality in this process. The careful listening and responding to creation's goodness issued in social and cultural structures—cities, kinship patterns, later, scientific advances, which are subsequently taken up into God's redemptive process. Already in the FT, God appears anxious not only to approve what humans do but to take credit for it! God shares in the human delight in discovery and invention. This is illustrated in a striking wisdom passage in Isaiah 28 that focuses on the patterns of sowing and reaping. God is speaking of the future, and his coming judgment and plans to lay in Zion a cornerstone that will bring about justice. Then he goes on to urge Israel to listen, pay attention: "Do those who plow for sowing plow continually . . . When they have leveled its surface, do they not scatter dill, sow cumin, and plant wheat in rows . . . For they are well instructed: *their God teaches them*" (Isa 28:24, 25, 26, emphasis added). Then later after harvest, he notes: "dill is beaten with a stick, and cumin with a rod. Grain is crushed for bread . . . *This also comes from the Lord of hosts*; he is wonderful in counsel and excellent in wisdom" (vv. 27-29, emphasis added)—even these human skills are a part of God's justice making. But wait, in fact, the farmer did not learn this from God, he learned it from his father, the miller from his mother. But here is the claim: this cumulative

---

39. Brueggemann, *In Man we Trust*, 17-24. For what follows, 46. He argues the influence of Augustine and Luther has been so strong that the church has not developed a proper theology of responsibility (61).

40. Fretheim, *God and World*, 57. He notes that the continuing creation is, in this respect, creaturely as well as divine.

human wisdom is also, at the same time, God's, or, better, it is Dame Wisdom's: "rejoicing in [God's] inhabited world and delighting in the human race" (Prov 8:31). Of course, there was nothing uniquely Jewish about this agricultural wisdom, just as there was nothing Jewish about the Wisdom of Amenemope that the writer of Proverbs borrowed in Proverbs 22. Its reliability reflected the fact that the wisdom God put in creation worked just as well in Egypt as it did in Israel, because all of it "comes from the Lord."[41] And God could rejoice in this wherever it showed itself, because all of it reflected not only the wisdom that God had built into the order of things, but the continued care and nurture that upheld this order. Though wisdom was human work, the created order, and by extension all that could eventually be made of it, was, at the same time, God's work.

The famous parable of the Sower in the Gospels offers a kind of New Testament commentary and even fulfillment of this FT theme. This parable by its placement as the first parable in all the synoptics (Matt 13:3; Luke 7:4; Mark 4:3) is obviously meant to play a central role in the teaching and ministry of Jesus. Jesus recounts a very common agrarian observation, the challenge every farmer faces in their pursuit of a harvest: what might be termed the constraints of "cultivation"—the basic human calling. As if anticipating the discoveries of new kinds of seeds, Jesus celebrates abundance, of good seed, good soil, and the joy of harvest—some thirty, some sixty, some a hundredfold. But here it gets interesting: scholars have pointed out that thirty and sixty might be possible, but a hundred? How do we have ears to hear this prediction? Here Jesus evokes his ministry, and, eventually, his resurrection from the dead that will unveil the hundredfold realization of creation's fertility, an anticipation of the extravagant renewal of the earth itself. This surely was Jesus' ultimate reference of what will grow up out of renewed soil and a renewed people; meanwhile, while we wait, we rejoice and celebrate the thirty- and sixtyfold increases that reflect human wisdom.

The wisdom heritage may have been widely shared, but what Israel made of this common store of wisdom was something special in large part because of the NT fulfillment it presaged. In Jesus' teaching wisdom was taken up into the disciples' covenant faith in a way that reframed and reordered it—just as eventually the kingdom reality would grow up in and through the accepted agricultural wisdom of Palestine. Here we see a pattern that was to be repeated throughout biblical history and beyond. As was seen most clearly in the work and ministry of Christ, though God will embrace human wisdom, God's creative program enhances it and gives it

---

41. See the discussion in Fretheim, *God and World*, 205, where he notes the continuity between regularities in the natural world and those in the human and social world.

fresh meaning—indeed, Christians believe, Jesus' teaching and ministry integrated wisdom into the saving work of God in a decisive way. This fulfillment theme was already evident in God's provision of the law. It is clear that the Law given by God to Moses on Sinai expressed legal imperatives that were widely shared in the Near East. Almost all the Ten Commandments are already evident in Genesis before the law was given to Moses; the law reflected a widespread near eastern sense of the way the world worked—honor God and parents, be faithful to your wife, do not murder or steal, and so on. In other words, these norms simply expressed a part of God's creational purposes that others had discovered and supported, and that God would endorse at Sinai. In giving the law to Moses God was placing on this a stamp of approval. As Terence Fretheim expresses this: "The specific revelation at Sinai . . . is thus seen to stand in *fundamental continuity* with the discernment of the will of God in and through *common human experience*."[42] But what God would eventually make of these instructions would extend their reach in unexpected ways, as our discussion of the Sermon on the Mount will show. God will not leave these instructions as they were. This common human experience now has been ratified and reordered by God's covenant promises and by his deliverance of Israel from Egypt, and, eventually, by the teaching and work of Christ. Something similar happens with the household codes in the New Testament. Often Paul ends his letters by listing behavior he encourages that has been clearly taken over from the Greco-Roman household codes. These were part of ordinary manuals of expected behavior in that culture: Fathers are to behave this way, wives that way, servants must do this, and so on. Their placement in Paul's letters, however, has the result of reframing these common instructions and making them serve the life that Christians are called to live in Christ by the Spirit.[43] This process of borrowing and reframing will become a pattern that I will highlight in the history of the church and that, I argue, is meant to characterize our approach to our own cultural situation. But here is what is already clear in the FT: learning from this biblical pattern, we should not have an overly fixed notion of what God is calling the church to do in any given situation, especially if

---

42. Fretheim, *God and World*, 137. His emphasis. He points out that much human law throughout history has this rooted and dynamic character to it.

43. This has long been recognized by NT scholars. P. H. Towner concludes his summary of the consensus by saying: "Paul's use of the Christian household codes reflects his (and the church's) sensitivity to wider social expectations. Moreover, the emphasis, especially in the Pastoral Letters, on behavior that is visibly respectable and appropriate would seem to imply that the apostle desired the church to meet those social expectations as far as possible." "Household Codes," 419.

this might limit the emergence of something new, indeed something that might herald the coming renewal of all things.

The Poetics of Wisdom

We have noted that the human creative ability to imagine and work toward what does not yet exist figures prominently in the search for wisdom. Moreover, the discovery of wisdom, the paying attention to what is there, results in delight—the same delight that God expressed at the creation and continues to enjoy in watching the human world. This is a delight that every scientist and every creative artist knows well. Such insights suggest that at the heart of wisdom, indeed at the heart of God's purposes for creation, lies what I have called the poetics of wisdom—"rejoicing in [God's] inhabited world and delighting in the human race" (Prov 8:31). People are shaped not only by what they know, but by what and who they love. They are in part products of the affective connections they forge with the created order, their love for the streaks of light at dawn, or the flight of the hawk, or the startling inversion of a Bach adagio. They are formed by the objects of their love and the projects that express this.

Important evidence for this resides in the singular fact that wisdom in the Bible, and indeed in the other cultures we have glimpsed, is invariably expressed in poetry. This is one of the reasons that the Wisdom literature was late in being appreciated in the last century—it fit uneasily with the developing emphasis on the history of Israel. As Robert Alter notes, poetry is not used to tell a story, though the narrative impulse emerges in juxtaposing images.[44] But as he goes on to show, biblical poetry has a special character of emphasis by parallelism, of two or three lines that shed light on each other. Biblical aesthetics is very different from our modern aesthetic sense. Othmar Keel notes that FT images placed in juxtaposition suggest a kind of emotional clash that increases their impact. In the Song of Solomon 4:4, the neck of the beloved is "like the tower of David" and in 6:5, her hair is compared to a "flock of goats, moving down the slopes of Gilead." Her teeth "are like a flock of ewes that have come up from the washing." Keel notes that the tower represents purity, pride, inaccessibility, and strength; hair flows like a flock and teeth speak of purity. All of these associations, experienced by all the senses over long periods and internalized, are brought together in a single

---

44. Alter, *The Art of Biblical Poetry*, 28. Narrative emerges, he thinks, in their minute articulations from one verse to the next. For what follows see 11.

memorable image, or collage of images. Modern images feature surface and finish; FT images present structure and character.[45]

More importantly, poetic images convey deeply felt emotional weight in a way that narrative cannot. Alter notes: "The poetic medium made it possible to articulate the emotional freight, the moral consequences, the altered perception of the world that flowed from monotheistic belief, in compact verbal structures that could . . . seem simplicity itself."[46] The impact of poetry can be seen for example in the way that the story of Job moves from narrative in the early chapters to poetry in later sections. Poetry highlights the stakes that increase as the book goes on, until finally God speaks "out of the whirlwind" (38:1), underlining the authority of the verses that follow in contrast to the conventional wisdom of Job's friends. This progression, Alter notes, expresses the "essential role poetry plays in the imaginative realization of revelation."[47] The poetics spark the response that leads believers to faith and trust, as Jesus indicates in his references to birds and flowers in the Sermon on the Mount.

Biblical scholars have long debated how much of the FT is actually poetry, because the modern distinction between prose and poetry does not always apply. But in any case, Craig Bartholomew and Ryan O'Dowd are surely right in saying, "in the Bible, poetry virtually dominates the OT 'curriculum.'"[48] But why is poetry a central vehicle of the FT story? The ability of poetry to convey deeply felt emotion is part of it, and the call of creation to take pleasure in the fullness of life that results (or lament its absence) is another factor. Humans are formed by what they become invested in, as Jesus' teaching stresses: "For where your treasure is there will your heart be also" (Matt 6:21). And such investments can best be expressed in image and metaphor—treasure, moth, rust, thieves. And the affective character of wisdom reminds us that proverbs and verse were oral performances before they were written down. Reciting wisdom in the market, home, or city gate was made easier and more memorable by its poetic character. Though the precise relationship between the sages and psalmists is unclear, temple musicians often incorporated wisdom materials into their psalms.[49]

---

45. Keel, *The Symbolism of the Biblical World*, 20.

46. Alter, *The Art of Biblical Poetry*, 113.

47. Alter, *The Art of Biblical Poetry*, 87.

48. Bartholomew and O'Dowd, *Old Testament Wisdom Literature*, 54.

49. Samuel Terrien suggests the musical poets who composed psalms were surely friends of the sages and scribes responsible for wisdom materials, though the oral context of both makes the exact nature of their relationship difficult to discern. "Wisdom in the Psalter," 54, 56.

But in their reframing of this body of material, Israel achieved something deeper. Remember that this material has been reoriented when it is finally incorporated into the covenant life of Israel. In this respect the poetry of Israel gestures toward something that poetry by itself can never bring about; it serves a higher purpose. On the one hand this poetry can point out Israel's differences from their neighbors. As Bartholomew and O'Dowd write: "The OT poetry always creates its point of view in distinct opposition to the cultures and religions of Israel's ancient neighbors."[50] Israel's poetry expresses what they call a covenantal urgency: what God is like our God?, Israel's sages asked. On the other hand, and related to this difference, FT poetry is pressed into service to point toward what does not yet exist. As we noted, it embodies the creative imagination reaching for a new world and thus it embodies an implicit response to God. In poetry, language is stretched to evoke what can only be imagined; it is the primary instrument available to humans to remake the world. And in the FT this instrument is eventually pressed into the service of a towering prophetic vision—what God actually promises about the future.

When Isaiah came to express his vision of the future of God's judgment and renewal, only the poetic mode suited his purposes. Indeed, its poetics is expressed as the direct voice of God, one laden with aesthetic language (Isa 66:17–19):

> For I am about to create new heavens, and a new earth;
>
> the former things shall not be remembered or come to mind.
>
> But be glad and rejoice forever in what I am creating;
>
> for I am about to create Jerusalem as a joy, and its people as a delight.
>
> I will rejoice in Jerusalem, and delight in my people;
>
> no more shall the sound of weeping be heard in it, or the cry of distress.

Michael Edwards's fine description of a Christian poetics, which we will explore in the next chapter, applies to this special use of poetry in the FT: "In one way or another the world is absented, so as to be represented and made anew"; poetry is the insistent attempt to use the broken materials available to us, "to deliver a new world out of the loss of the old."[51] Isaiah is drawn to poetry but he is also doing something new with this material.

---

50. Bartholomew and O'Dowd, *Old Testament Wisdom Literature*, 57.

51. Edwards, *Towards a Christian Poetics*, 146, 147. Significantly, he likens this process to one of death and resurrection.

Only poetry can carry such a vision, and only a poetry that is placed into the service of the narrative of creation and renewal.[52]

The Limitations of Wisdom

But the Prophets' particular use of wisdom also, inevitably, calls attention to wisdom's limitations. Though they made use of wisdom forms, and creational imagery, they also displayed at times a distinct distrust of the sages. Isaiah (eighth century) and Jeremiah (sixth century) both offer strong criticism of wisdom teachers. As David Penchansky points out, perhaps when Egypt was an ally one could incorporate Amenemope into Proverbs, but what happens when Pharaoh turns against Israel?[53] Isaiah makes clear what this means: "Alas for those who go down to Egypt for help, and who rely on horses . . . but do not look to the Holy One of Israel, or consult the Lord. Yet he too is wise and brings disaster" (Isa 31:1–2). There is irony in Isaiah's insistence that the Lord too is wise, because Yahweh's "wisdom" will bring destruction. Similarly Jeremiah two centuries on will lament the vain trust in wisdom: "The wise shall be put to shame, they shall be dismayed and taken; since they reject the word of the lord, what wisdom is in them?" (Jer 8:9). As we noted earlier, the one positive portrayal of a wisdom figure in Genesis is Joseph, but his wisdom is attributed to a special gift from Yahweh, who gives Joseph the interpretation of Pharaoh's dreams. For the prophets knew something that the sages often overlooked: that God will bring about the future the prophets saw, just as God, not Joseph, was the one who delivered Israel from Egypt.

Another part of wisdom's limitation became evident in the problem of suffering. Though in general wisdom led to success and foolishness to destruction this was clearly not always the case. As Roland Murphy has pointed out, the Bible consistently relates sin and suffering even if the relation is sometimes mysterious (as in Job), and, at other times, redemptive (as in Isaiah 53).[54] The moral order of creation promoted a general deeds-consequence understanding of human behavior. This was never completely convincing, even if it was never completely abandoned. The

---

52. Meir Sternberg sees this poetic impulse at work even in the narrative sections of the FT: "The biblical narrator is determined to operate as an artist even in the radical sense of courting danger and difficulty where he is most anxious for success as a partisan." As a result he often subordinates "expository to aesthetic coherence, business to pleasure." *The Poetics of Biblical Narratives*, 42.

53. Penchansky, *Understanding Wisdom Literature*, 17–18.

54. Murphy, "Israel's Wisdom", 7.

idea of the holy man who suffers, Murphy writes, hovers over the wisdom tradition like a cloud.[55] This paradox comes to special focus in the book of Job, which surely represents one of the oldest strata of Old Testament traditions—though it was probably composed after the exile. There Job's friends all argue, in various ways, that God would not afflict Job if he were in fact innocent—a straightforward deed-consequence orthodoxy. One can almost hear echoes of Jesus on the mountain: "You have heard it said . . ." But Job knows he is not guilty, and so he confronts God: "The terrors of God are arrayed against me" (6:4); "you have made me your target" (7:20); [God] "has torn me in his wrath, and hated me" (16:9). Who will deliver Job from this vicious cycle of affliction and lament?

There are many voices in Job, and its interpretation remains for many scholars, as Murphy says, a mystery. But it faces squarely the unavoidable fact that, too often, suffering appears in human life to have no discernible rationality. Though in the book Satan is incited by God to afflict Job (2:3), this is unknowable to Job (and indeed to his friends); Job's affliction is, like much evil in the world, a simple fact. So Job is justified in his laments. But there is also an echo, or perhaps a preview, of a liberating initiative in this long book. And it consists in two parts: the first is God's answer to Job in chapters 38 and 39, and the second in the epilogue (42:7-17). Many scholars argue that the book is to be read from the point of view of God's answer to Job in 38 and 39. Job has frequently called for God to hear him and answer, to respond to the charges made against him. And in these two chapters God does respond with evident authority: "Where were you when I laid the foundation of the earth?" (38:4). As creator, God has license to address Job; this voice anticipates Jesus' "I say to you." But there is a further anticipation of Jesus' sermon. God is not only creator but he is provider: "Who provides for the raven its prey, when its young ones cry to God, and wander about for lack of food?" (38:41). Matitiahu Tsevat has argued that making this speech the center allows Job to see that Yahweh's attention is wider than Job's, and, that God's provision is the only possible answer to Job's problems.[56] This alone enables Job to answer: "I had heard of you by the hearing of the ear, but now my eye sees you . . . I repent" (42:5, 6). In a sense these chapters anticipate Jesus' instruction: "Judge not so that you may not be judged" (Matt 7:1). Job has listened but also seen God in a way that reoriented his faith—and it centrally had to do with God's final purposes for creation and God's goodness displayed there. But

---

55. Murphy, "Israel's Wisdom," 12.
56. Cited in Penchansky, *Understanding Wisdom Literature*, 43.

a second liberation is proposed by David Penchansky.[57] He proposes that we read the book in terms of God's final answer to Job's friends in 42:7. There God addresses the friends, the orthodox sages, directly: "My wrath is kindled against you ... for you have not spoken of me what is right as my servant Job has." Offer sacrifice, Yahweh says, because Job has asked me not to deal with you according to your folly. Job has learned to forgive, and so he is rewarded; his friends are chastened but forgiven. Forgiveness then is both an anticipation and embodiment of the new creation glimpsed in these final chapters. Wisdom offers guidance that is often salient; but God alone is the deliverer and fashioner of creation and its future.

These ancient philosophical reflections lead one to wonder: can God approve of all that is written here? Job and Ecclesiastes emphatically leave many large questions unanswered: What meaning does suffering have? Does it have any meaning at all? This surely reflects further the astonishing degree to which God was willing to allow human investigation to go, to the extent of casting doubt on the fundamental meaning of things (Ecclesiastes), or even on God's own goodness (Job). This is like the laments of the Psalms that throw back in God's face, as it were, all God's promises that are implicit in creation and explicit in the covenant: God, you promised good to your people, and I have been faithful. What has happened? Where are you?

David Penchansky has characterized the whole terrain of wisdom materials as a site of conflict. One generation insisted that honesty generally pays off, the next doubted whether this works in practice, still another suggested that God may not even be good. In the later generations doubt and questioning were dominant in the material. But, Penchansky cautions:

> Expressions of doubt should not be confused with unfaithfulness or even sin. For the sage doubt and questions were an integral part of the wisdom enterprise. Without raising questions, even some really fundamental questions, even some *painful* questions, one would never find the truth.[58]

The sages were not only open to ideas from a variety of foreign sources, but they were also was willing to challenge received Israeli wisdom, even assumptions about God's own character.[59] Apparently, no question was off

---

57. Penchansky, *Understanding Wisdom Literature*, 48.

58. Penchansky, *Understanding Wisdom Literature*, 4. Emphasis original. He goes on to point out that "the contradictions in the text are those features that produce the meaning" (8).

59. Inevitably some of what was borrowed was also questionable. As Joseph Blenkinsopp notes, even the opportunistic ethics of Egypt were given "a Yahwistic 'baptism.'" *Wisdom and Law*, 26.

limits; it all could be part of the life of faith Israel came to live. And however ambiguous or even contradictory these elements appear, they were all embraced as part of the (inspired!) biblical canon. God continues to watch creation take shape with patience, and anticipation.

That wisdom incited questions about the reliability of the moral order or its ultimate meaning may, in the end, represent wisdom's most telling limitation—and thus its ultimate contribution. Walter Zimmerli says of the Preacher: "Ecclesiastes is the frontier-guard, who forbids wisdom to cross the frontier toward a comprehensive art of life."[60] Wisdom is not such a comprehensive guide; God needed to intervene, to deliver and to save. This reminded the Israelites that the God who acted with such unpredictable freedom in Job and Ecclesiastes could be trusted. In their worship they remembered how God had taken the initiative in creation, saved Noah's family from the flood, delivered Israel from Egypt, and preserved them during the exile. Because of sin God needed to intervene to finally bring about justice for Israel, interventions that anticipate the new creation. As Terence Fretheim notes, God needed to intercede to assure creation's future.[61]

But, here too, what Israel would make of these interventions was always up to them. God had to wait, to see how Israel would respond to their deliverance. How would they remember this liberation? Would they remember it at all? This is how God's sovereignty works: God invites an obedience that always involves a creative response to what is happening on the ground. And amazingly this creative response is not limited to what is done in the tabernacle or the temple, but extends into what happens in the market and even the bedroom. For the human who has fallen in love with Dame Wisdom and has been attracted by her power[62] learns to take delight in the gifts that creation has made possible, to pay attention to its patterns and colors and play along with them. And this playing along God allowed to help shape the performance and even the texture of the new creation.

Conclusion

From this brief overview what significance can be drawn from this collection of cultural wisdom? Wisdom is an important example of the human

---

60. Zimmerli, "The Place and Limit," 158.

61. Fretheim, *God and World*, 85.

62. Roland Murphy sees the erotic attraction of Dame Wisdom as an important counterforce to the seduction of the loose woman in Proverbs 9:13–18 and in previous chapters. "The Personification of Wisdom," 225. This is made clear in the inclusion of Song of Solomon in the Wisdom literature.

impulse to make human sense of the world—to enjoy its beauty and make something out of this. R. E. Clements points out wisdom's special role is making the world a friendly place, where one can escape taboos and fears of evil spirits.[63] Similarly the development of a method of inquiry in which intention and motives are central certainly did much to prepare the way for religion to be a matter of inward and personal reflection. The juridical guidance of the law could only do so much unless the inward orientation of the person was true. When the wise began to learn the lesson of Job—"Trust in the Lord with all your heart, and do not rely on your own insight. In all your ways acknowledge him, and he will make straight your paths" (Prov 3:5-6)—a new understanding of religion beyond sacrifices and the cult was in view. And, Clements notes, the focus on intentionality comes close to expressing what we think of as will—perhaps in the FT the "spirit" (Heb. *ruah*) comes closest to this.[64] These developments, so important to the New Testament, to say nothing of subsequent Christian history, would not have been possible apart from the wisdom movement of the FT.

The reference to the spirit calls for further elucidation. Throughout the FT wisdom is connected to God in the closest possible way—both a gift of God and, later, identified with the divine Spirit (Wis 1:7).[65] And yet wisdom, as we have stressed, is also a human achievement. One of the characteristic qualities of spirit (Heb. *ruah*) in the FT is the frequent difficulty of distinguishing the activity of the human spirit from God's spirit. As that part of the human person most open to God, the human spirit is the point of contact between humanity and God. So the occasional inability to distinguish divine and human agency is built into the (compatibilist) way God wanted the world to work. This has its counterpart in understanding the dual character of wisdom that we have proposed. Is the wisdom expressed in plowing the soil and reaping wheat a human or a divine work? Well, it is both. Is the call of desire to celebrate the joys of family and marriage merely a human affair, or is it God calling out? Again it is both. This is not to say there is no distinction between such working, but it is to insist that there is no separation. In the pursuit of fully developed human life, God takes an active interest. Nor does this mean that there is no possibility of these agencies being opposed to each other. That human actions, and the social processes these produce, can oppose God and God's work is all too evident in the FT. But the very possibility of the human spirit working

---

63. Clements, "Wisdom and Old Testament Theology," 275. He notes also the role wisdom played in ideas of education, in shaping Israel's literary tradition, even its approach to law.

64. Clements, "Wisdom and Old Testament Theology," 285.

65. Murphy, *The Tree of Life*, 45–46.

with God's spirit anticipates and indeed prepares the way for the more fully developed notion of the Spirit in the NT where, Paul says, "When we cry 'Abba Father!,' it is the Spirit of God bearing witness with our spirit that we are the children of God" (Rom 8:15–16). Here we recall the way the Spirit of God enables human participation even in what is finally God's salvific work, which we highlighted in chapter 2.

A second equally pressing issue is the motivation this study gives to rethink the whole traditional understanding of general and special revelation. In the popular conception these are distinguished by the connection with creation and redemption respectively. But this distinction in the material we have surveyed is often impossible to make; clearly there is a distinction, but no separation. In the first place it is clear that God not only approves of what the Egyptians and Babylonians have discovered about the way creation works, but God has endorsed Israel's practice of borrowing freely and generously from these traditions. Clearly the covenant life of Israel could not have developed or become what it was apart from borrowings of this kind. In this way the gentile nations contributed their gifts to making Israel what it was—and God watched the process with approval and even delight. And this is a process that will continue throughout Christian history. Secondly, we have seen time and again that there is extensive overlap between what humans find and what God has revealed. Where does the one begin and the other end? The wisdom tradition offers little guidance in this respect. So, I argue, a focus on cultural wisdom, as a gift of God that flows from the created order but that reaches beyond this, even to gesturing toward a new heaven and earth, provides a category of integration that allows a more holistic understanding of God's purposes. As we will see, even the redemption that Christ will bring is not in the end something different from what God brought in creation, but rather what the New Testament calls a new (fulfilled) creation. As Terence Fretheim says, "Redemption makes ordinary human life possible once again."[66] Not that they are equated, he notes, but the continuing creative acts, in the wilderness, during the exile, and finally in Christ, are the means, new creation is the end. "*Redemption is in the service of a creational end.*"

But for purposes of this book the conclusion to be drawn from this study is that God has an ongoing interest, even an investment, in what humans make of their world. If God was able to take delight in what Egyptians and Babylonians discovered about things, there is no reason to think that this interest flagged during the Mughal civilization in medieval India, or, say, nomadic culture in present-day Mongolia. In this respect at least

---

66. Fretheim, *God and World,* 125. Next quote is also from this page. Emphasis his.

we do not need to accept that revelation stopped with the biblical period. God's continuing indirect working in and through cultural wisdom continues to this day. We still are called to reframe our culture by the redemptive intervention of Christ. And this, I argue, is what offers motivation and warrant for our own cultural innovations, and encourages our openness to learn from the wisdom of our neighbors. All this merely adds to the glory of the creator and redeeming God.

5. Christ and the Wisdom of New Creation

"All things came into being through him, and without him not one thing came into being. What came into being in him was life, and the life was the light of all people. The light shines in the darkness, and the darkness did not overcome it." —John 1:3–5

WISDOM, WHAT PEOPLE WERE able to discover about the way the world worked, played an important role in the First Testament. The sages took delight in exploring the details of the created order, and puzzled over the mysteries of suffering and frustrated searches for meaning. God watched and approved, and though this wisdom could not provide the substance of covenant promises, it did influence the cultural shape this would take. And it was this culture that would provide the context for the teaching and work of Christ—reminding us that Christians must read the New Testament in the light provided by the First Testament.

When considering the NT development of wisdom, one is confronted with two issues that will be examined in this chapter. The first explores the contribution of Christ's teaching and work to our cultural responsibilities. What cultural practices, if any, follow from Christ's teaching? And from the Christ event? This is a critical question because, as we have seen in earlier chapters, Christians have too often seen the salvation Christ brings as a spiritual deliverance from sin and evil together with the promise of heaven—as though becoming a new creature diminishes our call to heal the earth. But I am convinced that this impulse is deeply mistaken, and I believe the work of Christ and the gifts of the Spirit call us to a deeper engagement with the work of tending and keeping the earth, and thus a closer identification with its joys and pains. This is not to say that Christ's death on the cross did not crucially address human lostness, becoming the new exodus from the slavery in Egypt—redeeming, covering sin, offering ransom and liberation from bondage, all that we call "atonement." But I want to resist *reducing* Christ's life and teaching to this single event. To this end I will develop what

Glen Stassen memorably called a "thicker Jesus" that includes his life, teaching, and miracles alongside his death and resurrection.[1] And this cannot be done apart from the rich perspectives offered by the FT. I will argue that alongside Christ's work as savior, he also opened up a new vision of life in God's good creation—what might be called the social and cultural gifts of the new creation. I offer this reading of Christ's work as a contribution to a more holistic wisdom theology that, I trust, may be allowed to stretch the categories of our received systematic theology.

But there is a second issue that arises when considering the NT treatment of wisdom: granted the NT inherits much from FT Jewish culture, what do the NT writers learn from the surrounding Greco-Roman culture? As we will see, the teaching of Christ rests firmly on the foundation of FT appropriation of their neighbors' wisdom that, in the later period, emerged as a distinctively Jewish wisdom. I will argue that the integration of that wisdom with the saving work of God, attempted during that Second Temple period, was accomplished finally and fully in the person of Christ. Christ as a teacher of wisdom—indeed as wisdom incarnate—in turn determined the structure of Paul's theology as well as other NT writings. But while there are important hints, a full evaluation of Greco-Roman culture is missing from the NT. What emerges initially in the light of the wisdom of Christ are the defects of that culture. As we will see in the next chapter, fuller appropriation of the strengths of classical culture would only arrive later—most influentially in the theology of Augustine.[2]

We recall that creation itself was God's good project intended to develop in ways God was eager to watch. The life of creation involves a forward movement: this is why the true profile of what would become of the image of God had to be worked out in the future—as Orthodox theology stresses. As created, the world was good, indeed its purposes were unspoiled. But as Colin Gunton notes, this was not goodness in the sense of completion. The created order was heading somewhere, and that goal is to be seen most fully in Jesus Christ; Christ opens up a new space and offers time for the creature to work by the Spirit toward creation's fullness. As we noted previously, Douglas Farrow put this even more strongly: with Adam's sin the forward movement of creation was turned backward, and headed in the wrong direction. In this sense Christ had to reorient the

---

1. This is developed in Stassen's last book, *A Thicker Jesus*.

2. It is true that Jewish wisdom had begun to show the influence of Greek philosophy. As Bruce Riley Ashford and Craig Bartholomew point out, "The melding of Greek philosophy and biblical theology had already taken place in Jewish thinking prior to the church fathers." *The Doctrine of Creation*, 58. They give the example of Philo. But the influence of this on the New Testament seems to be minimal.

created order—to change its direction, and in doing so, anticipate the end toward which creation tends.[3]

But how precisely does Christ accomplish this forward movement toward the perfection of all things? I will argue he does this by creating a larger space for God's purposes in creation to be realized and specifying, in his life and teaching, a particular poetics and practice that is to animate that space. As Colin Gunton explains, "Jesus Christ recapitulates our human story in order that the project of the perfection of all things may be achieved."[4] This description of Christ's work underlines the fact that God, in Christ, becomes human and in this way identifies with creation—is present in creation—in a very specific way, one that moves toward fulfillment of God's purposes for creation. As we saw in an earlier chapter, this movement speaks of God's enabling creation to exist and develop in its own way—giving it legitimacy and even eschatological importance. In taking on creation, Christ displays God's love and patience for what was made—Yahweh's presence in, with, and under, life in the created order, allowing it to become what it was meant to be. Further, it was Christ's great work to propose the shape of this forward movement and the pattern of its wisdom by embodying and teaching a new wisdom.

Christ the Wisdom of God

In the biblical account, though eventually wisdom materials were written down, they emerged in the oral give and take of everyday life. Christ's teaching finds its place in just such informal exchanges and it famously took the form of parables (*mashalim*), short aphorisms that were often extended into narratives that form the core teaching of the Gospels. As Ben Witherington reminds us, the unique purpose of the Gospels, as genres of literature, is to serve as "prompts or aids for the living voice and its proclamation."[5] Reflecting their origin as oral performances, these documents were meant to be read aloud in a communal setting. This collection of teaching was the basic source of instruction in the life of the early church. Those who became disciples of Jesus were those who heard and responded to this voice. Here, in the Gospels, Jesus' voice embodies the call of wisdom. Jesus not only employed wisdom forms, but presented himself as the living voice of wisdom—as wisdom in person.[6] It is a consensus of scholarship that Jesus'

---

3. Gunton, *The Triune Creator*, 201, 202.
4. Gunton, *The Triune Creator*, 202. Farrow, "St Irenaeus of Lyons."
5. Witherington, *Jesus the Sage*, 154.
6. Witherington, *Jesus the Sage*, 203–4.

teaching, especially as recorded in Matthew, reflects clearly the female figure of divine wisdom that is described in Proverbs 8:22–31. That enigmatic figure, Lady Wisdom, we recall, is described there as begotten ("possessed") of God, rejoicing before God, delighting in the human race, with God as a master worker in the framing of creation. This figure is frequently portrayed in Proverbs as calling out in the marketplace, perhaps as the sages themselves had done, and, according to the Gospels, it has now appeared in the form of a Jewish rabbi, teaching in the marketplace, to the crowds on the hillside, and addressing a woman at the well. Jesus not only teaches in the forms inherited from the wisdom tradition, but speaks as wisdom personified, with authority, demanding attention. As with the FT wisdom, the one who finds the wisdom Jesus teaches—has "ears to hear"—catches this delight and rejoicing, finds life.[7]

Jesus' teaching has a clear continuity with the FT—and especially Second Temple—traditions of wisdom represented by Sirach and the Wisdom of Solomon (200–100 BCE), but he also develops these in particular ways.[8] In Sirach (also known as Ecclesiasticus) wisdom is associated with the Torah, which now tabernacles in the Holy Temple (Sirach 24:8–12) in ways that anticipate John's reference to Jesus' identification of himself with the temple in John (John 2:19 and see 1:14). The Wisdom of Solomon portrays the reward of the righteous as a reversal of material fortunes in ways that anticipate the Beatitudes of Jesus and recall Mary's "Magnificat."[9]

First, in form, Jesus' teaching represents a prophetic appropriation of the *mashal* (or proverb) into a brief story. Rather than the usual prophetic formula, "Thus says the Lord . . . ," Jesus used these extended parables—they make up 70 percent of his teaching—as a form of indirect communication, saying in effect, this is what wisdom has said and it is also what I am saying. This dialectic becomes explicit in the Sermon on the Mount, when Jesus tells his listeners, "you have heard it said"—what his audience would recognize as traditional wisdom, but then adds, "I say to you"—in other words, "I am saying something about wisdom that you have not

---

7. Witherington, *Jesus the Sage*, 44–45. James Dunn, for example, notes that the fact that Jesus is given a role in creation in the NT is significant in that he is made to play the role previously ascribed to wisdom. Dunn concludes: Jesus as remembered in the synoptic tradition "made a claim . . . which in the event could only find satisfactory expression in the evaluation of this Jesus as 'Wisdom incarnate.'" "Jesus," 80 and 92.

8. Alan Winton has proposed that rather than thinking about the influence of a tradition we think of the NT "using theologically the traditions of the past to express [Jesus'] own understanding of present events." *The Proverbs of Jesus*, 19.

9. See C. T. R. Hayward, "Sirach and Wisdom's Dwelling Place," 38, 39, and Witherington, *Jesus the Sage*, 183.

heard before." So that, scholars conclude, by using this form of teaching he meant to present himself as a Jewish *prophetic* sage.[10]

Second, as well as wisdom taking on prophetic form, Jesus' teaching is placed within a distinct eschatological frame; it is oriented toward the fulfillment of God's created purposes. This was in marked contrast to previous teachers of wisdom (though not it should be noted the Wisdom of Solomon) and it took a form that went beyond even prophetic expectations. We recall Gunton's claim that Jesus' human life represented God's particular identification with the created order, especially in its movement toward perfection. In this sense Jesus' teaching was a prophetic appropriation of sapiential materials in an eschatological mode—that is, oriented toward the future of creation. James Dunn argues that the Gospels present Jesus as fulfilling "in substantial measure," in his ministry, the prophetic expressions of the age to come. And as Dunn recounts what was happening in and through Jesus' ministry, it becomes clear that Jesus, in his life and teaching, "transcended those [prophetic] expectations."[11] This is demonstrated by his casting out demons by the Spirit of God (Matt 12:28), his response to John the Baptist—the blind receive their sight, the deaf hear, and the dead are being raised (Matt 11:5)—and his frequent refrain, "I say to you." These together provide evidence, that, in Jesus' words to the Baptizer, "Wisdom is vindicated by her deeds" (Matt 11:19). That is to say the prophetic expectations are not simply announced, but they are "played out" in Jesus' ministry—in the healing, exorcism, table fellowship with the marginalized, all of which are often connected with wisdom sayings.[12]

A New Way of Seeing and Doing in Jesus' Teaching

Both the style and content of Jesus' teaching and ministry invite us to return to the themes that framed my description of wisdom: poetics and practice. I argue that these themes characterize the intention of Jesus' teaching and the result of his work, his miracles, death, and resurrection. Stephen Barton has argued that it is mistaken to understand Jesus' teaching as a body of knowledge that one must master; rather, he thinks, we should understand it as prompting a new way of "seeing."[13] That is to say, seeing the world in the way Jesus intends leads to a hermeneutic of wisdom, one that construes the world in poetic ways. Barton claims: "Insofar as it attends to what is

---

10. Winterington, *Jesus the Sage*, 155–58.
11. Dunn, "Jesus," 85–86. He calls this the "eschatological plus" of Jesus' teaching.
12. Winton, *The Proverbs of Jesus*, 163.
13. Barton, "Gospel Wisdom," 94. The quote below is also from 94.

hidden, wisdom is a way of seeing which has the potential for being innovative, paradoxical, ironic and subversive." The body of teaching, placed as it is in the context of a life offered in death and given again in resurrection, sparks a perception of the world that is at odds with reigning wisdom, yet, strangely, conversant with that wisdom. Jesus' teaching frequently focuses on seeing and feeling in new ways. This recalls Glen Stassen and David Gushee's insistence, mentioned earlier, that "Jesus emphasized seeing much more than most ethics does, and we believe that ethics needs to become much more self-aware and self-critical about how we perceive. Jesus often taught about how we see, or do not see, what God is doing."[14] They point to Matthew 6:19–23 as advocating this new way of seeing. In these verses Jesus is teaching about having a healthy eye, that is seeing rightly: "The eye is the lamp of the body. So, if your eye is healthy your whole body will be full of light; but if your eye is unhealthy, your whole body will be full of darkness" (Matt 6:22–23). Just before these verses Jesus has spoken about laying up treasures, which has to do with what we see, love, and are drawn to, insisting we should not "store up" (NRSV) earthly treasures that may be stolen or decay, but store treasures in heaven (which in Matthew is the sphere of God's rule, where God's will is done). We pay attention to things, Stassen and Gushee note, based on "where we have invested our money." These treasures are matters of the heart; and Jesus' teaching encourages seeing with pure or healthy eyes the eschatological era that is coming. Notice also that this passage comes just before the invitation to let enjoyment for the birds and the flowers supplant worry, thus drawing attention to the things we delight in and that embody a new order of things because they speak of the care provided by the heavenly father. To enjoy the lilies, or to see our neighbor's need, is to see with "pure eyes"; eyes that are healthy provide an imaginative vision for what God is doing, and enable us to see our city in the light of the new Jerusalem that is coming.

The Sermon on the Mount (Matthew 5–7), in which this reference to seeing with pure eyes is found, is the best place to look for Jesus' emphasis on the practice that follows from the new perception and the affections that result. And these chapters call for extended attention here. The two themes, poetics and practice, make consistent appearances in these chapters and in Jesus' teaching generally. On the one hand there is compelling reference to the beauty of creation and its processes, which figure prominently in his parables. Further, in many of his stories there is a call

---

14. Stassen and Gushee, *Kingdom Ethics*, 411. They note the significance of seeing in the teaching of Jesus and connect this with a central component of their ethical method "passions," which are the "stuff of virtue," citing Simon Harak. Another element of this method is "perception" (64). Following quote at 65.

to celebration and feasting, because the prodigal has come home, or the lost coin has been found. But on the other hand, there is the call to new practices: to the lawyer's answer about the law Jesus says, "Do this and you will live" (Luke 10:28) "Go, and do likewise" he tells listeners after the parable of the prodigal son (Luke 10:37); "Why do you call me Lord, Lord, and do not what I tell you?" he asks the crowd following him (Luke 6:46); and in Matthew 25 those who feed the hungry, clothe the naked, and visit the sick will inherit the kingdom.

Both of these themes are evident in what is arguably Jesus' core teaching, known as the Sermon on the Mount, in Matthew 5–7 (with parallels in Luke 6). In these chapters Jesus pictures the kind of wise living that is to characterize the new order he is introducing. The Matthew passage is set in the context of Jesus' expanding ministry throughout Judea and Galilee, and with reference to the crowds that followed him in these places. Gerhard Lohfink argues that the extended Sermon on the Mount is intentionally placed in this larger context to emphasize that "Jesus has announced the reign of God and made it present in both word and in mighty deeds on behalf of the afflicted members of God's people. In effect, the whole of Israel is assembled before Jesus."[15] Still the disciples are directly addressed in these chapters as representatives who are to hear and do what Jesus says.

This particular audience reminds us that Jesus, in fulfillment of First Testament prophecies and embodying its wisdom, came as the Jewish Messiah to the Jewish people. Though at significant points in his ministry Jesus reaches out beyond this audience—to, for example, the Syrophoenician women (Matt 15:21); the Samaritan woman (John 4); even describing the counter-intuitive "good" Samaritan (Luke 15)—it is primarily to the lost sheep of Israel that Jesus (and his disciples) minister. And significantly, though he can say good, even surprising things about these foreigners and their faith, he directs his strongest criticisms to the supposed leaders of Israel—its rabbis, especially the Pharisees—that is those considered the most zealous followers of the law (Mark 2:18; 7:3). "Woe to you," he tells the Scribes and Pharisees, "for you lock people out of the kingdom of heaven" (Matt 23:13); you are careful to tithe, he tells them, "but neglect justice and the love of God" (Luke 11:42). This points up the drastic expansion of God's purposes for creation and its peoples, as the Apostle John explains in his Gospel: "[Jesus] came to what was his own [or his own home], and his own people did not accept him. But to all who received him, he gave power to become the children of God" (John 1:11). But in Jesus' particular concern for women, the poor and marginalized and even sinners—his practice of

---

15. Lohfink, *Jesus and Community*, 36.

"justice and the love of God"—this expansion overturns even received ideas about religion itself. This becomes clear not in Jesus' litany of "you have heard," but "I say to you," to which we now turn in some detail.

The Sermon on the Mount: A New Wisdom

Beginning with the Beatitudes, the discourse (Matt 5–7) proceeds through a series of triads and concludes with a typical wisdom story about building one's house on a rock—a call to truly hear and practice what Jesus has taught. On one level the starting point of Jesus' teaching here is the conventional wisdom familiar to readers of the FT. Ben Witherington points out clear parallels with Proverbs 1–3, including the discussion of the narrow path, keeping the commandments, dealing with material goods, God's wisdom in nature, warnings about sexual impurity, and above all encouragement to hear the voice of wisdom.[16] But what Jesus does with this conventional teaching, as Glen Stassen has memorably argued, is to reveal the "ways of deliverance" consistent with the new order of things Jesus is introducing.[17] This new form of wisdom however does not overturn the received tradition so much as transform it, as Jesus makes clear at the outset: "Do not think I have come to abolish the law or the prophets; I have come not to abolish but to fulfill" (5:17).

The key to understanding these chapters, Stassen proposes, is to see the arrangement of material into fourteen triads (two groups of seven teachings). Each triad includes [1] the traditional teaching "You have heard it said," [2] the vicious cycles that invariably results from the attempt to follow this wisdom, and, finally, [3] the "transforming initiative" that consists of the new wisdom Jesus introduces (271–72). Stassen points out that the received wisdom doesn't include the imperative, it simply describes what everybody would have understood as the right thing to do. The second element describes the common dilemma of people seeking to do the right thing, and the third part offers a way forward, and an escape from the vicious cycle of human efforts. The Greek verb forms in the first two elements are always indicative; the only imperative in each triad is found in the third and final element. The call of lady wisdom now comes in the form of this new wisdom. Consider for example the triad about anger (6:21–26). It begins "you have heard it was said" followed by the traditional instructions,

---

16. Witherington, *Jesus the Sage*, 356.

17. Stassen's interpretation is laid out in detail in "The Fourteen Triads" and is summarized in *Kingdom Ethics*, 409–26. Pages in the text to follow are to "The Fourteen Triads."

that "you should not murder." But murder of course expresses anger, so that if you are angry, or call someone a fool, in fact you are on the road to murder. Now of course these feelings are common and result in the vicious cycle of anger, insult, and hatred—this is the common human response. But surprisingly the imperative is to "leave your gift at the altar; go first and be reconciled with your brother or sister and then come and offer your gift" (5:24). Your gift will not issue in reconciliation with God unless you are first reconciled with your brother or sister. This advice, Stassen writes, "spells out the normative practice of peacemaking instead of anger or murder" (271). This process of reconciliation becomes a *transforming initiative* delivering us from the inevitable cycle of anger and violence. Significantly throughout these chapters, Stassen insists, "Jesus' teaching should be read not as legalistic prohibition but a pointing the way of deliverance" (277). You have heard that you should not commit adultery, but looking at a woman sparks lust—this is the vicious cycle that simply describes the way things are. Deliverance involves taking drastic action.

Those willing to take the startling, positive action that is necessary—be reconciled; take action against lust; let your yes be yes, and no, no; love your enemies, pray for those who persecute you; watch the birds and flowers as signs of God's care; recognize the log in your eye—are hearing the voice of wisdom, but more than that they will be living out the new order that Jesus represents. But here's the key—by performing these transforming initiatives people will, at the same time, be experiencing God's grace. Such responses, Stassen insists, do not instill "human passivity, but rather delivers them into active participation in God's delivering love" (284). This is true because forgiving our brother and sister, letting debts go, giving to those who ask, express a central subtheme in these triads: that our reconciliation with God is tied to reconciliation with our brother and sister; you can't have the one without the other. This is how the new creation works; it is human work but it will flourish uniquely in the space that Christ's death and resurrection will open up, and that will be facilitated by the Spirit of Christ. Notice that this theme has to do with both enjoyment and sharing of the good things of creation, which God gives generously to all: we give to those in need, we carefully study the way flowers grow or birds are cared for, we ask God for our daily bread, because God intends the needs of all be equally provided for. Beyond this level of basic needs, as Stassen and Gushee write, possessions are "intrinsically insignificant." As Willie James Jennings puts this, Jesus' teaching is really not about possessions or lack thereof at all, but about "reciprocal devotion where followers will give themselves to one another" as they have given themselves to God.[18] In doing this they are discovering the joy and blessing of a new world.

Forgiving, trusting God, enjoying creation's goodness, all speak to Jesus' central concern with a *trustful, patient, nonviolent way of living*. This teaching comes to special focus in reference to the *lex taliones*—the law of retribution. This was a pillar of First Testament teaching intended to put a stop to the endless acts of revenge for wrongs done—it was a prompt in the direction of mercy. Jesus then takes this effort further by urging hearers to (literally) "not retaliate revengefully" (5:39).[19] To illustrate, Jesus proposes that when struck we offer the other cheek, when robbed of our coat we offer our sweater as well, when imposed upon, we go further than one would expect, and so on. This startling advice has the cumulative effect of reducing the pervasive soft and hard violence that characterizes human interaction—all forms of manipulation, subtle pressure, and oppressive structures are exposed and subverted.

In fact, *nonviolence* emerges as a keynote of Jesus' teaching and ministry, something that the early church appropriated in a remarkable way, as we will see. In this day of endless wars, it is important for followers of Jesus to recall his repeated teaching on this topic. Anyone familiar with the Roman Empire knows that fighting and wars were common throughout the empire, indeed emperors gained and consolidated their power almost exclusively by fighting wars. And it seemed common for ordinary people to carry swords. Peter famously had a sword during Jesus' trial and attempted to defend him by cutting off the ear of one of the high priest's slaves (Matt 26:51, cf. John 18:10). Peter here simply reflected the way of the world as he knew it—you threaten me and I will retaliate. Jesus' response was emphatic: "Put your sword back into its place, for all who take the sword will perish by the sword" (Matt 26:52). Later in his appearance before Pilate he explains this nonviolent posture: "My kingdom is not from this world. If my kingdom were from this world, my followers would be fighting to keep me from being handed over to the Jews. But as it is, my kingdom is not from here" (John 18:36). Interestingly, Jesus immediately goes on to claim his credentials as a teacher of wisdom: "I came into the world, to testify to the truth. Everyone who belongs to the truth listens to my voice" (v. 37). The voice of wisdom has called out to all who have ears to hear. Those who love wisdom, belong to it, will listen; Pilate's sarcastic "What is truth?" simply reflects his deafness.

18. Stassen and Gushee, *Kingdom Ethics*, 410–19. Jennings, *Acts*, 39.

19. Stassen and Gushee emphasize that this does not mean not to resist evil at all, but not to resist with violence and revenge, *Kingdom Ethics*, 198. The proposed translation is theirs.

Those who defend violence in the service of truth often point to Jesus' statement in Matthew 10:34: "Do not think I have come to bring peace to the earth; I have not come to bring peace, but a sword." But the consensus of interpreters is that the use of "sword" here is metaphoric, standing for the painful divisions that followers of Christ will suffer. The parallel in Luke 10:51 makes this clear. There Jesus says he has not come to bring peace but division. In both passages the emphasis is on the willingness of disciples to follow Jesus' way of the cross, the paradox of Christian life, that death—self-denial, nonviolence, and forgiveness—is the way to life. The teaching of these verses, then, offers training on living wisely; it is not an instruction for violence.

Similarly puzzling is Jesus' reference to the mission of the disciples in Luke 22. Though before they took no purse and lacked nothing: "Now," Jesus says, "the one who has a purse must take it, and likewise a bag. And the one who has no sword must sell his cloak and buy one" (Luke 22:36). From now on, like Jesus himself, because of the work Jesus will do, his disciples will be considered outlaws. Is this an instruction of the necessity of arming oneself? Joel Green denies such a reading. He argues in his commentary that Jesus is rather warning his disciples that, though they had previously been welcomed, now things would change: they should prepare themselves for hostility, even violence. But the implication that the disciples should respond with literal violence, Green insists, is unthinkable in the context and in Jesus' teaching generally. For only a few verses later when the disciples ask whether they should use the sword, and one of them cuts off the official's ear, Jesus responds immediately: "No more of this," and heals the severed ear (22:51). The sword here as elsewhere, Green claims, is a metaphor for the animosity that followers of Jesus should expect. The disciples' response about having two swords (v. 38), Green says, reflects their dullness, and Jesus' response, "It is enough," his exasperation with their lack of understanding.[20] In spite of their long association with Jesus they were not able to grasp the nature of the wisdom that would be appropriate in the new era that Jesus was bringing about.

New Testament Development of Wisdom

Both Jesus' teaching and work form the subtext of the extended wisdom teaching in the rest of the NT. But it was the Pentecost event that marked the beginning of the new era Jesus' life and teaching opened for his disciples. After the ascension, as the disciples gathered together during one visit to

20. Green, *The Gospel of Luke*, 611–612.

the temple, the Spirit fell on them. At once these distraught disciples began speaking boldly so that Jewish worshippers visiting from around the world—fifteen ethnicities are named!—"heard them speaking in the native language of each" (Acts 2:6). For our purposes two elements stand out. First, this is an empowerment that Peter claims was the fulfillment of God's promise through the prophet Joel that in the last days, "I will pour out my Spirit upon all flesh" (v. 17)—young, old, slaves and free, men and women, shall prophesy. That is, people from all over will announce the coming of a new (and final) era foreseen by FT sages and prophets. They will proclaim what Willie James Jennings calls "a new world order energized by the movement of the Holy Spirit, breaking through on all flesh and destroying social orders."[21] So as death comes through life, the new order comes, Jennings notes, through a collapse of the old order, and the emergence of a new one, where slaves speak and will be obeyed. But the second element to note is this display of power, Peter makes clear, is an embrace of—indeed an emphatic extension of—the ministry of Jesus of Nazareth. Peter describes him as "a man attested to you by God with deeds of power"; this man, Peter goes on so that it cannot be missed, was handed over to death but raised by God, and made both Lord and Messiah (v. 22, 23, 36). Now both the substance of Jesus' teaching and the power displayed in his death and resurrection has in some mysterious way been let loose, first here in the Jewish world, but eventually expanding to the ends of the earth (Acts 1:8). The question we address, then, is what might this event—the new era, centered on Jesus' teaching and work, with relevance to the ends of the earth—mean for the new wisdom Jesus brought? What might this wisdom mean for human culture? And how does the New Testament describe this?

Paul gives an important clue in his designation of Christ as the second Adam. This underscores Christ's connection with creation's purposes, and highlights the fact that the destiny of the first Adam, and the creature more generally, is bound up with Christ. Christ's victory over sin and death, signaled by the resurrection and the pouring out of the Spirit, is bound up, Paul explains, with the renewal of all things (Rom 8). But Paul also stresses that this renewal is carried by the Spirit who raised Christ from the dead, and who will mediate Christ's continuing presence (Rom 8:3–5). Henceforth the work of the Spirit will be intrinsically related to what we have been tracing as wisdom: first wisdom became incarnate in Christ, now enabled by the power of the Spirit let loose on all flesh—the call of Lady Wisdom will be the voice of the Spirit.

---

21. Jennings, *Acts*, 34–35.

5. CHRIST AND THE WISDOM OF NEW CREATION

As we noted earlier, references to the "image of God" outside of Genesis 1 are rare,[22] but now in the New Testament it takes center stage. But now it is Christ who is the true (human) image of God. The worldly gods have blinded the minds of unbelievers, Paul writes in 2 Corinthians 4:4, "to keep them from seeing the light of the gospel of the glory of Christ, who is the image of God." Colossians 1:15 describes Christ as the "image of the invisible God, the firstborn of all creation." And it is into this image that believers are transformed by the work of the Spirit (Rom 8:29; 1 Cor 15:49; 2 Cor 3:18; Col 3:10). As Paul will stress: For those God called "he also predestined to be conformed to the image of his Son" (Rom 8:29). We learn about the image of God then, not only from Genesis, but from the story of Christ. For there we see the true image of God. And this image deals with all the problems associated with our stewardship of the goods of creation, and with our relations, both in the family and the larger society; all that is involved with the fundamental human calling to be stewards and neighbors—to walk wisely. This renewed wisdom has been definitively laid out in the teachings of Jesus.

All of this rests on the radical identification of Christ with the materiality of creation—this "man" (Acts 2:22, Gr. *andra*) that Peter announced was "attested by God." This enfleshment will be the consistent emphasis of the Eastern tradition from Irenaeus to Athanasius and John of Damascus; it is the central condition for the reorientation of creation toward the future. As Douglas Farrow says of Irenaeus's notion of recapitulation, "what the savior gathered up and 'commenced afresh' is the very creation that we are," and that God had prepared for this coming.[23]

New Testament wisdom surely represents something new, but this is also a renewal of all things—what the NT calls new creation, and human wisdom is clearly among the things renewed. It is clear from Jesus' life and work that we cannot redraw the dichotomies between the spiritual and material, and between some form of Christian culture and all other cultures. To be sure, human wisdom as an expression of human creation in God's image is often problematic. The creative impulse that reflects God is always in danger of going off on its own, creating its own visions of the good life. Human wisdom, we recall, can reflect the multiple ways peoples and cultures have appropriated God's good creation, but it can also confiscate this goodness in the service of what we are calling the trajectory of death.

---

22. After Genesis 1, Genesis 9:6 and James 3:9 are the only two appearances of the image that do *not* refer to Christ.

23. Farrow, "St. Irenaeus of Lyon," 343. Farrow goes on to remark this ties creation and redemption together with ties that cannot broken.

We are not surprised that Paul sees serious problems with Greco-Roman culture. The first-century version of this distorted wisdom is clearly laid out in Paul's treatment of wisdom in 1 Corinthians 1, one of the central NT passages on wisdom. There Paul appears implacably opposed to the wisdom of this world. Quoting Isaiah's opposition to the counsel proposing smart alliances with foreign powers, Paul says "I will destroy the wisdom of the wise" (1 Corinthians 1:19 quoting Isaiah 29:14). Rather, Paul says, God has proposed through the foolishness of the cross to save those who are perishing. God has unexpectedly chosen to define life through death, power through weakness, in Jesus Christ, "who became for us wisdom from God and righteousness and sanctification and redemption, in order that, as it is written, 'Let the one who boasts, boast in the Lord'" (1:30–31).

Biblical scholars have debated whether Paul's argument here represents a blanket rejection of human wisdom or a reframing of it within Christ's life and teaching. Richard Hays has argued strongly that Paul offers here a total repudiation of human wisdom.[24] Hays believes Paul draws a stark contrast between human wisdom and the word of the cross, because this word, this logos, offers, he thinks, an apocalyptic vision of something entirely new (114). "Rather than confirming what the wisest heads already know," he argues, "[the gospel] shatters the world's systems of knowledge" (115). Wisdom now lies in the primacy of God's actions, confronting and overturning human wisdom (122). Human wisdom, Hays argues, is necessarily oriented toward self-seeking and death.

But is this Paul's intention? A better reading is to see Paul addressing the particular Greco-Roman distortion of human wisdom, its particular alliance with the culture of death. This reading proposes that the wisdom of the cross that Paul describes is a truly human (and cultural) possibility that is potentially an instrument of life. As David Ford points out, to insist on an absolute disjuncture between divine and human wisdom would make human intellectual activity "competitive" with divine revelation, something we have consistently resisted in this book. As Anthony Thiselton writes: "It is not wisdom as such which Paul attacks, but that which is status seeking, manipulative or otherwise flawed in some way which diverts it from the purposes of God." Further evidence for this lies in the fact that Paul not only makes ample use of wisdom language, but he also employed in positive ways the wisdom of the Greco-Roman culture that he inhabited. Ben Witherington argues that "Paul draws on late sapiential handling of Hebrew Scriptures when he uses the Old Testament to make a point." Witherington goes on to show how Paul makes use of wisdom hymns, language, acts-consequence schema, and creation

---

24. Hays, "Wisdom according to Paul." Pages in the text are to this source.

theology.²⁵ Moreover, almost every one of Paul's letters makes use of Greco-Roman household codes to describe the Christian's calling to reflect Christ, even if these codes are radically reframed within the narrative of Christ's death and resurrection. So it is more consistent with all of Paul's thought to argue that 1 Corinthians 1 reflects a reframing of wisdom within the new eschatological plan of Christ's death and resurrection. This is a wisdom that is from God, one that transforms but does not overturn human wisdom. This is consistent with the final appeal that underlines Paul's purposes here: "Let the one who boasts, boast in the Lord" (1:31).

What is overturned here are the unique distortions that characterized Greco-Roman wisdom: the search for a higher (and secret) knowledge, and the haughty assumption of cultural power and superiority that Roman citizens displayed. What follows in this letter (and in 2 Corinthians) makes clear that Paul did not seek to overturn the wisdom inherent in God's created goodness, even if he did want to remind them that it is God's work in Christ that saves, not wisdom. Still the cross and resurrection, I want to argue, make way for a new kind of wisdom, a vertical wisdom that enhances and transforms all inherited horizontal wisdom. It is a wisdom, as James writes in his letter, that is "from above" (Jas 3:17).

The New Wisdom and Its Greco-Roman Context

While it is clear that Paul was able to adopt elements of his Greco-Roman context, influence in the other direction—from Paul to his culture—was a nonstarter. We can safely say that citizens of Rome found nothing in Paul's description of Jesus' teachings to imitate. This is made clear in his Letter to the Romans, though one has to read carefully to see the contrast (and in fact most modern readers miss it entirely). One who has helped us see this is S. K. Stowes. In his discussion he points out that the issue of self-mastery loomed large as a backstory of Romans.²⁶ In classical Roman ethics, influenced by Stoicism, desires were dangerous, prone to break free of rational control, and goods were limited and in short supply (47). In response, just before the Christian era, Octavian (also known as Augustus), claimed to associate himself with Apollo, and "created an ethic and ideology of imperialism rooted in the ancient ethic of self-mastery" (53). This ideology of self-mastery was subsequently propagated in literature, art, and even religious practice. In marked contrast to the Antony's dissipation in Egypt, Octavian

---

25. Ford, *Christian Wisdom*, 180. Thiselton, *First Epistle to the Corinthians*, as cited in Ford. Quote from Witherington, *Jesus the Sage*, 331.

26. Stowes, *A Rereading of Romans*, 42–82, pages in the text are to this source.

promoted courage and ascetic self-discipline, and promotion of the elites over "inferior" classes—who, like women, were those who "obeyed" (56). Even Jews, Stowes points out, accepted these values and came to offer the law as a means of self-mastery (he thinks Philo adopted these values)—something that Paul confronts in Romans 2. In that chapter Paul argues that since gentiles do the right thing without the law, why do Jews boast in the law? Paul goes on to insist that the dominion of death holds all alike captive; the law is no guarantee of self-mastery. Only the death and resurrection of Christ, and a life modeled after Jesus' faithfulness—"acquiring the capacities of the Spirit" (71), liberates one from sin's dominion (Rom 5:21); only in the body of Christ is a true (and communal) self-mastery available.

It is not hard to see that Jesus' teaching of mutual service and forgiveness would be seen by the Roman elite as an expression of weakness rather than strength. Indeed such prejudices account for the early Roman association of Christians with women and slaves. And this provides the background of Paul's criticism of reigning wisdom in 1 Corinthians 1. There he is emphatic that the cross itself displays a new kind of wisdom. John Barclay picks up Paul's claim and argues that the crucifixion itself, when seen against the backstory of Roman culture, can be understood as a wisdom event.[27] Christ's work located in the midst of the oppressive dominance of the imperial power of Rome links political power with foolishness and wisdom with weakness. The social categories of power and knowledge had colonized the language of wisdom in Greco-Roman culture—wisdom had become a tool of power. In this respect the wisdom of the cross, Barclay believes, is not just an alternative wisdom but an anti-wisdom, "refuting and subverting what normally would be taken for granted. . . . disturb[ing] its claims . . . confront[ing] its hegemony" (5). In the mind of Greco-Roman elites the cross was the epitome of foolishness, associated with slaves to such an extent that it was called "slave punishment" (6). Thus the cross poses the stark contrast between the imperial power of Rome with its privilege and power, and the worthless outcasts represented by what was left of Jesus' followers, so that, Paul is saying, we have to totally rethink our system of values. Jesus' teaching and death is proposing a new way of looking at the world and a new of living and acting in that world (14). But though Paul emphatically rejects this wisdom of self-mastery of the Roman elites, he will insist that the alternative, the power of mutual service, is also a form of wisdom. When he goes on to instruct Roman Christians in chapter 12 to associate with the lowly, not repay evil with evil, approve what is good, feed your enemies, and "do not be overcome by evil, but overcome evil with good" (vv. 14-21), he

---

27. John M. G. Barclay, "Crucifixion as Wisdom." Pages in the text are to this source.

is describing another form of wisdom. Though taken almost verbatim from the Sermon on the Mount, this also resonates with much First Testament wisdom. It is the wisdom incarnated in Jesus and meant now, by the Spirit, to be extended, Acts shows, to the ends of the earth.

But here, in the light of our larger argument, a question arises. We have defined wisdom as something that humans have "discovered" about the created order, but what Paul is developing in these letters is what the Spirit of God has "revealed" to him. But over the course of our journey we have seen evidence that these categories are not mutually exclusive. On the one hand, as we saw in the previous chapter, God is the source of wisdom: "For the Lord gives wisdom; from his mouth come knowledge and understanding" (Prov 2:6 and cf. Eccl 2:26). And on the other hand, Jesus implies that the new wisdom from above is meant to be widely available, even to infants—it is discoverable (Matt 11:25). Clearly the wisdom from above was "revealed" to Paul, but the apostle's unique background and training suggest his own reflections had much to do with what he made—discovered—of this revelation. Moreover, Paul's presentation of this will offer a pattern of human life that would prove to widely influential in subsequent history. And it is this pattern that we want to develop in what follows.[28]

The Cross and Resurrection as Wisdom Events: A New Testament Cultural Vision

The world says in the midst of life we die.

The Christians says, no, in the midst of death we live.

—Martin Luther[29]

We have considered in some detail the wisdom profile of Jesus' teaching because we wanted to resist the impulse to move too quickly to the passion narratives and from there to Paul's explanation of the meaning of Christ's death and resurrection. Removing the passion narrative from its context in Jesus' teaching and miracles (something in fact that Paul himself does not do) risks reducing his death and resurrection to cosmic transactions that have little to do with the social and cultural lives that most people live, leaving us with a thin Jesus. Of course, the Lord's teaching and ministry should likewise not be taken out of the events associated with his death, resurrection, and the gift of the Holy Spirit. Indeed all ethical instruction, any

---

28. I am dependent here on the discussion of these things in Avery Dulles, "Revelation and Discovery." I owe this reference to Robert Johnston.

29. Cited in Oberman, *Luther*, 330.

proper construal of virtues and goals of human life—those central aspects of wisdom teaching—only make sense within some particular narrative that connects them to the creation and its natural processes. Recall that God gave the law on Sinai in the context of God's deliverance from Egypt: "I am the God who brought you out of Egypt, therefore [you should do these things] . . ." (Exod 20:2). The law could only be properly understood in that context of deliverance. And wisdom itself made sense within the covenant story that included this deliverance and God's gift of the land. Similarly, in the NT, Jesus' teaching needs to be integrated into the events of his miraculous birth, his death, and resurrection. In the context of our argument these events should be understood as wisdom events. They are the historical shape given to the teachings, indeed they have been called parable events in the world.[30] The significance of this, I am arguing, is that these events are new creation events; they create the historical space for the church—indeed for everyone—to work out the wisdom that is from above, which Jesus taught and embodied in his work.

But what does it mean to consider the cross and resurrection of Christ historical and social "parable events"? The theological tradition has understood that these events accomplished the redemption of creation—a covering of sin, a defeat of the powers, and the inauguration of a new creation. These truths stand at the center of the Christian faith and its creeds. But what if, in addition, taking these events as historical "parable events" had implications not only for the forgiveness of sins, or for personal and social ethics, but beyond this for the human cultural mandate? What if these events not only created the historical and cultural space for the church to live out a new order, but also provided a pattern for that order that could eventually be instructive beyond the church?

I believe the New Testament clearly suggests such a pattern. In fact I want to argue that these events and their careful New Testament development have enormous implications for our human cultural calling, both for its poetics and its practice. To develop the consequences of this pattern for cultural renewal let me return to the two trajectories of creation: that of bounty and limit, of life and death. In Christ these trajectories are also taken up and lived out. But notice in the Christ story there is a radical inversion of these trajectories, a reversal that changes everything for our cultural engagement. Recall that the original Genesis account starts with life, the fulsome display of fertility and growth. All is perfect except for a limitation and a warning: All goodness is available except for restrictions placed on the tree in the middle—the constraints that enable growth

---

30. See Leander Keck, *A Future for the Historical Jesus*.

and development, and the menacing prediction that eating of the tree of knowledge carries a death sentence. First, creation, life, then, after Adam and Eve disobey, a promised death. Now notice: in Christ this order is reversed, in Christ's life and ministry, in obedience to God, there is first a death, then resurrection life. As Jesus famously put this to his disciples, "If any want to become my followers, let them deny themselves and take up their cross and follow me. For those who want to save their life will lose it and those who lose their life for my sake will find it" (Matt 16:24–25). New Testament wisdom suggests, strangely, that the path to life is through death. If, as Douglas Farrow laments, the fall turned creation in the wrong direction, Christ has now reversed the orientation.

This is, in fact, the way the Gospels tell the story. From the beginning of his ministry Jesus sets his face to Jerusalem, which means he will endure a terrible death on the cross, and be raised on the third day. The story tends to life, but it is a *via dolorosa*, one that leads through death to life. To fully appreciate this however we need to recall the theme of the bounty of God's goodness in creation. Again, rather than beginning the story with the fall and sin, we begin with creation, and its original goodness. Christ came not only to forgive our sins or even to conquer the power of evil, though he did both of these, but he came also to introduce us into the creative life of God, something that is realized by his resurrection from the dead. And this resurrection is not simply a historical event in the past, a lived parable, but, because of the gift of the Spirit poured out on believers, it is an ongoing victory over death and its power in the present. It makes possible a new way of living in a broken creation. New Testament wisdom is a resurrection wisdom. As Paul writes: "Just as Christ was raised from the dead by the glory of the Father, so we too might walk in newness of life" (Rom 6:4). And it is precisely because of this resurrection newness that the transforming initiatives Jesus proposed in the Sermon on the Mount can actually work in peoples' lives.

The Wisdom of the Cross: Nonviolent Service

But how does Jesus' death offer a pattern for human life? And for its poetics? To answer these questions I want to return to the image borrowed from John Calvin that I employed in an earlier chapter. You will recall that the Reformer begins the first book of his *Institutes* with the image of the human person poised as a spectator before the glory and splendor of the created order. All the beauty and splendor of that order have a single purpose: to call that figure, indeed all those who look on this dramatic vista, to the praise of its creator, and to gratitude for its many gifts. In Calvin's telling, though the human fails to offer such praise, and even worships the creature rather than the creator, in Christ that ability to praise and right worship is restored.

But how is this poetic? Indeed, how can death ground a Christian poetic? Michael Edwards, picking up Calvin's appeal, points out that creation, despite its grandeur, fails in its intended purpose; it leaves us stupid. For, he notes, "we have an accumulation of faulty sight."[31] Edwards's description of a Christian aesthetic offers suggestive categories for this aesthetic of death and life. He believes the creativity of religious art begins with darkness rather than light, and moves from darkness toward light. In the artist's work, he argues, "in one way or another the world is absented, so as to be represented and made anew . . . the process, one realizes, is one of death and resurrection" (146). Great art replays, in a different key, Edwards thinks, the biblical impulse to deconstruct a broken order and make it anew. The wisdom of all art with deep religious sensitivities must reckon with the darkness and work, in hope and expectation, toward light. Art's visual impulse derives from this dialectic of unmaking and remaking (207). The process is poetic because in seeking to transform the world, new possibilities of seeing and delight are birthed.

This process of unmaking to make new on Jesus' account reflects the fundamental human calling: it begins by giving up one's autonomy, abandoning a false sense of self-mastery—a dying to self. Moreover, the NT claims this calling emphatically rests on, and is correlated with, the facts of Christ's death and resurrection. It represents the new wisdom of the cross. If as we recall after Genesis 3 the human figure is "turned backward," then the solution is to be turned around, which is the literal meaning of "repentance." Such a turn might allow us to acknowledge and even savor our modest place before creation's splendor and before the loving creator of these gifts. In other words, the human calling, in a broken order, is to turn to God, to live in love and praise before the face of a loving God. This involves, it is already clear, a kind of death. As T. S. Eliot puts this in his "Journey of the Magi":

> . . . this birth was
>
> Hard and bitter agony for us, like death, our death.
>
> We returned to our places, these Kingdoms,
>
> But no longer at ease here, in the old dispensation.[32]

---

31. Edwards, *Toward a Christian Poetics*, 205 and pages listed in the text.
32. Eliot, "The Journey of the Magi," 99.

But here is the relevance for my larger argument. This process involves, I argue, a specific constellation of virtues: humility, patience, and a close and loving observation of the beauty and terror of the world. These comport with the gifts that the New Testament attribute to the Spirit, but they also fulfill and enrich First Testament wisdom of humility, trust in God, and above all a patient waiting for the realization of God's purposes.

The classic passage that deals with Christ's role in this complex of virtues is Philippians 2:5–10—which likely was based on an early Christian hymn. Paul is concerned here that the squabbling Philippians come to a common mind, being "in full accord," as the NRSV translates this. How is this possible? Only when the mind of Christ, the true image of God, determines their way of relating to each other. Christ, who, though he was God, did not think equality with God something to be grasped—exploited. Here the temptation of the garden, explicitly repeated by the devil's bogus offer to Christ, has been reversed. Rather than claiming what was his by right, he was willing to give this up—to take on the form of a servant, become obedient unto death, even the death of the cross. Beyond its reference to the First Testament sacrificial system the cross lays out a clear social and cultural pattern. In Christ's life among us "as one who served" we find an image of what God wanted the first Adam to be and what, by God's grace—that is as a gift—we can become. What is interesting about this passage is the use of the verb "to grasp"—the same word used in the Greek myth of Prometheus,[33] which captures perfectly the contrast Paul expresses here: rather than seeking to claim, like Octavian, what belongs to the gods, Christ who is God gave up his claims and took on the role of a servant, even to death on the cross. But notice that scholars have agreed this passage probably constituted an early Christian hymn, that is, this Christlike way of living was not something believers argued about, but a pattern that moved them to sing. It was about a new way of acting together, but it also became a central part of early Christian poetics.

This first step, then, in the trajectory of life in this new order of things, is that of limit, and of rupture and death—in other words of repentance. In the original account of creation recall that difference is a gift; limits are protections. Day is separated from night; sea from land, a tree in the garden is set apart, to spark the realization that these gifts were a product of God's word and the limits an expression of grace. And then the serpent's conflicting advice distorts the picture introducing a power imbalance that altered the created order. Notice the language prominent in Genesis 3:15–19: enmity, bruising, pain, rule. The way is open for the goods of creation

---

33. See William Lynch, *Christ and Prometheus*.

and the most intimate relationships to become commodities, hostages to power struggles.

But here is the irony: the perennial human inclination is to see these power plays as a means to life, as wisdom, when in fact they lead to death. What the world regards as "knowing how to get ahead" is all a working out of the disobedience of our first parents; "The getting of treasures by a lying tongue is a fleeting vapor and a snare of death" (Prov 21:6). Paul puts this more directly: in Adam we all die (Rom 5:17). We see this death-dealing at work even among Jesus' own disciples, and interestingly, in Mark it is placed in the context of Jesus' prediction of his death.[34] In Mark 10 the disciples begin to wonder where they will end up in the new order that Jesus has announced. James and John want to know if they will continue their special relationship and the others become angry. Such political negotiations have become such a normal part of our life that we are not surprised at this exchange—in fact we see it all around us. But that is just the point, as Jesus indicates: "ordering people around" (v. 42 CEB) is the usual way of gentiles, it represents the world we take for granted—it is our traditional wisdom, our vicious cycle. But that must change, we need deliverance. As Jesus goes on: "but that's not the way it will be with you. Whoever wants to be great among you will be your servant" (v. 43 CEB). And why is this? Because of the cross: "For the Son of Man came not to be served, but to serve, and to give his life a ransom for many" (v. 45). Notice that Jesus gives his most prominent prediction of his death in the context of his reordering human power structures. This is because with Christ's death there will be a new way to think about relationships that reflect a giving up of status, not the pursuit of it, a willingness to suffer rather than to inflict suffering. This is a liberation that is to be celebrated in song and culture.

But Paul makes clear this new way of being is not a deliverance from the struggles of the world, but rather summons us to go more deeply into the yearning of creation for its liberation. One cannot participate in God without sharing in the groaning of creation to be free from decay and death and brought into the liberation of God's children (Rom 8:21). God is often found in the darkness as the mystics have taught us, and among the outcasts and vulnerable. This movement is a deeply theological one: in going deeply into the created order—both confronting its pain and considering deeply the lilies and birds of the field—we are, at the same time, encountering the creator. When fourteenth-century mystic Julian of Norwich marveled that the small hazelnut can survive and grow, God tells her, "It lasts, and ever

---

34. An earlier prediction in 8:31 is also closely connected to the challenge that all who want to save their lives must lose them, they must "say no to themselves" (v. 34 CEB). That is, the death of Christ implies also our death.

shall last, because God loves it. And in this fashion all things have their being by the grace of God."[35]

This Christian imaginary, opened up by the parable events of Christ's death and resurrection, reframes social relations as arenas of mutual service rather than power plays. From the beginning differences were meant to be part of the natural covenant God intended. The devastation of Genesis 3 and the outworking of this in human society introduced the power differentials and resulting violence with which we are familiar. But Christ came to overturn that order of violence and death, making possible for us to have what Paul calls the mind of Christ. Because of this reversal, ethnic and gender differences become gifts to be savored and shared, not problems to be solved. All this seeks to embody the reconciling love of God revealed in Christ in actual social relations. This is possible only because we have learned to see (and enjoy) the world differently, in the light of death and resurrection as the original nonviolent intervention.

The Wisdom of New Creation: The Economics of Grace

After death comes life. Already much in Christ's ministry references the trajectory of the original good of fertility and permission, and recalls God's loving generosity: "Of all the trees you shall freely eat . . ." The Gospel accounts emphasize the openhandedness of Jesus' healing power and his provision—"All the crowd were trying to touch him for power came out of him and he healed all of them" (Luke 6:19); the miracle of the feeding the multitudes with baskets left over; the miracle of the draught of fish that they were not able to haul into the boat. Christ reminds us that the disruption of Genesis 3 did not thwart this richness—the earth still produces its plenty; the rain still falls on the just and unjust. This abundance is a central theme of his teaching because it points to the central events of his life, death, and then life. Even his death, Jesus describes in terms of creation's bounty: "I tell you, unless a grain of wheat falls into the earth and dies, it remains just a single grain; but if it dies it bears much fruit" (John 12:24). After death new life, and much fruit. Our claim is that the resurrection of Jesus and the gift of the Spirit at Pentecost has enabled a new set of cultural practices. The mind of Christ is correlated with a new kind of human relations—nonviolent service. This is a great gift, but we must not stop here. For limiting Christ's work to a renewal of relationships with God and each other leaves out the critical relationship: the human connection to the earth and its goodness. What does Christ's death and resurrection have

---

35. Julian of Norwich, *Revelations of Divine Love*, 88.

to do with these relationships? I want to argue the work of Christ and the continuing presence of the Spirit makes possible new ways of exchanging the goods of creation and even new ways of thinking about those goods. This is the wisdom of a new order: the economy of grace.

Having this new perception of things—the mind of Christ—we are enabled, again, to set about cultivating the earth, working on the trajectory of life. The problem of course is that though the earth still produces its bounty not everyone enjoys it equally. It is appropriated by one or another power; it is distributed as a commodity and becomes a scarce resource. How can this impetus of fertility and plenty be recovered? The New Testament account has an answer: Only by the intervention of the new economy of grace introduced by Jesus Christ, by the power of his resurrection given to the world by the Spirit. Accordingly, central among the signs and wonders in the first Christian community was a new set of practices: "All who believed were together and had all things in common; they would see their possessions and goods and distribute the proceeds to all, as any had need" (Acts 2:44–45).[36]

This impulse reflects something central about Christ's life and teaching: the recovery of the original connections implied in the human creation in God's image. Many traditional societies have a notion of mutual exchange of gifts, where the goods of creation are used to promote community. But as Kathryn Tanner points out, this is not at all equivalent to what God does for humans in Jesus Christ, for though these exchanges continually support communal relations—and there is much we can learn from them—they must be endlessly repeated. In the gospel version of grace, God offers an unconditional gift, even or especially when we fail; debts are forgiven not paid, prodigals are welcomed home not punished, and without boasting or fanfare enemies are blessed and welcomed. It turns out that God's giving outgives—a hundredfold—even the fertility of the created order.[37] Still there is something in this notion of prevenient, undeserving, and profligate giving that suggests a new pattern for human cultural practice.

Frances Young and David Ford have termed this possible graceful exchange a "new economy." And they have argued that this new economy is the organizing metaphor of 2 Corinthians.[38] Further, they proposed that there is an actual connection between real human economies and "the economy of God." The basic argument of the epistle, according to Young and Ford, is that God is the central provider. This is emphasized in key passages:

---

36. Much of the following section appeared earlier in my article "Poised between Life and Death." It has been extensively revised here.

37. Tanner, *Economy of Grace*, 56, 62–63.

38. Young and Ford, *Meaning and Truth*.

2:14 uses the imagery of God leading us in Christ in a "triumphal procession"—such as the emperor processing with the spoils of victory through the streets of Rome; in 5:18 after announcing the "new creation" in Christ, Paul emphasizes "all this is from God"; and in 9:15 he sums up the central argument of chapters 8 and 9, with this doxology: "Thanks be to God for his indescribable gift!" And what is this gift? The overflowing grace of Jesus Christ poured out by the Spirit (1:22; 3:6).

This gift is elaborated in chapters 8 and 9, where the specific connection is made between the exchange of God's grace and the sharing of finances.[39] Based on the argument of chapter 5 where enmity, through Christ's reconciliation,[40] has been replaced with friendship—what Paul calls *koinonia* (partnership, sharing, fellowship)—Paul uses the literal collection he is making among the Macedonian believers for the impoverished saints in Jerusalem as a metaphor for the new economy of abundance that Christ has introduced. The collection (which Paul calls literally *charis*/grace, or gift of grace) specifically subverts the traditional patron-client understanding of benevolence, where specific returns were expected, and even the mutual gift giving of traditional societies. Rather it expresses a new understanding of economic abundance, embodied here in the exchange between Macedonian abundance and the needs of the poor in Jerusalem. In itself this involves a reversal, where a relatively poor area, Macedonia, is asked to support Jerusalem, ordinarily supplied with abundant imperial resources. But this too illustrates that this new economy overturns all normal expectations. Young and Ford comment: "This money seems to function like a sacrament both of the unity of Jews and Gentiles in the Church and the validity of Paul's apostolate in relation to the original apostles in Jerusalem."

But what is the basis of this exchange? It is theological. Paul writes: "For you know the generous act of our Lord Jesus Christ, though he was rich yet for your sakes he became poor, so that by his poverty you might become rich" (8:9), and this means that "God is able to provide you with every blessing in abundance, so that by always having enough of everything, you may share abundantly in every good work" (9:8). The point Paul makes here is that this profound divine identification with human need, in addition to its salvific power, has enormous economic and social implications.

We must be careful not to see this as a text supporting the notion that the gospel somehow promises material blessings. Nothing could be further

---

39 Young and Ford see 1:3–11 and Paul's exultation in chapters 10–12 as also key to developing this metaphor. *Meaning and Truth*, 174, 175.

40. Young and Ford point out that the original meaning of reconciliation (Gr. *katallage*) was an exchange of money, a money lender's profit, or merchandise. *Meaning and Truth*, 176. Quote which follows at 180.

from Paul's intention in this passage. We are dealing here with a mutual exchange of gifts that flows from and reflects the boundless grace extended to us in Christ, and indeed the unconditional giving that characterizes the Trinitarian life of God. Moreover, none of the participants Paul addresses were wealthy by any standard. Indeed the Christians in Jerusalem were in dire straits due to a recent famine; and most Christians in Macedonia were anything but rich. The point, Paul stresses, is not that one should suffer at another's expense, but that through a mutual sharing and the multiplication this allows, all might have enough. As Paul describes this community of mutual benefit: "I do not mean that there should be relief for others and pressure on you, but it is a question of fair balance ['a matter of equality,' CEB, Gr. *isotatos*] between your present abundance and their need, so that their abundance may be for your need so that there may be fair balance [Gr. *isotas*]" (8:13–14). That is the grace of sharing which models itself—replicates and lives off the grace extended in Christ—and is an extension of the resurrection life of Christ (though it also reprises God's provision of manna in the wilderness, as Paul goes on to remind them in 8:15). The gifts of creation find their highest purpose in being offered in the service of one another. The point is to allow the goods of creation to be taken up into a eucharistic offering: blessed and distributed, in memory of the one broken for us—creation offered in the service of communion. This in itself may not constitute an economic program, but it does suggest an impulse that would transform our thinking about the just distribution of the earth's resources.

Here is the significance of Paul's illustration. The reality introduced by Christ's teaching and work is not an abstract or theoretical possibility for human society. Nor is it only an anticipation of the future kingdom at the end of time. Paul's example shows that this work is capable of social instantiation now in this period of history—what Paul calls the end of the age. This is why Paul is able to speak of a new creation, because, in Christ, creation has been renewed. Christ's teaching then is not simply about personal ethics, about making people better, though it does that as well. It is about culture and society, the created order that God made and continues to love. This grace (*charis*) can be made visible, even by people who themselves are not believers in Christ. And further, it can allow us to look at the earth with a resurrection imagination and ask: what if the earth itself can be renewed?

The Wisdom of the Resurrection: Regeneration of the Earth

We have proposed that possessions have to be reconceived as assets in the service of building a community of love and mutual benefit, and that this must come to social expression in an actual economy. But what about our work with creation itself? What if that can be remade? What if we treated the earth not as a possession to be hoarded and exploited, but as a gift to cultivated and shared? What would that look like? Here I want to propose that the resurrection imagination suggests that our cultivation of the earth might move beyond even sustainability, to imagine human projects that are regenerative.

This is a further implication of dying to live that is built into the created order but has been given new importance by Christ's own death and resurrection. In John's Gospel, just after the triumphal entry into Jerusalem on Palm Sunday, Jesus tells his disciples: "The hour has come for the Son of Man to be glorified" (12:23), making a clear reference to his coming passion. But then he goes on: "Very truly I tell you, unless a grain of wheat falls into the earth and dies, it remains a single grain, but if it dies, it bears much fruit" (v. 24). He goes on to tie this to his central teaching that those who love life lose it, but those willing to give it up, keep it (v. 25). Mostly we take this as a metaphor for Jesus' resurrection, but what if we looked at it the other way around? What if it is the fertility of the earth that is foundational, and Christ's new life is not simply an alien intrusion into the created order, but an enhancement and sign of the transformation of that order? If something like this is possible we ought to be able to engage the earth and its processes with a resurrection imagination.

There is evidence again in Paul, in Romans 8 and 1 Corinthians 15, that early Christians had such an imagination. In the former text, Paul specifically connects the renewal of creation with the resurrection of Christ. In Romans 8:11 Paul writes: "If the Spirit of him who raised Jesus from the dead dwells in you, he . . . will give life to your mortal bodies." Only a few verses later he connects this new life to the restoration of creation itself: "The creation itself will be set free from its bondage to decay and will obtain the freedom of the glory of the children of God" (v. 21). In 1 Corinthians 15 Paul famously lays out the implications of Christ's resurrection for our resurrection: "For this perishable body must put on imperishability, and this moral body must put on immortality" (v. 53). But this implies something more: death itself will be "swallowed up" by the victory of new creation (v. 54). And this, Paul says, has great implications for our work: we can be immovable, knowing "that in the Lord, your labor is not in vain" (v. 58). That there is evidence for all these possibilities in our own day we will argue in a later chapter.

Conclusion

To this point my argument has tracked with the general Christian assumptions that this teaching, and this pattern of life, are the special gifts of the Spirit, possible primarily for those baptized into Christ's death and raised by Spirit to "walk in newness of life" (Rom 6:4). But what if this teaching and the imaginative vision it promotes could be influential beyond those believers? What if this wisdom could be embodied in the larger culture? I believe the biblical trajectory of FT creation-based wisdom, and the NT teaching about the new creation that Christ's work anticipates, both open up this possibility. In fact I would put this even more strongly: sacrificing for a needy neighbor, forgiving your enemies, not repaying evil for evil, caring for the earth, represent true wisdom, these are cultural practices that allow people, communities, and the earth itself to flourish. Moreover, places influenced by these ideas are demonstrably healthier than those where violence is the norm. These virtues offer a kind of vertical wisdom from which others can learn, and that often leads people to find their source in the gospel teachings of Jesus. In the Introduction I hinted that in fact virtues of this sort resonate with recent responses to the pandemic, racist violence, and environmental challenges. In a later chapter I will argue that these themes resonate in contemporary Western culture precisely because of the long term influence of the Christian gospel. Nonviolent intervention as a moral strategy, connected to Martin Luther King and Gandhi, may in fact be the most important social innovation of the twentieth century, one that fueled the civil rights movement, and has reappeared in the current Black Lives Matter movement. But for many leaders of these movements the foundation was the life of Christ who came not to be served but to serve. Gandhi learned this not only from his Hindu heritage, but from his careful reading of the New Testament he always carried with him, just as King absorbed this from his Baptist tradition of ministry.

Self-sacrificial and nonviolent service, formation of (economic) communities of mutual benefit, and a regenerative perspective on our bodies and the earth are not completely unknown in twenty-first-century America. One sees variations of such themes in many forms. But, historically, that fact itself turns out to be quite remarkable. As I will argue in chapter 7, the very openness toward such world-changing practices—what might be termed the social capital deriving from long-term exposure to the gospel—may in fact reflect how deeply Jesus' teachings have penetrated into our Western culture. But before thinking about our own time, we need to consider the drastic contrast this New Testament teaching offered to the violent, xenophobic, and misogynistic culture of the Roman empire. To this we turn in the following chapter.

Part Three: Wisdom and Theology in Historical Perspective

6. From Wisdom to Theology in the Early Church

"By His Incarnation, the Word deposited His eternal truth in vessels which history fashions in every period for [those] who must keep it in their hearts and then hand it down in the words their own civilization has taught them."
—Jean LeClercq[1]

IN OUR EXTENDED ATTEMPT to unpack the category of wisdom—our revised version of common grace—to make sense of the human response to God's creation, we have now come to the point when the good news of Christ presented in the New Testament writings (let's call this the gospel) has been launched amidst the wealth and power of the great Roman Empire, and into the larger history of the world. The challenge the early believers would face was how to faithfully live out the gospel, wisely, in this world, and, eventually, how to comprehend reigning political and intellectual currents in light of that good news. During this period what, from a modern perspective, we would recognize as "theology" will begin to emerge—that is the systematic process of understanding God, creation, Christ, and salvation, in light of the values and assumptions of various places and times. We're calling these assumptions the facts on the ground. These facts, or some version of them, confront everyone who seeks to follow God, or indeed, attempts to work out what a good life looks like. They are, for everyone, the starting point of all practical, spiritual, and intellectual projects. They represent the wisdom humans, in various places and times, have made of God's good creation.

In the First Testament, wisdom largely was the human project of seeing clearly and carefully these facts on the ground. From the beginning of the Hebrew Scriptures, we have seen how wisdom played a role in God's purposes for Israel. Wisdom moved them to explore carefully God's world—to see it clearly, and it gave them a language that oriented them to this world. But at least at the earlier stages its connection to the

---

1. Leclercq, *The Love of Learning*, 258.

saving work of God was unclear. While wisdom materials appear in many places in the FT, the main wisdom writings (Proverbs, Job, and Ecclesiastes) contain no direct reference to God's liberating work. Still, what could be learned by careful attention to the way creation worked was both motivated and oriented by the covenantal love of the creator God. As a result, the development of these traditions—wisdom and God's liberating work—exhibited an ambivalent relationship, by turns supportive and opposed, until a constructive integration was attempted in the later Second Temple period. This chapter explores a similar process of integration, in this case between the gospel—God's saving work in Christ—and the facts on the ground in the first centuries of the church.

As we saw in the last chapter, Jesus' ministry picks up on the later stream of wisdom initiated in the Second Temple period; he continues and completes the integration of the saving work of God with FT traditions of wisdom. What is missing as the contour of the gospel appears is any deep interaction with the surrounding Greco-Roman culture. Here it is necessary to remember that though the First Testament writings reflected a period of eight or ten centuries, the New Testament writings were all composed within a single century, and they often refer to events taking place at most a generation earlier. So there was not time for the early Christians to begin the process of exploring and explaining their relationship to the surrounding cultures' wisdom. There are important hints of course: the Apostle John, as is well known, made use of the critical idea of creation by the "Word" (Gr. *logos;* John 1:1, 14) as part of what may have been an early Christian hymn. As Marianne Meye Thompson points out, this is surely derived from the Greek philosophical tradition, particularly the Stoic view of *logos* as the rational principle of the universe. But significantly, as Meye Thompson notes, John's use of the word here more closely resonates with the biblical descriptions of God's creation of all things by God's word (Ps 33:6) and by God's wisdom (Prov 8:27–31).[2] Paul also makes use of Greco-Roman thought and culture in his address on Mars Hill (Acts 17) and in his references to household codes in his letters, but, as with John, these are subordinated to his presentation of God's saving work in Christ. It is the gospel that is center stage in the New Testament. Thus the more appropriate question for a student of wisdom, at this early stage, is not to ask how New Testament writers appropriated Greco-Roman wisdom, but rather to inquire into the cultural implications of the gospel. What might the gospel *contribute* to wisdom? It will be recalled that, in the last chapter, we proposed three such cultural patterns: the social program of nonviolent

---

2. Meye Thompson, *John*, 28.

service, the economy of sharing within a community of mutual benefit, and promotion of the earth's capacity for regeneration.

These—what we might call gospel themes—offer a possible outline of the resources early believers could appropriate to live wisely in their culture. Though one sees Greco-Roman culture in the background of the earliest descriptions of the gospel, it was the Jewish tradition—and Jewish wisdom—that had more direct influence both on Jesus' teaching and its elaboration in New Testament writings. Aside from the not incidental references to the wisdom of this world, which we noted, Greco-Roman culture and thought are not addressed in any systematic way in the New Testament. And though it is not possible here to provide any detailed explanation of how such exploration developed in the first four centuries, in this chapter we explore first the emerging profile of the gospel as a uniquely Christian form of wisdom, and then later the way believers began to appropriate the resources of their context to understand, live out, and communicate that gospel.

Christians in the Empire

The fact that Greco-Roman culture represented a very different way of interacting with God's creation than the Babylonian or Egyptian cultures reminds us that wisdom takes multiple twists and turns over time. As with these earlier traditions, Greek philosophers were offering advice on how a wise person goes about reflecting and living in the world—how to become a lover of wisdom. But since they were adding their own reflections on the nature of God and God's (or the gods') relation to the created order, sooner or later Christian believers would have to come to terms with that wisdom and seek to integrate it into their faith in Christ—or, at least, to distinguish it from that faith. It also important to remember that wisdom is not simply an aggregation of discovery and insight. It is, for better or worse, cumulative. Later sages often build on what went before, as when Plotinus rereads Plato for his third-century Roman world, or when scholars of the Renaissance (1200–1500 CE) appropriate the wisdom of the Greeks that had been preserved for centuries by Muslim sages. But cultures also inherit patterns that prove destructive over time, as when European powers carried medieval notions of holy wars with them in settling the New World. In the Introduction I noted that one of the weaknesses of discussions of common grace is the failure to critically locate characterizations of common grace in their (changing) historical settings. Accordingly in this chapter and the next I will embed my discussion of wisdom in some historical particularities, as modest examples of how we might learn from a critical reading of our history.³

Early Christian Wisdom

In what follows then I want to ask: what became of wisdom after the New Testament period? My thesis is that a particular kind of wisdom developed in the first three centuries that enabled the church to flourish in the face of a hostile and violent imperial political culture. There we will see the gospel, represented by Jesus' teaching and work, offered a unique form of wisdom that responded both to the persistent persecution by the political authorities and to the growing gnostic heresies. With the conversion of Emperor Constantine in the early fourth century, an evolution and a reconstruction occurred in Christian expressions of wisdom. In that critical period new possibilities opened up as theologians began interacting with philosophical traditions in more substantial ways, with the gains and losses those traditions made possible. Rather than attempting any review of that complex and endlessly fascinating later period I will focus on the North African Bishop of Hippo, St. Augustine, and the particular notion of wisdom that he developed. I want to argue that his understanding of human life as a journey of the affections, in his particular cultural (and political) context, represents a new understanding of Christ's work, one called forth both by his reading of Paul's letters and by his Neoplatonic context. From these sources, Augustine was able to shape views of desire and sin that have been influential up to the present. With the Bishop of Hippo, I argue, Christian wisdom has become Christian theology.

Wisdom, remember, in Scripture, is always the human attempt to find life and live wisely in God's good creation. As we have seen, it is always a response to God's work of creation and, now after the coming of Christ, to Christ and the new creation, as these events were laid out in the Hebrew and Christian Scriptures. The work of God, and God's continuing presence in creation and recreation, is always and everywhere the nurturing womb of human wisdom. But the particular circumstances of believers—the facts on the ground—determine the shape that wisdom takes as it interprets the creation and the gospel for its place and time. These facts, remember, are human projects, and similarly, the subsequent shaping of the gospel in light of these facts is also a human project. In chapter 4 we saw that biblical wisdom came in a wide variety of life-forms and media. It was discerned in

---

3. I have sketched briefly what a critical rereading of history might look like, in a general sense, in Dyrness, "Listening for Fresh Voices."

6. FROM WISDOM TO THEOLOGY IN THE EARLY CHURCH

the home and family, among the elders by the city gate, and, eventually, in the royal court where the sages sometimes competed with the prophets for attention. These expressions of wisdom rested on the order and potential of God's creation, and on the Spirit's continuing and active presence there, as their necessary condition.

Similarly when we turn to the development over time of a uniquely Christian wisdom, we need to keep in mind this variety of forms and media. Though in this chapter we now are glimpsing the appearance of "theology" in some developing sense, what we will be tracing is really a new permutation of the search for wisdom, now with the resources embodied in the gospel. David Ford, in his fine book on wisdom, has summarized this connection between wisdom and theology as *Christian Wisdom*. As he notes, throughout history, "God is the One who blesses and loves in wisdom . . . [and] theology is for all who desire to think about God and about reality in relation to God." But, he notes, this wisdom has a wider application than for Christian (or religious) believers, because "the overall meaning and discernment in specific situations involve God."[4] Though theologians intentionally consider God's presence, everyone seeking to live wisely, whether they realize it or not, does so before the face of God. Our journey through the development of biblical wisdom has made it clear that we should think of theology and emerging theological traditions as different ways that believers in their places and times have sought to live wisely and faithfully in light of God's purposes for creation and, later, Jesus' teaching and life and the gift of the Spirit. I want to resist the tendency to isolate theology from the everyday life of people; though theology is talk about God that is based on biblical materials, it is also, at the same time, a human project shaped, in part, with human materials and framed by human perspectives. And as this chapter will show, its human character reflects the fact that theological assertions, even those central to our faith, are always framed in the light of some particular cultural wisdom—some specific facts on the ground. And, in the human search for wisdom, these facts are both ambivalent and inescapable, both assets and liabilities. The gospel always changes the way these facts are seen, but our human construal of that gospel also plays a role in a developing Christian wisdom.

---

4. Ford, *Christian Wisdom*, 4–5.

Patience and Nonviolence in the Early Church: Christian Wisdom before Theology

What shape did wisdom take in the earliest centuries? To get at this we need to recall that the Scriptures of the earliest Christians were basically the First Testament, though gradually collections of Jesus' teaching and Paul's letters began to circulate. These two sources, early Christians believed, preserved the prophetic testimony to Christ's coming (in the FT),[5] and the apostolic witness to his life and teachings (the Gospels and Paul's letters—first orally conveyed and later written down). These two sources were understood as completely consistent with each other. As Christian leaders, first the Apostolic Fathers then the Greek Apologists, wrote down the teachings current in the churches, little by little an unwritten tradition began to emerge that represented the developing consensus about interpreting these two sources. It is to this tradition that one must look for an emerging systematic reflection. During this early period, one is impressed that even for the most reflective of these writers, Irenaeus or Origen for example, the appearance of Stoic or Platonic ideas are mostly incidental (or oppositional); their thinking is primarily dependent on biblical materials.[6] The gospel and Jewish wisdom in its biblical form continued to hold sway.

The surrounding Greco-Roman culture could not be ignored entirely, of course. Anyone educated in the prevailing educational centers would have been exposed at some point to the inherited classical wisdom. This mostly took the form of handbooks that summarized this wisdom, the textbooks of the day. A major source was by a certain Artius, dating to the time of Augustus, which contained "lists of the views of philosophers and schools, summarized and arranged under sub-headings."[7] This focused on questions that today we call science (What causes the Nile, or the tides, to rise? Where is the birds' winter home? What lies beyond the oceans?), but also addressed larger questions such as the existence and power of the gods. Such sources served to keep alive this wisdom for the early Christians and their leaders.

Still, what is most remarkable about this period of history was not the churches' emerging doctrine, but their developing liturgical and communal life. Though initially reflecting the small and struggling communities

---

5. Most early Christians would have read this testament in its Greek version, called the Septuagint (LXX), translated in the second century before Christ.

6. An authoritative description of this process is J. N. D. Kelly, *Early Christian Doctrines*, 29–51.

7. See Grant, "Irenaeus and Hellenistic Culture," 41. Artius was edited by Plutarch in the mid-second century CE.

glimpsed in the New Testament, the Christian church eventually grew until at the beginning of the fourth century it probably numbered between five and six million believers, comprising 8 to 12 percent of the population of the Roman Empire. From the modest beginnings described in the book of Acts, this represents a remarkable rate of growth. There have been many attempts to account for this growth, but a deeply researched reflection by Alan Kreider has argued recently that the most important factor was a lifestyle modeled after the character of God as reflected in Jesus' life and teaching. Kreider argues this teaching led believers to a particular kind of wisdom he calls "patience": a life not given to worry or haste, and a nonviolent and hopeful habitus.[8] This resulted in an emerging social profile—a wisdom—that proved deeply attractive to their contemporaries. Kreider observes that prior to the fourth century we have relatively little detailed information on what believers were taught—their catechesis—before their baptism.[9] It was in the fourth and fifth centuries of course when the great ecumenical councils debated the nature of Christ's deity and humanity, the Trinity, and the role of the Holy Spirit, and confirmed the content—the canon—of the New Testament. By a careful review of scattered evidence of the first three centuries, however, Kreider has put together a short list of what was taught. This is what he found: early believers sought a change in behavior from old habits to those of Christ; one that avoided all kinds of idolatry; sought peace; and above all, was founded on the narrative and the details of Christ's teaching.[10]

This focus on Christ's teachings was to have profound influence on the life of early believers, and eventually on the theological reflection that would develop. But initially it issued in a new kind of gospel wisdom. This could be summarized by saying that for early Christian teachers Christ reflected and taught what the very character of God looked like in human form and this provided a model for believers to follow. Additionally, from their knowledge of the Hebrew Scripture, they knew that the God revealed in Christ was also the creator of all things, and so learning about wisdom involved perceiving the way the world works. This First Testament perspective gave them a particular way of interpreting Jesus' teaching. Recall that central to this teaching in the Sermon on the Mount was Jesus' instructions not to worry, but "consider," reflect on, the birds and flowers (Matt 6:15–33), that

---

8. Kreider, *The Patient Ferment*. He gives the statistics of growth at 8. His description of patience is at 35.

9. As Everett Ferguson notes, by the end of the second century, "the catechumate as an organized, formal institution took shape . . . and 'catechise' acquired a technical sense," but, while there were common themes, during this early period "there was no fixed content to the instruction." *The Early Church*, 2, 21.

10. Kreider, *The Patient Ferment*, 157–59.

is to pay close attention to these—"see how they grow" (v. 28)—a creational emphasis that characterizes Jesus' parables as well. Paying close attention to birds and flowers, watching how they find their food, how they grow and flower, universally has provided aesthetic satisfaction of course. But paying attention in this way does something else: it reflects a letting go of worry, and eventually a trust in the provision of a loving creator. Positioned in the center of his teaching, I argue, this posture represents a complex of virtues that came to characterize Christian living in these early centuries: close perception of life as a means of discerning God's presence and protection, a refusal of anxiety, and a letting go of hatred and violence.[11]

The consistent focus on Christ's teaching led to particular products and treatises that have survived from this period and that reflect both an emerging theology and an early Christian poetics. Prominent among this early work is the careful exposition of Scripture—the First Testament and writings that became the NT—along with a focus on practical Christian living. Of these writings I consider briefly examples of early Christian reflection from the Eastern Church (what we call today Eastern Orthodoxy), an early work by Irenaeus, the hymns of the Syriac Church, and then treatises on patience by Tertullian and Cyprian (and eventually another by Augustine, all from the church of North Africa). We recall from our discussion of creation that the Eastern Church is known for stressing the original good of creation, and this is an emphasis that became visible early in its history. By the end of the first century churches were flourishing in Asia Minor—what is today Turkey—and Syria. The latter, Syriac-speaking churches, were centered in Antioch. These Syriac believers reflected the influence in particular of Matthew's Gospel and the *Didache,* an early collection of teachings that is often a transcription of Matthew's record of Jesus' teaching.

Irenaeus: *Against Heresies*

We begin with Irenaeus of Lyon (125–200), a Greek-speaking native of Asia Minor who spent most of his life as a missionary to the Gauls, in Lyon (in what is now France). His work *Against Heresies: On the Detection and Refutation of the Knowledge so-called* is one of the most important expressions of Eastern Christianity from this period. It was written to defend the gospel against the Gnostic heresy represented by the teaching of Valentinus (d. c. 160). Valentinus taught that ordinary Christians

---

11. It is significant that the core meaning of the Greek word "to forgive" in the NT (*aphiami*) is to let go, or send away, suggesting that letting go of hatred and anxiety reflects a life of trust in God.

needed to achieve additional knowledge that would allow them to move through levels (or aeons) of reality to escape the hold of the material world and join the pleroma—the fullness of God. One can see already in the New Testament the hints of this view when Paul talks about seekers after "knowledge" in 1 Corinthians, or his references to thrones, powers, and dominions in Colossians 1. Irenaeus's response to these heresies in this treatise represents one of the first detailed interactions with the surrounding Greco-Roman philosophical culture. Robert Grant has found evidence of Irenaeus's dependence, in a more general sense, on the handbooks of Greco-Roman culture we mentioned earlier. Grant notes references to art, hunting, natural philosophy, music, and even medicine in *Against Heresies*. But, though Irenaeus did not think his education was mistaken (and he noted his opponents lack of learning), with the Skeptics and Stoics, Grant thinks, Irenaeus "inclines toward skepticism" about this teaching. His interest in this material was more rhetorical than philosophical.[12] Perhaps it was the heretics' appropriation of this tradition that inhibited Irenaeus from making constructive use of what he learned in school.

Valentinus had been a Christian pastor, but when he was passed over as a bishop, he left the apostolic church and formed separate groups of believers that spread rapidly. Irenaeus's response (written about 180), was framed as a "refutation [of Valentinus] with the Lord's words." It constitutes one of the earliest treatises of Eastern theology, reflecting and shaping its sensitivities. Like the treatises on patience that we survey, it emphasizes practical Christian living. As Irenaeus wrote, though no one can measure God's wisdom, "those who obey him always learn that it is he who by himself created and adorned and contains everything. This 'everything' includes us and our world."[13] The focus on the goodness of creation is often reaffirmed, an emphatic response to the escapist teachings of the Valentinians. Famously, Irenaeus argues that God was not without hands to create the world, "For always with him are his Word and Wisdom, the Son and the Spirit through whom and in whom he made everything freely"—the two hands of God. This ensures the material order is good. Since humans are made in God's image, Irenaeus insisted, the very substance of the creature, as well as its pattern, derives from God himself (114).

---

12. Grant, "Irenaeus and Hellenistic Culture," 46–50, quote at 46. Grant concludes: Irenaeus "represents the confluence of Hellenism and Christianity no less distinctly than the apologists do. And he is choosing from the maelstrom of Greek thought what he thinks will adaptable to the Christian religion" (51).

13. "Against Heresies," in Grant, *Irenaeus of Lyon*, containing Grant's translation of the five books of "Against Heresies," 113. Pages in the text are to this source.

His summary of Genesis to Revelation is crowned by a reference to the Spirit of wisdom that founded the earth (referring to Proverbs 3:19 and 8:27–31). Therefore, the Greek father goes on, since the Spirit enables us to serve God in holiness all our days, humans "will see God in order to live, becoming immortal by the vision and attaining to God" (115). Bearing a diversity of gifts "like a well composed and harmonious melody," God's people are allowed to advance through the "economies" toward the sight of God—wisdom constituting for him a new way of seeing. He writes: "For the glory of God is the living man, and the life of man is the vision of God. If the revelation of God by the creation already gives life to all the beings living on earth, how much more does the manifestation of the Father by the Word give life to those who see God" (116).

The gnostic theology of Valentinus represented one of the first expressions of a Hellenized form of Christianity—that is, a Christianity formed under the influence of the surrounding culture. Its distinctive feature for our purposes is the identification of evil with a cosmic ontology— the goodness of the human spirit needed deliverance from an evil material world. The significance of this, as Douglas Farrow points out, is moving sin and evil out of its relational context of God's loving promises in the old and new covenants, and making it part of cosmic order.[14] Irenaeus by contrast speaks of Christ's work of recapitulating the disobedience of Adam in his bodily life, and so reconstituting the creation that "we are." As we will see, a later influence of Platonism will become critical for the theological reflections of Augustine, and indeed for the subsequent Christian tradition. The model of creation's imperfection, capable of forward movement by the Spirit, not its bondage to evil, becomes Irenaeus's most significant contribution to this tradition.

So, Irenaeus concludes, the gnostic claim to a knowledge "superior to the truth" cannot surpass "the wisdom of God by which he saves men" (129). He goes on quote Proverbs 1:21: "At the busiest corners [wisdom] cries out; at the entrance of the city gates she speaks." Against the spiritual journey of Valentinus, Irenaeus stresses the resurrection of the body, and the coming of the New Jerusalem to the renewed earth (138). The focus throughout is on the practical renewal of life in the flesh, and the renewal of creation based on the gospel, issuing in a life of justice and peace. Irenaeus is insistent that Jesus' teaching, which he believes he is handing down as it was given to him, provides the basis of his refutation of Valentinus.

---

14. Farrow, "St Irenaeus of Lyon," 336. Farrow notes, "If the created world is *inherently* flawed, it can only be rejected or done away with" (336, emphasis original). Subsequent quote at 343.

Syriac Church: Odes of Solomon

From the developing worship life of Syriac churches during this same period, a collection of hymns survives that reflect the early Christian complex of virtues: exhortation toward a peaceful, trusting life that walks in the way of truth. These hymns, called the Odes of Solomon, were written over the course of the second century. Recalling the Song of Songs, they translate that sensitivity into a Christ-centered mode, portraying the incarnate Lord as both savior and model. The collection begins: "The Lord is on my head like a crown" (1.1).[15] And hymns soon focus on God as creator of wisdom: "He who created wisdom is wiser than his works" (7.8). From this grounding in the creator as Lord, the Odes move to celebrate God's work in Ode 16, what could be called a New Testament-inspired Psalm:

> (1) As the occupation of the plowman is the plowshare, and the occupation of the helmsman is the steering of the ship, so also my occupation is the psalm of the Lord by his hymns.
>
> (2) My art and my service are in His hymns, because His love has nourished my heart, and His fruits He poured unto my lips.
>
> (3) For my love is the Lord; hence I will sing unto Him.
>
> (5) I will open my mouth, and His Spirit will speak through me the glory of the Lord and His beauty
>
> (12) And He fixed the creation and set it up, then He rested from His works.
>
> (13) And created things run according to their courses, and work their works, for they can never cease nor fail.
>
> (10) And the worlds are by His Word, and by the thought of His heart.
>
> (20) Praise and honor to His name. Hallelujah.

These hymns constitute paeans of praise; each one ends with a shout: "Hallelujah." Significantly, like the New Testament itself, the odes offer theological reflection in an aesthetic mode: in the form of hymns sung in worship. Centuries before the careful doctrinal definitions the relations of the Trinity are clearly laid out in poetic form:

---

15. James H. Charlesworth, "The Odes of Solomon." The translation of the Odes is his. Numbers are of the Odes and their sections.

> A cup of milk was offered me,
>
> and I drank it in the sweetness of the Lord's kindness.
>
> The Son is the cup, and the Father he who was milked,
>
> And the Holy Spirit she who milked him. (Ode 19:1–2)

The Spirit here takes on the image of Lady Wisdom, who urges believers to "walk in the knowledge of the Lord, [so that] you will know the grace of the Lord generously, both for his exultation and for the perfection of his knowledge" (23.4). Here, appropriately, knowledge is connected with the practices of praise sung in worship; wisdom is a fruit of liturgy. Though often ignored in the study of theology, this early Christian poetry surely had a widespread influence in that region, even on the sensitivities reflected in the Quran, and it resonates with the later medieval mystical writings.[16]

An Emerging Practical Theology of Patience

During this early period pastoral concerns focused on strengthening these early communities, and providing defenses against gnostic heretics and the developing persecution, but, with some notable exceptions, they offer little in the way of formal theological reflection. Alan Kreider points to another lacuna among early Christian writers: no treatises survive on evangelism, mission, and church growth. Still, he notes, the church continued its amazing growth. What accounts for this? Kreider proposes one answer: What almost all early leaders did write about was, oddly enough, "patience." "Arguably," Kreider concludes, "a significant reason for this growth was the Christians' patience."[17] As evidence for Kreider's claim we examine briefly work by Tertullian (c. CE 200–203) and Cyprian (c. 256), and later compare these with Augustine's work on this topic (d. 430). Interestingly, all three come from North Africa. More particularly, Tertullian and Cyprian come from the indigenous Berber population of that region, suggesting this early Christian wisdom reflected learning from indigenous wisdom as well as from Christ's teaching.

Tertullian is known for his controversialist writings—as in his challenge "What has Athens to do with Jerusalem?"—but appears in this treatise on "Patience" as a quiet, careful thinker and pastor. Converted later in life, around 197 (he was born c. 150), he subsequently joined the radical

---

16. The fluid boundaries between Islam and Syriac Christianity is described in Michael Philip Penn, *Envisioning Islam*.

17. Surveyed in Kreider, *The Patient Ferment*, 13–36, quote at 36.

sect known as the Montanists, which have sometimes been compared to modern-day Pentecostals. But he wrote his treatise on patience between 201 and 203, before making that move.[18] Though the passionate Tertullian admits at the outset that patience is "a virtue that I am utterly unfit to practice" (1.1), he is emphatic that "patience has been given such prominence in matters pertaining to God that no one can fulfill any precept or perform any work pleasing to the Lord without patience" (1.6). It is the highest virtue possessed supremely by God who sheds light on all and "by his patience [God] hopes to draw them to himself" (2.3). As we have noted above, God displays a particular patience in the unique relationship to time expressed in Christ—his birth, maturing over time, bearing reproach, suffering temptation and death, which Tertullian describes in detail (3.2–4). Jesus showed patience, Tertullian notes, even in the healing of Malthus's ear, thus cursing "for all time the works of the sword" (3.2). Patience is the mother of mercy and obedience (4.5).

Impatience then must come from God's adversary (4.3), Tertullian reasons; the origin of evil is especially shown in the first disobedience (4.7). Thus, Tertullian goes on, "what sin previous to this sin of impatience can be imputed to man?" (5.13), leading as it does to murder, hatred, and greed. In what is surely one of the earliest reflections on the origin of sin and evil, Tertullian concludes: "Impatience is, as it were, the original sin in the eyes of the Lord. For . . . every sin is to be traced back to impatience" (5.21). Echoes of Christ's Sermon on the Mount are everywhere: revenge belongs to the Lord, do not judge, blessed are the peacemakers, all of which Tertullian sums up by noting "nothing undertaken through impatience can be transacted without violence," which brings its own destruction (10.8), while patience forgives seven times seven and gives hope because of the resurrection (12.1). Patience, like love to which it is connected, is a theological virtue, as Tertullian concludes: "When the Spirit of God descends, patience is his inseparable companion" (15.7). Such teaching in the context of the frequent persecution of Christians, was not an idle proposal, but an embodied call from Lady Wisdom.

That this became an accepted part of Christian teaching becomes clear when we see what use Cyprian, a North African bishop, would make of it half a century later. Cyprian wrote "The Good of Patience" (257) during a wave of persecution that began around 250 with an imperial edict that required everyone to offer sacrifices to the Roman gods in the presence of a state official. Cyprian would himself suffer martyrdom only a year later. Many of the basic ideas from Tertullian are developed in a highly original, if

---

18. Tertullian, "Patience." Chapters and verses of this treatise are noted in the text.

convoluted, manner. He laid out his pacific views in a famous letter accompanying this treatise: "We do not contend on the subject of heretics, with our colleagues and fellow Bishops we keep with the divine harmony and the peace of the Lord."[19] Cyprian's originality is evident from the very first paragraph of the treatise when he observes that the word of God and the way of salvation are only "effectively learned, if one listens with patience to what is being said" (1). Patience then is an embodied practice that underlies everything that Cyprian will teach in this treatise. Like wisdom itself, it is performed, as Cyprian goes on to say: "We . . . beloved brothers, are philosophers not in words but in deeds . . . we do not speak great things but we live them" (3). As with Tertullian, patience comes from God, who gives to all in abundance (5): "whoever is gentle, patient and meek is an imitator of God (5)," Cyprian says, quoting Matthew 5:43–48. Patience makes possible all the other virtues. Cyprian goes on to connect patience to the trajectories of life and death—patience partakes of the directionality of wisdom. For patience not only makes possible the good, but it repels what is evil (15). Patience encourages turning the cheek, forgiving seven times seven, by offering a shelter from the clamor of life:

> For if a Christian has withdrawn from the fury and contention of the flesh as from the storms of the sea, and has now begun to be tranquil and gentle in the harbor of Christ, he ought not to admit into his heart either anger or discord, for it is not right for him to render evil for evil or to hate (16).

Impatience meanwhile is connected to sin, an "evil of the Devil" (19). Adam was impatient, indeed the Jewish people were impatient and faithless; but we should not avenge ourselves but await the vengeance of the Lord for which the martyrs cry out (21). So "let us think of [Christ's] patience, beloved brethren, in our persecutions and sufferings" (24). One senses the loving voice of a pastor urging believers along a particular spiritual path, one that Jesus had taken and urged upon his followers. We don't know in any detail how these treatises were received, but the growth of the church gives some sense of their attraction and the spiritual community they made possible.

---

19. The basic question that tormented the church was the question of rebaptizing those baptized by heretics, something Cyprian opposed. Cyprian, "The Good of Patience." Cyprian's letter is quoted from the introduction, 258. Numbers in the text are chapters noted in this source.

War and Nonviolence

As one strand of evidence for what this emerging poetics meant in practical terms, I want to consider briefly the Christian attitude toward war and violence during this early period. Over the last century there has been a vigorous debate between those who argue Christians have from the beginning of their history supported war—or participation in killing in defense of the state, and those who felt this was initially forbidden.[20] In general, however, most scholars concur that, though it was never understood in an absolute way, Christians felt participation in state-sanctioned killing was forbidden. John Driver, though recognizing exceptions, concludes: During this period "no Christian writer, to our knowledge, approved of Christian participation in warfare."[21] Clearly, by the beginning of the third century there were Christians serving in the army, though often in roles that did not involve killing, reflecting a growing diversity of views. Still, Origen's views were typical of those Driver surveys. That theologian, writing early in the third century, insisted that the church could perform its priestly role in society only through nonviolence, and that Christians must resist evil by "spiritual resources of prayer and non-violent resistance." This led to the strong tradition of steadfast endurance and resistance without doing violence to evildoers that was central in Jesus teaching and in the treatises we have reviewed. There is little doubt that in this respect as in many others, things were to radically change in the fourth century when Christianity became not only an approved faith but, soon, the dominant religion of the Empire. The Synod of Arles (CE 314), called by Emperor Constantine, allowed that, for the good of all, Christians may accept civil appointments, or join the army as noncombatants (though some Christian leaders objected even to this at the time). But, inevitably, attitudes gradually changed, until in 416 a ruling required all soldiers must be Christians; by this time, nonviolence was relegated to clergy and monks.[22] For a variety of reasons, by the early fifth century Christians had come to a mutual accommodation with the powers of the Empire.

---

20. The debate and issues are surveyed in Alan Kreider, "Military Service." He summarizes early attitudes: "The theologians of the Pre-Constantine church vigorously, and with considerable unanimity, forbade killing in its many guises" (424).

21. Driver, *How Christians Made Peace*, 14, 20, Origen quote at 47. Driver notes the situation was complicated by the fact that serving in the Roman army required offering sacrifices to the Roman gods, so resistance to serving might have reflected opposition to idolatry rather than to killing.

22. Driver, *How Christians Made Peace*, 73–75.

Still there can be little doubt that the impulse to patience in the face of evil, and a prejudice toward humility and nonviolence was the default mode of Christian wisdom in the Roman Empire during the early centuries. And equally clear is the source of these impulses in the widespread emphasis on following the teachings of Christ. Many of these early pastoral treatises, like Jesus' teachings themselves, were designed to instill—to prompt—a certain structure of feeling expressed in the complex of virtues we have surveyed. What holds people together—or indeed what separates them—in communities and families are deeply embedded structures of feelings. From the tradition of biblical wisdom as interpreted by Jesus, this involved a trusting and caring response to the goodness of the earth as evidence of God's presence and love, and an openness and solidarity with others in a community of mutual benefit. On the biblical account this was the purpose God had in mind for the human community.

Constantine and the Imperial Church

Following the famous vision of Constantine of the cross during the battle of Milvian Bridge in 312, the Emperor issued the Edict of Milan, which formally recognized Christianity.[23] This was to result in major adjustments in the church in its attitude toward culture. Still, initially at least, much of the humble lifestyle we have described continued to characterize Christian communities, and it even found its way into Constantine's household. Lucius Lactantius (260–325), who was later appointed by Constantine to tutor his son Crispus, had written in his *Divine Institutes* that empires are inherently aggressive and grow only by robbery and violence. Followers of Jesus, he argued, must abandon wealth and power; if killing is wrong how can there ever be a just war?[24]

A further piece of evidence for this continuity with earlier sensitivities lies is the development of the iconography of Christian art. In the early period, reflecting the poetics we have described, sculptors in the third century focused on images or symbolic portrayals of Christ as the good shepherd, or the salvation symbolized by Jonah's deliverance—often in the mode of Greco-Roman styles. But what is interesting is the way Christian artists adapted

---

23. The church historian Eusebius is the source for the vision. Kreider discusses the process of Constantine's attraction to and acceptance of Christianity and his eventual baptism just before his death in CE 237, in Kreider, *The Patient Ferment*, 251–53.

24. Lactantius's work is described in Karen Armstrong, *Fields of Blood*, 154. Lanctantius was one of the first Christian writers to use classical rhetoric in the manner of Cicero.

and even subverted these classical styles after the conversion of Constantine. A previous generation of scholars, represented in particular by Andre Grabar and Ernst Kitzinger, argued that artists simply continued to borrow from their imperial surroundings and portrayed the story of Christ with imperial iconography: Christ is the new emperor, and he reigns over all as the earthly emperor reigns over the earthly political system. In other words, artists simply sought to contextualize Christ's work within the dominant imperial structure. But more recently Thomas Mathews has challenged this view, pointing out that, while there are some superficial similarities, there is an important contest being carried on, what he calls a "clash of the gods." Artists were able to shape the pagan forms in a way that showed Christ challenging not only the power of the emperor, but that of all other mediators of spiritual power. Moreover, they did this in a way that pointed in particular to Christ's humility, in contrast to the trappings of power displayed by the emperor. These artists actually subverted the expectations set up by the contemporary imagery. In contrast to the coming of the emperor in splendor, for example, Christ comes into Jerusalem riding on a humble donkey, sidesaddle (a decidedly nonmilitary, even feminine, posture), making the lowly ass a collaborator of God's work.[25] Though contemporary forms—the artistic facts on the ground—are appropriated, they are adapted to express the Christian understanding of Christ's work.

In fact, according to Mathews, this processional model of Christ entering Jerusalem is the closest thing to a program of imagery in the early church. Early Christians would have been familiar with military and imperial processions in their daily lives. But now processions were being appropriated to serve a new Lord and express a new journey. In the construction of church spaces and the images they contained—which would have been very public and visible to people—everyone was being invited to join the procession of saints and heavenly beings and bring their gifts into the church and lay them at the feet of the savior. As the tradition of the Eastern (or Byzantine) Church developed, this processional theology was central both to the liturgy and to the artistic program. These reflect then both the inherited artistic forms and traditions and the developing Christian sensitivities.

---

25. Mathews, *The Clash of Gods*, 41, 43, 48. Mathews notes there were at least twenty-eight sarcophagi depicting Christ's entry into Jerusalem. Many of the later images show Christ riding sidesaddle. I have elaborated this history in more detail in my *Visual Faith*, chapter 2, from which this account is drawn.

Augustine: Greco-Roman Wisdom and Theology

It is not our purpose to explore and evaluate all the effects that resulted from Christianity's integration into late Roman imperial life. But to continue our focus on early Christian wisdom, we consider finally the case of Augustine of Hippo (CE 354–430), converted at age thirty-three, ordained priest at thirty-six, and made bishop in North Africa at age forty-one.[26] His massive theological output represents one of the first attempts to achieve a synthesis between the gospel and the cultural values and assumptions of his time. Augustine's contribution was to make constructive use of the inherited religious and philosophical language—to shape the Christian gospel in the categories of his day. His challenge was to provide a Christian reading of the Neoplatonic tradition and Plotinus and to propose an accompanying Christian behavior in light of empire.

To understand his constructive synthesis, we must consider briefly Augustine's biography.[27] In many ways Augustine's spiritual journey may be described as a search for wisdom. He was brought up with the ancient learning of Roman culture represented by Cicero and the Stoics, a *paideia* (formation) expressed in courtesy and self-control that would shape much of his understanding of Christianity. In his *Confessions* he recalls the impact of Cicero's advice not to study this or that sect, "but to love and seek and pursue and hold fast and strongly embrace wisdom itself, wherever found."[28] Later he would integrate this search for wisdom into a framework shaped by his reading of the Platonists. Because of his classical formation, it was a great disappointment when, early in his life, he was directed by Christians to seek the meaning of wisdom in Scripture. What he found there reflected nothing of the "cultivated and polished" virtues he sought.[29] But when a group of Manichaean missionaries arrived in North Africa he was immediately attracted to their radical dualism of the kingdoms of light and darkness, where light attracted the spirit upward and the corrupting force of the physical and the material pulled the person down, and he soon became a "hearer" of this faith.

Though Augustine's conversion is dramatically portrayed in his *Confessions* as an illumination sparked by reading Romans 13:14, "Put on the Lord Jesus Christ and make no provision for the flesh," the implications of this

---

26. Augustine's continuing influence on the Western Christian tradition may justify this focus, but, regrettably, it leaves out a number of representative thinkers from the Greek Eastern tradition that might also have been considered.

27. The best introduction to his life is Peter Brown, *Augustine of Hippo*.

28. Augustine, *Confessions*, 39. The quote is from Cicero's *Hortensius*.

29. Brown, *Augustine of Hippo*, 42.

for reflection on his context emerged over time. When he came to Milan, where his conversion took place (c. CE 387), he encountered the Christian Platonists and began to read Plotinus (CE 205–270). Their views replaced the radical dichotomy of the Manichaeans with an active sense of God, the highest being "processing" outward, with its corollary of the human response "turning inward." In his late imperial context, it was impossible for Augustine not to be attracted by this philosophical framework.[30] As Peter Brown points out, this Platonic framework was as natural to his time as the idea of evolution is to ours—its thinkers represented the intellectual "aristocrats."[31] It was from the perspective of this background formation that, after his conversion, he began his own reading of Scripture and made his constructive contribution to a theology of sin, desire, and virtue.

As we have seen, earlier church fathers were ambivalent about the contribution of classical sources; Augustine was one of the first to make constructive use of them. Peter Harrison has argued that this ambivalence reflected the fathers' "affirmation of the ends of philosophy, but skepticism about the means."[32] As Pierre Hadot has pointed out, the universal goal of classical philosophy was the formation of learners into a communal "way of living."[33] Augustine felt that goal reflected God's providential presence in this tradition and thus he was one of the first to claim Christianity represented the "true philosophy" that formed believers into a new moral community. This advance of Augustine, best represented by the monastic community and order that he founded, was one of his most consequential contributions to medieval Christianity. Harrison goes so far as to say that Aristotle's idea that the highest human activity was contemplation (*theoria*) was "subsumed by the Christian contemplative tradition, and his three speculative sciences found themselves mapped onto the three stages of mystical theology (*purgatio, illuminatio, unitio*)."

Augustine's struggle over desire and enjoyment as morally formative led to both his deepest and most enduring insight, and the one that has sparked consistent critique. For Platonists the life of the senses was not evil in itself. But the very quantity and insistence of these drives threatened to keep one from the contemplation of God. After his conversion through his

---

30. In the *City of God,* Augustine wrote that God had revealed the truths these philosophers taught. He says of them: "they have declared that God himself, the creator of all things, is the light of the mind, which makes possible every acquisition of knowledge" (VIII.9.311).

31. Brown, *Augustine of Hippo,* 98.

32. Harrison, *The Territories of Science and Religion,* 40–41. Quote later in the paragraph at 42.

33. Hadot, *Philosophy as a Way of Life.*

study of Scripture, Augustine came to see that it was in the experience God's love and his own love for God—as both attraction and bonding—that the secret of desire was to be found. This experience offered him the terms of a Christian interpretation of the Stoic search for the good life and the Platonist taming of desire. During this time Augustine began work on his manual of doctrine, *On Christian Teaching* (CE 395–406), where he develops further his views of desire. In Book I of this treatise, he described the journey of the Christian life: We are on a journey to God, he tells his students, but it is not a physical journey from one place to another, but a journey of the affections. On this pilgrimage we need the character and integrity that we can only get from the wisdom made flesh in Jesus Christ, who offered a "pattern for living," a wisdom made accessible to us via the foolishness of preaching. This wisdom and pattern represents both our homeland and our journey to that homeland. For Augustine this tour on the journey of the affections involved a single-minded attachment to the truth of Christ and a growing ability to love all things in God and God in all things.[34]

Augustine's conception of this lifelong pilgrimage he develops from Jesus' teaching in Matthew 22:37–40 (you shall love the Lord with heart, soul and mind and your neighbor as yourself), but also from the tradition of moral formation represented by classical philosophy. The centrality of this love guiding the affections challenged the eudaimonism (the search for the good life) that he inherited from the Stoics. As Nicholas Wolterstorff points out, for the Stoics the only thing worthy of love is oneself, or better one's own virtue.[35] Augustine here develops and transforms the worldview he inherited from the Stoics and Plotinus: complete virtue is not sufficient for happiness. The problem with eudaimonism, Wolterstorff points out, is that it is agent-oriented, and it was only Augustine's encounter with Christ that liberated him from this fixation on self-mastery.[36] This liberation also freed him to love others as created and loved by God. As Wolterstorff put this, our concern for the physical well-being of family and friends "is not to be ascribed to our fallenness but to our created nature. God made us thus. To try to undo this dimension of ourselves . . . is to try to undo the work of the Creator." The love of self and neighbor then, is not simply the love

---

34. Augustine, *On Christian Teaching*, 12, 13, 25, 34–35.

35. Wolterstorff, *Justice*, 194. He notes that the Stoics did not refer to love in these terms, but with Augustine's argument in mind, he thinks "that is surely the right way to describe it" (194).

36 Wolterstorff, *Justice*, 194–204, quotes which follow at 199 and 360 respectively. Wolterstorff will go on to argue that it was this liberation that allowed the notion of humans as valued and loved by God, and therefore having certain rights, to develop in subsequent history—something that today we take for granted.

of souls, but of embodied persons who suffer and desire a flourishing life. In the developing Western tradition of human rights as normative social relationships, Wolterstorff argues, Augustine plays a key role in recognizing the ultimate value of humans based on God's continuing love for them. As he summarizes this conclusion:

> If God loves, in the mode of attachment, each and every human being equally and permanently, then natural human rights inhere in the worth bestowed on human beings by that love. Natural human rights are what respect for that worth requires.

The resources of Augustine's context could prove a handicap as well as a blessing, as we will see. But clearly in his teaching on God's love as the source and goal of human desire, and formative of moral communities, he made a contribution to Christian wisdom that has influenced the Western tradition to this day. Contemporary critics, as we will see, are apt to diminish his contribution because we can no longer inhabit his Neoplatonic framework. But, quite apart from whether he had a real choice in the matter, in the process of reading his Platonic heritage in the light of Christ and Scripture, one might claim Augustine saved Plato for the Christian tradition. Whatever one's philosophical framework, one must acknowledge that some of the central achievements of Christian thought and practice (its wisdom!) owe a great deal to this platonic reappropriation—from medieval mystical theology, Pseudo-Dionysius, Thomas, Dante, to the Enlightenment recovery of Plato, for example, in Jonathan Edwards, even to the contemporary rereading of the Greek Fathers, the Catholic Nouvelle Théologie, and Radical Orthodoxy, to say nothing of the continuing luminous presence of Eastern Orthodoxy.

Augustine's reading of Scripture was necessarily a contextual one; he sought to reframe the Stoic and Platonist wisdom in Christian terms. But this context could be constricting as well as productive. Though he formally abandoned the Manichaean teachings of the radical dichotomy between the forces of light and darkness, he struggled all his life to come to overcome the suspicion the Manichaeans (and his Platonism) carried toward the material world and its desires. In his many discussions of creation and God's purposes there, he returned to this question again and again. When Augustine turns subsequently to write his *Confessions,* this yearning for God becomes the driver of the narrative. He struggles to understand how this rugged landscape of desire opens the way to God. In that treatise he frequently lays out the paradox of desire:

> When I love you what do I love? It is not the physical beauty nor temporal glory nor the brightness of light dear to earthly eyes, nor the sweet melodies of all kinds of songs nor the gentle odor of flowers and ointments and perfumes, nor the manna and honey, nor limbs welcoming the embraces of the flesh; it is not these that I love when I love my God.[37]

Yet, he knows, this physical beauty does awaken desire. And, somehow, this desire directs him to love God. Throughout he struggles to see how God is related to this physical beauty, and more broadly, how God is related to time and space. He is able to describe this gulf eloquently in the *Confessions*: "A person singing or listening to a song he knows well suffers a distention or stretching in feeling and in sense perception from the expectation of future sounds and the memory of past sounds." No one, before or since, has better described the experience of musical beauty. But he goes on: "With you [God] it is otherwise. You are unchangeably eternal, that is the truly eternal creator of minds."[38] Why must it be "otherwise"? Because enjoying the good of music takes time and patience, and God's eternity places him outside of time. Here Colin Gunton believes Augustine's view of God's eternity and impassibility makes it impossible for God to relate meaningfully to time—to act in time and with time. But this is just what God did, Gunton insists, in taking on human flesh in Christ; it was this Jesus who encouraged his followers to contemplate the beauty of creation and endured with patience the suffering on the cross. But for Augustine, because all God's acts are timeless, the days of creation mean nothing; creation cannot take place over time. But if this is so how can God express the patience the New Testament ascribes to him—patiently calling and wooing the creature? Gunton concludes: for Augustine "the fact that activities and events take time is a sign of their fallenness."[39] But it is also a sign that Augustine was struggling to understand the ineffable God he inherited in relation to Scripture's teaching of the creation.

This ambiguity is shown clearly in Augustine's own contribution to the early Christian reflection on *Patience*.[40] Patience or long-suffering, Augustine says, is a virtue of the mind by which "we tolerate things with an even

---

37. Augustine, *Confessions*, 183.
38. Augustine, *Confessions*, 245.
39. Gunton, *The Triune Creator*, 83. The absolute separation of God's eternity from human time also suggests a determinism that Scripture does not support. See his discussion at 71–86. Still, in reading Gunton's critique one must keep in mind the positive contributions of Augustine's inescapable Neoplatonism.
40. Augustine, *Patience*. The date of writing this is uncertain. Numbers in the text are to the chapters of the treatise.

mind" (1). Here the ancient Roman wisdom is reborn in a Christian form; patience becomes a cultivated virtue of the mind, exercised in the body (4). Patience, Augustine believes, is a gift from God, but is not experienced by God as in us. For God is impassible and his patience ineffable: "For if we conceive of [jealousy or wrath] as they be in us, in Him are there none. We, namely, can feel none of these without molestation: but be it far from us to surmise that the impassible nature of God is liable to any molestation" (1). God's patience is literally incomparable.

Moreover, the good of patience is conditional: it must be exercised for a cause good for the soul (5). And this virtue is emphatically not something expressive of human agency, which would lead to pride, but only as the Holy Spirit makes it possible. So it becomes not the wisdom of human life, but a fruit of salvation, a gift of grace not of works (17). Augustine's view of original sin cannot allow any human agency toward goodness, anything suggesting that "there can be in the will of man somewhat of good" (24). This struggle poses a dilemma for Augustine:

> For we must take heed lest haply, if we affirm that patience to be the gift of God, they in whom it is, should be thought to belong also to the kingdom of God; but if we deny it to be the gift of God, we should be compelled to allow that without aid and gift of God there can be in the will of man somewhat of good (24).

But his view of sin and desire cannot allow him to concede such goodness, and this failure was in turn a deeply theological one. Augustine struggled to reconcile God's impassible patience with the God who suffered on the cross. He of course believed that God took human form in Christ, but it was a sign of God's humility: God is humbled; humanity is not raised. The wisdom associated with Christ's humility is the unique possession of believers. But it is unavailable to everyone else, they are restricted to the realm of knowledge (*scientia*) derived from temporary realities; Christ is wisdom and knowledge only for believers, who draws forth truth of eternal things.

We have seen this absolute dichotomy expressed before in some interpretations of the wisdom of the cross in 1 Corinthians chapter 1—which we judged to be mistaken. But Augustine did much to make this the default understanding of Christian wisdom, as an internal matter of the will which is entirely dependent on God's grace for choosing the good. But we have already seen in earlier chapters that the natural covenant which God instituted between creation and the human vice-regent suggests that a continuing moral order does reward good choices; Lady Wisdom extends her call to all with ears to hear. To deny the human ability to choose the good, Augustine seems to deny any relevance to Christian teaching for public policy and our human pursuit of the common good, even for notions of human flourishing—a rigorist view he modified in his later work the *City of God*. The view of God Augustine inherited from his philosophical heritage, at least at this stage of his life, led him to draw a sharp line between Christian and human wisdom; an eternal and impassible God could not sustain a deep (internal) relationship with the good creation. This surely had much to do with the deterministic and predestinarian theology that he was to develop. As Colin Gunton has shown, this is a theological error, one with long-term consequences in the Christian tradition. Because, Gunton notes, it is the Spirit "who enables the creation to be truly spatial and temporal by relating it to God the Father, through the one who took our time and space to himself in order to redeem it."[41]

Augustine and Violence

Another transformation during this time was the developing Christian perspectives on political power and its associated violence. Augustine's role here, practically speaking, may be as consequential as his theological contribution. As we have seen, Christians living in the Empire soon made their peace with the violence and war of the Empire. Augustine lived in a violent time. The shock of the Visigoths' sack of Rome in 410 led many to blame the Christians and their failure to honor the traditional Romans gods for the catastrophe, something that prompted Augustine to write his monumental apologetic work the *City of God* soon after. In that work he contrasts the City of God, based on the love of God, with the human city, based on self-love. He recognizes there that the miseries of warfare are allowed by God for reasons that remain mysterious to us and that killing under proper authority is justified.[42] As Kreider notes, this attitude was in continuity with some strands of thought that preceded the Empire, especially among the

---

41. Gunton, *The Triune Creator*, 86. An alternative interpretation argues Augustine struggled to define God's eternity in a way consistent with Scriptures, and portrays this in *Confessions*, XI, where God's eternity collects both past and present into itself. See Taylor, *A Secular Age*, 56–57. But a careful reading of book XI, I would argue, shows that though human notions of expectation and memory exhibit this kind of "distention," God still exists in a separate sphere in which we find our "rest." So he writes at the end of Book XI: "You are my eternal Father, but I am scattered in times whose order I do not understand. Its storms of incoherent events tear to pieces my thoughts, the inmost entrails of my soul, until that day when purified and molten by the fire of your love, I flow together to merge into you." Augustine, *Confessions*, 244.

42. Augustine, *City of God*, 31,32, 216–18. It is here that the idea of "just war" makes its first appearance.

laity.⁴³ But his inward focus on virtues of the mind led to a unique (and revisionist) interpretation of Jesus' teachings. In a treatise responding to a Manichaean leader, written around 398, he gave one of his most complete teachings about war and violence. There he asks:

> What is the evil in war? Is it the death of some who will soon die in any case, that others may live in peaceful subjection? This is mere cowardly dislike, not any religious feeling. The real evils in war are love of violence, revengeful cruelty, fierce and implacable enmity, wild resistance, and the lust of power.⁴⁴

In this section he goes on to inquire into Jesus' teaching about resisting violence by turning the other cheek (Matt 5:39). To this Augustine responds: "What is here required is not a bodily action but an inward disposition." Augustine here effectively overturns the force of Jesus' teaching by denying what that teaching was meant to emphasize. Jesus insists feelings are invariably expressed in bodily action—feelings and actions are connected; Augustine makes the kingdom Jesus' teaches into a future and spiritual project, not a present call of wisdom.⁴⁵

It is possible this spiritual reading of Jesus' teaching had something to do with Augustine's support for the violence later unleashed on the Donatist church. From the Berber population of North Africa—which Cyprian and Tertullian represented—a more radical opposition had arisen to restoring lapsed priests to their ministry, a controversy that had led these Berber believers to schism during Augustine's life. Denying Christ during persecution cannot simply be forgiven; according to Berber spirituality such sin infected the person and influenced their subsequent actions. And so lapsed priests could not be appropriate vessels to serve the body of Christ in the Eucharist. As the Nigerian theologian Mercy Oduyoye points out, the root problem was that Augustine's Catholic (and Roman) tradition could not comprehend the Berber spirituality: "To the Berbers, sin (in this case apostasy) was contagious and should not be trifled with. The Church is *de facto* holy, that is made up of good women and men."⁴⁶ By contrast Augustine's training in Roman law led the bishop to a different

---

43. Kreider, "Military Service," 435.

44. Augustine, *Contra Faustum Manichaeaum*, book 22, section 75, consulted online. He goes on to cite John the Baptist's advice to soldiers, noting he did not tell them to throw down their arms (sections 74–76, quote at 513).

45. See Driver, *How Christians Made Peace*, 81.

46. Oduyoye, *Hearing and Knowing*, 23. Oduyoye argues that it was in part because Christianity could not be made compatible with this indigenous intuition that it was destined to disappear from North Africa when Islam appeared on the scene.

understanding of guilt and forgiveness that could not accommodate the Donatist focus on purity. This misunderstanding was to have tragic consequences. Early in his career Augustine refused to allow force in encouraging belief, or conformity. He had written: "I am displeased that schismatics are violently coerced to communion by force of any secular power." Later he changed his mind, something which is reflected in his notorious interpretation of Luke 14:23. There in Jesus' parable the master instructs his servant to go out to the highways and "compel people to come in" to his banquet. If Jesus encouraged such violence, Augustine notes, who are we to hesitate? As a consequence in his *Retractions*, written at the end of his life, he admits his earlier views were mistaken: "And truly, at that time such coercion displeased me because I had not yet learned how much evil their impunity would dare or to what extent the application of discipline would bring about their improvement."[47] Force became appropriate, Augustine concluded, because it worked. In such an environment, Alan Kreider asks plaintively, what future would patience have?

This particular controversy may reflect a further weakness of the developing church life of this time. Everett Ferguson in his survey of the catechetical teaching of the fourth and fifth century churches, and of Ambrose and Augustine in particular, notes a distinct movement away from a moral and biblical emphasis toward a doctrinal and liturgical focus. He writes: "Being a Christian was now defined primarily in terms of doctrine, and not in terms of behavior. It was left for the monks to maintain the witness to a distinctive Christian lifestyle. Was all this the price of becoming the church of the Empire?"[48]

It was in response to the Donatist challenge that Augustine formulated his famous theory of the just war. In this he combined the Greco-Roman notions of causes and ends with the Christian idea of intent. From Aristotle he borrowed the goal of peace, from Cicero the idea that it is "the injustice of the opposing side that causes the wise man to go to war," and from Roman lawyers he took the idea of a proper authority. Notice how these traditions, in this reading, overshadowed Paul's actual instructions in Romans 13, to say nothing of the Sermon on the Mount. This teaching on war continues to resonate up to the present. In the Medieval period, when taking up the cross to follow Christ came to be identified with joining a crusade to destroy unbelievers (or heretics), many appealed to

---

47. Augustine, *Retractions*, 129. This was written c. CE 427.

48. Ferguson, *The Early Church*, 51. He suggests this preoccupation with doctrinal controversies (especially when placed alongside the inability to understood the indigenous sensitivities) may account for the failure of Western Christianity to "penetrate more deeply into the behavior of the people."

Augustine's "application of discipline."[49] Christopher Tyerman says of this period, and of Augustine in particular: "The Beatitudes had to be reconciled with human civilization, specifically with the Greco-Roman world, or, to put it crudely, ways found around the Sermon on the Mount. Being extravagantly well versed in the highest traditions of Classical learning, the Church fathers did this rather well."

As one of the first to seek a Christian wisdom that learned from both Scripture and the facts on the ground, Augustine's influence is both critical and instructive. As we have seen, Augustine's theology of desires, and his views of virtue and affections, even in their Christian rehabilitation, reflect the ancient Stoic understanding of virtue, and of classical philosophy as formative of a moral life. Indeed, Augustine's theology offers a brilliant exposition of Pauline wisdom for that setting, and there is much for us to learn from his synthesis. But one of the primary learnings should be the contextual nature of all theology. Augustine's work, whatever its brilliance, and however influential, is not a timeless word from God. No theology will have the last word precisely because theology itself is part of the human search for wisdom. It always consists of located attempts to hear the words of Scripture and obey them in the light of one's time and its intellectual, social, and political resources; the layers of theology on offer will necessarily reflect all these influences. We will continue to read and learn from Augustine. Though we no longer wrestle with Stoic eudaimonism, we have our own version of this search for the good life. But we honor and learn from Augustine, not as a universally applicable reading of Scripture for all time, but as an instance of a vital contextual theology. In this role Augustine becomes one of the layers of inherited wisdom from which Christian theology must learn.

---

49. See Christopher Tyerman, *God's War*, 33–34, quote that follows at 29.

7. The Poetics and Practice of Contemporary Wisdom

[Genesis and the Gospel of John] dare us to believe that the universe runs by the logic of creativity, goodness, and love. The universe is God's creative project, filled with beauty, opportunity, challenge, and meaning. It runs on the meaning or pattern we see embodied in the life of Jesus. In this story, pregnancy abounds. Newness multiplies. Freedom grows. Meaning expands. Wisdom flows. Healing happens. Goodness runs wild.[1]—Brian D. McLaren

IN THIS FINAL CHAPTER we turn our attention to the contemporary situation and ask: where is wisdom to be found in twenty-first century America? How do we understand our own facts on the ground? In the previous chapter we have seen the way God's work in Christ, what we are calling the gospel, began to make its way in the Mediterranean world. Initially the small Christians communities formed themselves largely by means of the teachings of Jesus; only later did leaders begin to make use of the intellectual categories of Greek philosophy to understand and teach God's saving work in Israel and Christ. Augustine was one of the first to integrate the gospel and this intellectual heritage. While indigenous forms of wisdom continued to make appearances, in the medieval period Augustine's synthesis proved enormously influential and, as a result, what passed as wisdom during that period—the facts on the ground—bore the mark of Augustine's synthesis of classical culture and the gospel.

It is easy to overlook what a major innovation this represented in the developing relationship between the human project of seeking creation's wisdom and God's project of saving and redeeming the world. Recall that in the First Testament the relationship of these projects was sometimes troubled, only being integrated in its later period (and even then, only in

---

1. McLaren, *We Make the Road*, 14.

apocryphal writings). Christ embodied in his teaching and work a fully integrated vision of the life of wisdom and faith in God's delivering love. Still, in the New Testament, Rome remains in the background of the development of Christianity. Though Jesus' vision featured prominently in the teaching and life of the early Christians, initially, the imperial culture and its classical heritage—the facts on the ground during this early period—mostly appeared in heretical movements, as something early believers needed to resist. This is true even though the fate of Christianity would turn out to be more closely tied to the Roman Empire than either Judaism or Islam. Only in Augustine's time were those facts considered, constructively, as resources for developing Christian wisdom.

With the synthesis of the medieval period there was no longer any question that the gospel provided a pattern for cultural and political life; for better or worse, what we call Christendom had become an established fact in world history. No one doubted that the reigning political and cultural institutions were "Christian"; but, as Dante's journey in the *Divine Comedy* shows, neither could anyone doubt the classical heritage could be given a Christian gloss (even if the divide between Virgil and Beatrice—reason and revelation—was unbridgeable). But now, with the hindsight of the centuries since the Reformation, when we look back on that experiment, though we love the art and culture of the period, many of us do not like what we see. We are repulsed by the violence associated with the crusades, as this infected subsequent colonial projects, and the violent subjugation of indigenous peoples and the slavery that supported this.[2] But, though the evils represented by Christendom may safely be relegated to the past, the continuing influence of the political and cultural project of that period still resonates. As Oliver O'Donovan puts this, "there is a legacy still apparent in the institutions of Europe and America. Even if Christendom is not our tradition . . . it was our great-grandfathers.'"[3] So that even in our current twenty-first century setting the question presses upon us: what do we make of this legacy?

---

2. Cf. Enrique Dussel: "It is a single process. It was the same Latin, Hispanic Christendom which came to America." *The History of the Church*, 15. There is of course a vocal minority that laments the *loss* of the medieval synthesis at the Reformation: See Brad S. Gregory, *The Unintended Reformation*, along with the vital movement called Radical Orthodoxy.

3. O'Donovan, *The Desire of Nations*, 226.

Modern Culture and the Gospel

Earlier, at several points, I have called attention to the transformation that took place at the Reformation. In this chapter I want to show how these changes opened the way to the modern world we take for granted.[4] Both Luther and Calvin sought to move the focus of Augustine's spiritual journey out of the confines of church and monastery and into the lived world, what Calvin called the theater of the world—"This magnificent theatre of heaven and earth, crammed with innumerable miracles, [that] Paul calls the 'wisdom of God.'"[5] This space, which Calvin believed was animated by the drama of sin and salvation, became an early expression of what we know as the shared public sphere. Further, Calvin's proposal of the human figure as the responsible spectator and participant in this drama called attention to the human role in exploring this divine wisdom. Both this emerging sphere and human responsibility within it, I will argue, have vastly transformed modern conceptions of the facts on the ground

In this chapter then I want to reflect on the situation that resulted—the reigning character of wisdom in which we find ourselves today, especially as this relates to our inherited versions of religious (and Christian) truth. The development traced in the preceding chapter argued that, with Augustine, wisdom had become theology—that is informal notions of right living in the early church began to take on a developed, systematic, framework that we call theology. In this chapter I want to extend the story of the relation between wisdom and theology into the present.

A generation ago it would still have been possible to argue that the major societies of Western Europe and North America were largely post-Christian and secular; this view is increasingly difficult to sustain today. In fact in this chapter I will argue that in many contemporary Western cultures, including prominently the United States, Christian values, even those central to the teaching and work of Christ, are increasingly influential.[6] Indeed one might say they have so permeated the culture that they are no longer questioned. Every culture is shaped by various patterns of belief and practice, most of which have their sources in forms of religion.

---

4. It is important to note that the Reformation and Renaissance, especially in the area of theology, were as much a development of medieval ideas, as a radical departure from them, even as the cultural and political project was decisively reframed during that period. On this period see Dyrness, *The Origin of Protestant Aesthetics*.

5. Calvin, *Institutes*, II.vi.1.

6. Given that Christian wisdom inherited Jewish traditions of wisdom, and Jesus came to "fulfill" those traditions, this is also to recognize the continuing influence of the Jewish religion.

While the Enlightenment had given people the illusion that they had been liberated from such superstitions, scholars over the last generation have recognized the continuing role of Christian values in modern Western cultures. Max Stackhouse notes in the conclusion of his book (and series) on globalization that a responsible analysis of any context must include its intellectual and religious sources and in the Western context this includes the culturally formative influence of Christian theology.[7] Oliver O'Donovan traces this influence to the time of the Reformation. During that period, he thinks, habits and practices worked to form a constellation of social and political ideas formative of the modern liberal society common in Europe and America. Among these ideas he notes the rise of responsible government, the authority (Latin *ius*) of rulers deriving from the law of God, and free subjects able to speak and act freely, which has led to a legal-constitutional conception of the state that is "the essence of Christendom's legacy."[8] Though, as we observed, this legacy has been tarnished by the violence done in its name, the role of religious traditions, both negative and positive, in cultures is increasingly recognized.[9]

In spite of these recent reflections, it needs to be said that the academic work of sorting out the precise role of theology in forming cultural patterns, at least in this neo-Weberian form, is in its infancy.[10] Though this chapter will address this question in a North American setting, it represents the merest sketch of what that might look like. One who has pioneered this conversation is Robin Gill. He has proposed we follow Max Weber and speak of transposition rather than secularization. He presents the current situation (in modern Western cultures) in these terms:

> Western society is embedded in Christian virtues to such an extent that it can scarcely even detect these virtues. According to this [transpositional] view, Christianity has been astonishingly

---

7. Stackhouse, *Globalization and Grace*, 231.

8. O'Donovan, *The Desire of Nations*, 226–40, quote at 240. O'Donovan believes it is the rule of Christ and his victory over the powers in the resurrection that has transformed the way we think about government. This view, while true so far as it goes, tends to overlook, and thus belittle, the creation/new creation dynamic I am tracing as the larger context of resurrection.

9. See Jennings, *The Christian Imagination*, and Robert Woodberry, "The Missionary Roots," for the negative and positive influences respectively. And for the implications of this for theological education see Pui-Lan Kwok et al., eds., *Teaching Global Theologies*.

10. The opposite question of the role of culture in developing theology has had a longer run, thanks to discussions of "contextualization" over the last century, though the problem is still hotly debated. See Dyrness, *Insider Jesus*, chapter 1. My argument in this chapter also has that conversation in mind.

successful in converting Western society, so successful in fact, that it is difficult to tell Christians apart from non-Christians within it.[11]

In describing this integration as part of the accepted wisdom—the facts on the ground—of these places, as I am doing, one can avoid the problem of deciding whether people formed in this way are Christians or not. Remember, wisdom is a resource to good living; it is not salvific. Still I am arguing the fruit of this saving work—the goals of unselfish mutual care and peacemaking, communities of mutual benefit, and environmental renewal—has been made available to everyone in these gospel-influenced cultures. This reading of theological influence might also provide a response to those eager to show how societies can become highly developed and peace-loving without any particular faith in God.[12] The truths of the gospel can be worked so far down into the warp and woof of society, as Gill points out, that their origin is no longer noticed. They become a part of the accepted wisdom of these places.

The Poetics and Practice of Our Contemporary World: Fullness and Reform

In working toward an understanding of the contemporary, gospel-infused context, I will again highlight our dual themes of poetics and practice—what people love and what they do with these loves. We begin with the foundational role of poetics, that is the need to have eyes and imagination to discern the affective wisdom of our era, and then move to the resulting practice, the universal impulse to construct a better world. These reflect, we recall, our human response to the goodness of creation and its call to perform and enact that goodness, but, in this period, I will argue this has been influenced by the social and cultural pattern laid out in the teaching and life of Christ. In both cases—seeing and doing—we consider ways in which, following the biblical precedent, these are consistent (or sometimes not) with the biblical witness to Christ and the new creation.

Just as integration of human wisdom and the liberating work of God in the First Testament took some centuries to work out, similarly, the implications of the new creation, what Jesus termed the "kingdom," would take some centuries to be framed in terms of prevailing wisdom, something that

---

11. Gill, *Society Shaped by Theology*, 57. Other important contributions to this conversation are Michael Gillespie, *The Theological Origins*, and Dominic Erdozain, *The Soul of Doubt*.

12. See, for example, Phil Zuckerman's study of Denmark, *Society without God*.

Augustine was one of the first to attempt. The Reformation, it seems clear, released the gospel into the culture in a fresh way, and subsequent centuries little by little made attempts, more or less successful, to read culture in light of this gospel. One way of describing this period might be to portray the growing attempts, halting and often opposed, to apply the social and cultural patterns of Jesus' teaching and work—what we are calling the social gifts of the new creation—to the larger culture. My argument in chapter 5 was that those gifts, enabled by the Spirit's power poured out on believers in Acts 2, are not limited to the church or to baptized believers, but have been made available more broadly; non-violent social relations based on unmerited love and service, the possibility of forming economic communities of mutual support, and regenerative practices anticipating the renewal (the resurrection) of the created order are concrete expressions of the gifts of New Creation, made available in places where the gospel is preached. From the New Testament teaching it is clear that real fulfillment of these ideals is a gift of God's grace, given as a new life in the Spirit at baptism. But I argue that, because these ideals are grounded in God's larger purposes for creation and the goals proposed for that creation by the biblical prophetic tradition, it is possible for those who do not confess faith in Christ to embody such virtues, to "seek the peace of the city" (Jer 29:7). This means that Jesus' teaching and the great parables of his life, death, and resurrection embody virtues relevant to a constructive cultural strategy, one that has, I argue, in various ways, been influential in modern Western culture.

To help illumine this contemporary integration, I turn again to Charles Taylor, and borrow two central themes from *A Secular Age,* what Taylor calls the contemporary *search for fullness,* which he places against the background of the modern *quest for reform.*[13] These are arguably the motivating poles of Taylor's magisterial work and they serve, I will argue, as useful descriptors of our contemporary search for a good life. We will examine Taylor's use of "fullness" in the context of the nineteenth century Romantic movement, and develop Taylor's notion of "reform" in the context of events subsequent to the Reformation. This background provides the relevant historical context for understanding the contemporary wisdom of fullness and reform, but it also suggests ways in which a specifically Christian response and engagement with the current facts on the ground may be framed. As we noted in the first chapter, for Taylor this historical background has resulted in a shift in consciousness, in which we perceive possibilities for human flourishing not in terms of belief or unbelief but of a fragilized belief. Though this means we have left behind previous assumptions of a

---

13. Taylor, *A Secular Age,* quote that follows at 304.

shared faith—what everyone would have believed in 1500—it also means our choices are contested, challenged by the knowledge that others think differently. The interchange and increased exposure to other beliefs resulting from media technology and globalization have made available unprecedented choices for us. The result, Taylor writes, is "differences become more insistent: why my way and not hers?" This background condition, as Taylor terms it, constitutes the context in which our two impulses play out in our common life, and in which our cultural wisdom emerges.

These two conceptions—fullness and reform—express something central about contemporary wisdom from which we may learn, and in which, I argue, the call of Lady Wisdom can be heard. This is not to say the longing for fullness our contemporaries feel, or the desire for reform, are necessarily framed in Christian (or religious) terms; seekers after wisdom often pay little attention to religion or even spirituality. But I argue that these longings reflect the creative impulse of our contemporaries' creation in God's image and the unique sensitivities of our particular historical moment, sensitivities that have, in part, been formed by the particular influence of Christianity. Since they are part of the given life world we necessarily inhabit, these facts on the ground cannot be ignored. The desire for fullness, in its various forms, expresses a movement of the soul that may be directed toward God. But it also provides opportunities for peculiar and characteristic distortions—our contemporary versions of the false wisdom Paul attacked in 1 Corinthians 1. Desire, as Augustine saw, is a necessary motivator, but it can be enlisted in the trajectories of life or of death.

The Poetics of Fullness

To develop this thesis I turn first to Taylor's description of fullness. Time and again in the 800-plus pages of *A Secular Age*, Taylor returns to the theme of the contemporary search for what he calls "fullness." He introduces the notion early in the book in this way:

> We see our lives, and/or the space wherein we live our lives, as having a certain moral/spiritual shape. Somewhere, in some activity, or condition, lies a fullness, a richness; that is, in that place (activity or condition), life is fuller, richer, deeper, more worthwhile, more admirable, more what it should be. This is perhaps a place of power; we often experience this as deeply moving, as inspiring.[14]

---

14. Taylor, *A Secular Age*, 5; quote that follows at 313.

Sometimes, Taylor goes on, we experience this at a distance, at other times it takes definite shape before us. This idea is critical to Taylor's argument; though people today live in a secular age where both faith and unbelief are fragile and threatened, there is, Taylor thinks, a widespread search for this moral and spiritual fullness. Taylor goes on to articulate and explore this notion in two ways, both of which are relevant to the argument of this chapter. First, this quest has its roots historically in the Romantic movement of the nineteenth century, where artists and poets reacted against both the sterile rationalism of the Enlightenment and the revolutionary violence of political and industrial developments. Second, the energy behind these movements lay in the belief that aesthetics was the privileged means to a richer life. In the Romantic period the ideal was that surroundings should be "transfigured by the sense of their higher significance. The ideal is thus a fusion of ordinary desire and the sense of a higher goal," an ideal that came to be identified with beauty. This, Taylor thinks, animated an expanding terrain in which aesthetics and experiences of joy and delight—fullness—that, for many of us, have become a central life goal. One might argue this search for fullness constitutes our modern version of the ancient Stoic quest for the good and pleasant life. But for Christians attuned to the teachings of Jesus, this fusion of desire with something higher recalls Jesus' admonition to pay special attention to the gifts of creation—the lilies and sparrows—as signs of God's loving provision and the call to seek first God's righteousness.

Taylor shows how the Romantic century represented multiple reactions against Enlightenment rationalism and the mindless violence associated with late eighteenth-century revolutions (and, before that, the Wars of Religion). Poets and artists led this revolt, which included the confidence that human moral efforts could be encouraged without transformation and grace—part of the larger movement toward Reform that we turn to below. But central to the search for fullness was the growing assumption that aesthetics was a sphere in which human flourishing was uniquely encouraged. Artists in the nineteenth century saw art not as mimesis (imitation), as Aristotle had taught, but as creation; not as a mirror, but a lamp. So while the universe of traditional beliefs might have been shrinking, the space in which one was invited to pursue spiritual options was expanding. In the English-speaking world, Taylor notes, aesthetics became an ultimate and self-sufficient universe. But since it could open up the world to transcendence (as in Gerald Manley Hopkins) or it could point to something within oneself (in Walter Pater), this achievement, like religious faith, was fragile. For as art—in, for example, Mozart or abstract art—created its own world, Taylor notes, "we have something like the essence of the response without the story." Since it was disconnected from the previous narratives—of religion or national glory—its "ontic commitments are unclear." Unclear, but not closed. For such art can refuse any narrative meaning, as in Schopenhauer, but it can also disclose very deep truths about the nature of creation, as with Hopkins.[15]

Taylor's point in his extended development of these themes is that the search for fullness remains intensely relevant even for people living in a so-called secular age. The search for fullness has left an indelible mark on our culture that Taylor finds remarkable. In longing for fullness and searching for it in various poetic projects—artifacts and objects that embody our life goals—Taylor claims we are all Romantics now. Though many people do not consider themselves artists or see their projects as poetic, if Taylor is right about the longing for fullness, everyone has a desire to make something not only meaningful, but attractive of their lives, their homes, and their work.[16] And for many of these, the idea of creativity, making something new, as this is celebrated above all in artworks of all kinds, hovers over them as a paradigm case, a kind of inspiration, for what they would like to make of their lives. They want to write texts, or text analogues, that tell their story, with patterns or surfaces that spark admiration or desire, an impulse that is encouraged by the various forms of social media.

This contemporary desire for fullness, as Taylor saw, is a consistent aspect of human motivation, but it also shows itself in unique moments, even in the midst of great suffering and loss. Consider the following example. At about 4 PM on May 27, 1992, one month after the Siege of Sarajevo began, several mortar shells fell on a line of people waiting to buy bread at a bakery, killing twenty-two. The next day Vedran Smailovic, a cellist in the Sarajevo Symphony, came to the same square outside the market at 4 PM and played Albinoni's Adagio in G Minor. He returned every day at 4 o'clock for twenty-two days and played the seven-minute-long adagio. Soon crowds, despite the risk of snipers, gathered in the square in silence and contemplated their loss as the cellist played his adagio. The siege, one of longest in modern history, lasted until February 29, 1996, when allied bombing finally forced the rebels to lift the siege. It left 10,000 dead and 50,000 wounded, and destroyed 23 percent of the city.[17] What makes this such a moving story is that

---

15. Taylor, *A Secular Age*, 404; quotes at 355 and 356, respectively.

16. This idea is developed in greater detail in Dyrness, *Poetic Theology*, chapter 1. In chapter 4 of that book I argue that even these Romantic aesthetic developments were sourced, in part, in Christian pietism and, behind this, medieval mysticism. The increasing importance of aesthetics in contemporary America has been shown by many studies. See Robert Wuthnow, *All in Sync*.

17. The event was made known to the world by the fictionalized account of the cellist, by Steven Galloway, *The Cellist of Sarajevo*. He recounts the historical details in

music, usually thought of as a special set-apart performance in a concert hall, is here thrust into the savagery of modern warfare with its incredible firepower and into the racial accelerant that can drive it. It becomes a form of protest, testifying to the longing of people for fullness in the midst of unspeakable suffering. The dramatic impact is increased by knowledge that this particular Adagio of Albinoni was salvaged from a library in Dresden that was almost completely destroyed by another allied bombing in March, 1945. A composer named Grazotti found the blackened pages of part of the manuscript and arranged it into its present form. Perhaps there can be no better example of the human attempts to bring life out of death, to seek fullness in the midst of pain.

Examples of this contemporary prominence of aesthetic practices could be multiplied. During the 2019 protests in Hong Kong, participants began to sing an anthem that highlighted their desire for freedom. During the 2020 coronavirus lockdown people used music in various ways to encourage hope and to celebrate front line workers. In Italy, during the lockdown, songs and spontaneous performances broke out on balconies and out of windows—including Maurizio Marchini, lead violinist of La Scala, performing on his balcony beneath a banner reading: "Let's not give up, we will make it."[18] Perhaps the most moving image is the now famous sight of Andrea Bocelli, on April 12, 2020, standing alone on the steps of the deserted Milan Cathedral, singing some of his favorite songs, including "Amazing Grace"—something that has been watched by millions on YouTube. Bocelli's performance recalls watching President Obama in the Charleston, South Carolina church still reeling from the tragic killing at a Bible study, as he softly began singing "Amazing Grace." As with Bocelli, millions heard, were moved, even joined in singing along.

But why are these intrusions of art and beauty in times of pain a reflection of wisdom? They surely reflect the human ability of using aesthetic artifacts to make it through times of suffering and loss. But in addition, this impulse surely reflects something fundamental about how God has made the world—one intended to prompt expressions of awe and joy as at the creation. Further, in Western societies, it may also reflect something of the hope of the gospel—that life can come from death, light from darkness. In times like these, works of art and the response they evoke, allow the suffering to be a crack in the darkness, letting light shine through, suggesting a world—broken and beautiful—reflecting on itself. The process in this gospel-inflected tradition may even echo a God who suffered the world's

---

the Afterword to the novel.

18. Jason Horowitz, "Italians find 'a moment of joy.'"

brokenness while creating a new order out of the old. In any case these incidents point to poetic pursuits as a fundamental way that humans reflect the creator God—watching the world become itself.

The Wisdom of Nonviolence

But to connect this discussion with themes of wisdom we have explored in earlier chapters, let me linger on the historical context of the contemporary sensibilities constituting this search for fullness. Taylor develops this moral (and aesthetic) sensibility in terms of an expanding commitment to "benevolence."[19] I believe this sensibility, lying on the border between the poetics of fullness and practices of reform, lies behind (and fuels) modern movements toward peacemaking and nonviolence.

In *Sources of the Self* Taylor traces the modern virtue of benevolence to the Scottish Enlightenment and to Francis Hutcheson (1694–1746) in particular. The Presbyterian divine Hutcheson argued for a strong connection between beauty and virtue, as ideas he believed presented themselves to us as immediate and necessary, and grounded ultimately in the character of God. Beauty he believed is the pleasure sparked by seeing the harmony and order of an external object; the moral sense is the equivalent internal sense of order that directs our actions. The Author of our Nature, Hutcheson argued, "has given us a Moral Sense, to direct our actions and to give us still nobler pleasures, so that while we are intending the Good of others we undesignedly promote our own greatest private good."[20] These reactions to beauty and goodness can't be further defined, they are natural to us; they do not function in respect to any external interest.

Taylor believes this tradition has come to define the modern social imaginary. As seekers after benevolence, people influenced by these teachings have moved beyond care for their family, or tribe, to see their good as tied up with the good of all. In fact, many of us, Taylor says, have come to think this is a natural expression of our human nature; it has become part of the world we take for granted. But in many places in the world this idea is anything but natural. Where this universalism exists, Taylor insists, it is a Christian import, a version of New Testament agape (unmerited and unconditional) love demonstrated in the life and teaching of Jesus, especially as this is shown in the story of the Good Samaritan. The victim on the road to

---

19. He makes this argument strongly in his earlier book, *The Sources of the Self*, though it is also explored in *A Secular Age*.

20. Hutcheson, *An Inquiry* (1725), 99. He goes on to point out that this sense flows from some affection (101).

Jericho could make no claim on anyone passing by, apart from his suffering; still the Good Samaritan felt sympathy and stopped. Taylor develops the NT context of this: "And the paradigmatic stepping beyond of agape, the incarnation and submission to death of Christ, is not motivated by a pre-existing community or solidarity. It is a free gift of God."[21] Though ideas of benevolence were soon incorporated into a vague Deism, and, later, highjacked by a utilitarian calculus, and in our own century, assumed by an exclusive humanism, as Taylor shows, their source is to be found in the teaching and story of Christ. We have come to believe that society could approximate the model of mutual benefit, and it is "agape" and "benevolence" that funds this belief. Taylor writes: "Charity was part of the ideal of personal conduct; good social order must involve care of all members of society and the proper inward dispositions of a decent man included charitable ones."[22]

This contemporary impulse toward benevolence could be illustrated in many different ways, from the universal support of the White Helmets in Syria's recent civil violence, to the growing support of humanely raised free-range chickens and grass-fed beef, even the refusal of vegans to eat animal products of any kind. But here I want to focus on one particular evidence of benevolence in the growing embrace of nonviolence as a larger social (and political) good. In the chapter on Christ's influence on wisdom, I noted that one of the twentieth century's most impressive achievements may well have been the development of nonviolent movements for social change, deriving from Gandhi and Martin Luther King, and their proliferating contemporary heirs. Two hundred years ago the violence of the French Revolution, which no one knew how to stop, fostered the quest for nonviolent solutions that the Romantics often framed in aesthetic terms. Today there are parallel reactions against the endless wars with their indiscriminate suffering, against cruel immigration policies, and the police violence against Black bodies—the contemporary responses I noted in the Introduction.

But it is the heirs of Martin Luther King promoting nonviolence that I want to highlight as ongoing evidence of the contemporary wisdom of benevolence. Part of this growing movement results from the awareness that modern warfare, waged with increasingly powerful weapon systems, has made irrelevant traditional notions of a "just war," with its tenets of proportionality and the need to discriminate between combatants and noncombatants. The growing percentage of noncombatant deaths in war over the last

21. *A Secular Age*, 245–47, quote at 246. Taylor notes that this "caring" even extends to concern for animal rights.

22. *A Secular Age*, 247–48. Interestingly, fullness is clearly connected to benevolence in *A Secular Age*; in his earlier book *The Sources of the Self*, however, fullness makes no appearance in his development of benevolence.

hundred years shows a rise from 42 percent in World War I, to 67 percent in World War II until during the 1990s (in Iraq and Afghanistan) the percentage reached 90 percent. Meanwhile, almost perversely, efforts have been made to protect military combatants, so that American deaths in Afghanistan decreased as civilian deaths continued to grow.[23] Viewing these statistics, people might be forgiven for wondering: are American husbands, fathers, or mothers more valuable than Afghani sons, mothers, or fathers?

All of this has suggested that a growing cultural consensus—its accepted wisdom—has concluded the idea of just war is something of a contradiction of terms. During the 1980s voices were raised in support of nuclear pacifism—the notion that nothing could possibly justify the use of this magnitude of violence. In the 1990s this protest became more narrowly focused on finding nonviolent alternatives to the calculus of just war. During this time a generous grant funded Glen Stassen and a group of twenty-three scholars from diverse traditions who met regularly over a period of six years. These discussions resulted in a strategy they called Just Peacemaking, a description of which was subsequently published.[24] These scholars made the case that we needed to move beyond the polarities of just war and pacifism toward a nonviolent and active paradigm they called Just Peacemaking. The practices proposed included supporting nonviolent direct action, proactive intervention to reduce threat, cooperative conflict resolution, taking responsibility for injustice, promoting democracy, and sustainable economic development. These scholars have shown that, historically, countries that mutually engage each other in these ways have never resorted to war. What is immediately striking in these holistic and practical proposals is that none of them are religious in any direct sense and indeed many have been embraced by people of no faith. Moreover, there is evidence that, apart from the reduction of violence, participation in the active processes of peacemaking forms people in ways that markedly contrast with those involved in war. After watching Gandhi's program of nonviolent intervention for many years, the famous Christian missionary Earl Stanley Jones made this observation: "In wars carried out by physical arms the men who are engaged in it are brutalized—the more so, the more efficient. On the contrary, I have found that the men who threw themselves in with Gandhi and really practiced his program were spiritualized; it deepened their sense of moral values and made them self-sacrificial."[25]

---

23. A responsible attempt to calculate and evaluate these losses is Valerie Epps, "Civilian Casualties in Modern Warfare."

24. See Stassen, *Just Peacemaking: Ten Practices* (1998), and Stassen, *Just Peacemaking: The New Paradigm* (2008).

25. Jones, *Christ of the Indian Road*, 97.

A recent offering by the Catholic scholar Lisa Cahill has framed similar practices in terms of "peacebuilding."[26] Cahill notes the deep wounds and divisions that violence leaves in its wake. Drawing on the precedent of the civil rights movement, and nonviolent revolutions like that in the Philippines in 1986, she suggests that the gradual, multidimensional, and fallible processes available for building peace are infinitely preferable to state-sponsored violence. Significantly, she argues that aesthetics often provides the motivation for social peacemaking: "Song, story, art and ritual can be powerful vehicles of conversion and change in which the participant re-envisions not only their relation to their former enemy but also their own identity." Above all, Cahill shows that Augustine was wrong: violence does not work; nonviolent resistance does.[27]

One example, often cited, is the peaceful revolution that succeeded in overthrowing Ferdinand Marcos in the Philippines in 1986. In a recent book dedicated to recording its history, written by major participants of the revolt, the contrast between this revolution as reflecting the consistent teachings of Jesus and various Marxist revolutions is highlighted—the one nonviolent and the other drenched in bloody conflict.[28] One missionary participant, Adrian Helleman, pointed to some of the obvious challenges to just war theory we have cited, and concludes that warfare today is hard to justify for any cause. He describes what he calls the template for nonviolent revolt that emerged in the EDSA revolution.[29] There the general populace streamed onto this main highway and gathered by the large Manila military base where the troops were being mobilized. Churches activated pop-up kitchens to feed the growing crowds and the people appealed to the soldiers to join them in the revolt. Reflecting on this event, Helleman proposes elements of a possible peacemaking theory: first, success is based on an active pursuit of change over a long period, one that mobilizes a large and visible section of the population. Second, peacemaking features visible practices of sharing, in which diverse groups provided mutual support in multiple ways. Third, successful efforts for social change involve in some way symbolic reversals, reminiscent of the prophet's description of beating swords into

26. Cahill, *Blessed Are the Peacemakers*; quote at 332.

27. The relative success of nonviolent efforts has been shown in a number of empirical studies. See the literature cited in Andre Henry's blog "Is Non-violence a Viable Choice?"

28. See Maggay, ed., *To Be in History*. Internationally the book is distributed by Langham Global Library under the title of *Dark Days of Authoritarianism*.

29. Helleman, "A Non-Violent Revolution." EDSA (Epifanio de los Santos Ave) is the main peripheral highway in Manila on which the confrontation between the people and the army was played out.

plowshares (Isa 2:8). The most famous image of such symbolism, during the EDSA revolution, involved a nun in her habit placing a flower in the giant gun-barrel mounted on a tank. Helleman recalls in this context the Magnificat of Mary where the poor are exalted and the rich brought low. Finally he proposes that such changes can become harbingers, or down payments, of the larger personal and social changes that are needed. This example of concrete nonviolent social change provided models that other places followed in the revolutions in 1989. These impulses have spawned substantial efforts toward peaceful reconciliation such as the influential Fellowship for Reconciliation, or more local efforts like the Los Angeles-based Interfaith Communities United for Justice and Peace, founded (and meeting weekly) after 9/11.[30] None of these has brought about the complete transformation we all yearn for—they are simply expressions of cultural wisdom after all—but all of them provide evidence that working toward the resurrection of all things, wisdom promoting the trajectory of life, can be a realistic dimension of human wisdom in our period of history.

My argument is that the sensibility these practices reflect is firmly rooted in the general Judeo-Christian wisdom tradition, but more specifically it lives off of the particular teachings of Jesus. One sees evidence of new perceptions that "consider the lily," or efforts to "turn the other cheek," or more generally to let go of enmity and anger. Perhaps more specifically Christian practices like forgiveness or prayer do not figure prominently in discussions of nonviolence, but they are hinted at. Forgiveness may prove difficult, since lasting peace demands progress in the direction of actual justice (something that is being addressed by a growing movement toward "restorative justice").[31] Still the perceptions encouraged in these processes gesture in that direction. Indeed one might argue that nonviolence is a central precondition for trust, and the practices of paying attention—of listening to one's life, are prerequisites of prayer. Clearly there is a strong connection between nonviolence and prayer.[32]

---

30. See forusa.org and icujp.org.

31. On restorative justice see http://restorativejustice.org/#sthash.7l3KsEkU.dpbs. After the Rwandan genocide against the Tutsi, forgiveness was seen as a slow and contested process, that when successful, was often rooted in religious faith. See Donald E. Miller and Lorna Miller, *Becoming Human Again*, 153–68.

32. That Jesus' instructions on prayer appear in the center of his Sermon on the Mount that teaches nonviolence suggests that the practices of nonviolence and prayer are deeply connected to one another.

Practices of Reform: Building a Better World

It has become clear as I have tried to develop the impulses of poetics and practices that the line between them is difficult to draw. Poetics involves practices of imagining and making; practices need guiding images and affective motivation. Indeed the sensibility that I have described using Taylor's term *benevolence* occupies a territory that sits squarely between these impulses. Taylor shows frequently that the desire to be good, often expressed in aesthetic categories, necessitates doing good, and this necessity involves having some sense of human purpose, some corporate life goal. Taylor refers to this goal, as it has appeared in the modern period, as "reform."

Like fullness, reform is a central category in *A Secular Age*. Taylor describes the vast scope of the idea in one of his first references to the term. The transformation of the medieval to the modern world picture, often called "disenchantment" involved, Taylor believes,

> a movement which gathers steam in the late medieval period, and which aimed to remake European society to meet the demands of the Gospel, and later of "civilization." It would not be wrong to apply the overworked word "revolutionary" here, because this drive to Reform was the matrix out of which the modern European idea of Revolution emerges.[33]

The reference to late medieval trends is significant because, as we have hinted, the Reformation itself inherited calls in the preceding centuries to abolish abuses and allow a wider participation in human society; the Reformation, Taylor thinks, merely finished the abolition of the old hierarchy of ordinary Christians and Super Christians: All Christians could be equally dedicated (77).

The Reformation is a fruit of the reform spirit and also an accelerant of this.[34] But as we have argued in several places, the unique contribution of the Reformers to this project of Reform was to move the focus of religious life out of the sacred space of the church and monastery into the larger world. This is where the Christian is to find her active vocation. This influence is seen in what Taylor describes as the gradual rise of the disciplinary society, consisting in two steps (90–145). The first reflects the Reformation focus on everyday life I have highlighted, and the resulting interest in and exploration

---

33. Taylor, *A Secular Age*, 61. Subsequent pages in the text are to this source.

34. Peter Wilson makes the point that the reform of manners was not wholly a product of the Reformation; "police measures" date back to the thirteenth century when Aristotle was translated and authorities seeking good order had the right to regulate social behavior. *The Heart of Europe*, 534–38.

of nature itself. This led, Taylor thinks, to an increasing confidence in human ability not only to manage this nature, but to transform themselves (121), which led in turn to the scientific revolution and the Enlightenment. The second move involved what Taylor calls the "great disembedding," which entails escape from the confines of medieval faith (and its picture of the world as open to the transcendent) to a purely immanent world. This led to what Taylor calls the modern moral order: a growing public sphere, where people meet through various media, where the vision emerges of "we the people" as sovereign, and "where the constituting factor is nothing other than common action" (194). With this achievement, a modern social imaginary emerges, Taylor writes, and what we know as secularity appears. Though all of this bears marks of the Reformation, the consequences are both intended and unintended—faith is possible but fragile. What is new is an increasingly widespread belief that it is possible to work toward a world the Reformers thought more nearly reflected the values of the gospel. As Taylor reports, for the 300 years after John Locke, "the underlying idea of society as existing for the (mutual) benefit of individuals, and the defense of their rights takes on more and more importance" (160).

But is there any real evidence—in our history—for the influence of these values? Our social imaginary, as Taylor calls it, is of course a vast and various terrain to map out, but much of it, he argues, reflects a general impulse for reform—the general modern desire to build a better and more inconclusive, less violent world, one fueled by the longing for personal and social fullness. In the modern West the equivalent of the sages would be its philosophers, medical and social scientists, and students of economics and ecology. Is there evidence in these sectors of the influence of the gospel? To answer this question let's take a brief, nonscientific tour of our current cultural wisdom.

The Multiple Forms of Contemporary Wisdom

Consider an example from contemporary *philosophy*. We have already signaled our dependence on the widely acclaimed work of the Catholic philosopher Charles Taylor. Together with Hubert Dreyfus he has recently described a realism that assumes the goodness and order of creation.[35] They argue we have direct and reliable contact with the world that we know intuitively; our experience is not, as Descartes believed, mediated by ideas or

---

35. Dreyfus and Taylor, *Retrieving Realism*, quotes at 18 and 36, and for what follows see 118. They do not use the language of creation, but the implications are there for us to draw.

frameworks. Thought and knowledge, they argue, needs to be "re-embedded . . . in the bodily and socio-cultural contexts in which it takes place." Our immersion in the physical world makes possible the perception and agency we have argued for in this book—it offers a reliable environment in which we learn and grow. It naturally structures experience. We are moved intuitively to certain kinds of actions and perceptions. They write: "this environment hems us in, that allows us to move; another one frustrates us, another one again facilitates what we want to do. Or things can show up as attractive or repulsive, pleasant or grating, soothing or anxiety arousing." We need our body, they say, to make sense of the world. And though our experience of this world is mostly unconscious, formed by habit, we are able to respond to its promptings and critically manipulate it in order to express our creative agency. How we modern Americans perceive and respond to our world feels natural to us, but it does not feel natural to visitors, say, from China. What is natural to us depends both on our physical environment and the cultural shape we have given to this; the world is a safe and ordered space in which human agency may be exercised.

In understanding this "naturalness" I have been helped by reading work in *cognitive psychology*—a recent branch of the social sciences. Justin Barrett, for example, has been engaged in research exploring what he calls the natural cognitive functioning of people in relation to religion.[36] In a 2011 book he describes this "naturalness" as what has become automatic and fluent, and that characterizes normal cognitive functioning in a given cultural situation. The general argument is that across human cultures, normal cognitive functioning expresses a "natural" religious impulse that often includes a sense of a designer, unseen agents, ritual and sacred places, and so on. (He does not want to call this "hardwired," as though it were resident in our genes, but describes this as a cultural capacity that develops under normal circumstances.) His research has shown that across many human cultures religious ideas are natural to human cognitive functioning. As he says: "Humans have a natural propensity toward believing in some kind of God."[37] I find his description of normal cognitive functioning

---

36. Barrett, *Cognitive Science*, 28, 131, quote at 161.

37. In another book, Barrett argues that children are naturally inclined to believe in God or gods as a part of their normal cognitive development. See his *Born Believers*. Though Barrett based his conclusions on empirical studies, he appropriates the ideas of nineteenth-century Scottish Common Sense Realism of Thomas Reid in developing his ideas (a further fruit of the Scottish Enlightenment). Reid proposed that our normal cognitive functioning "should be given the benefit of the doubt and their deliverances should be treated as true and justified until sufficient reason are mounted to supplant them" (*Cognitive Science*, 155). Barrett also cites Alvin Plantinga's argument that humans are disposed to be convinced of God's existence, as that philosopher develops this

a helpful description of what I have been calling cultural wisdom and its relation to religion. A people's normal functioning provides resources with which they get a grip on things, manage social relations, cultivate natural resources, and even, as Paul says in Acts 17, seek after God. If my comparison of normal cultural functioning to wisdom is fair, Barrett's connection of this to the inclination to practice some religion offers a helpful way to describe, for example, the great religious traditions of the world. They display various forms of wisdom that have developed over time and have become resources in a given culture. One can admire these and learn from them without claiming they are salvific.

But here I want to call attention to what Barrett calls "anchor ideas," which contribute to widely accepted cultural narratives, whether understood in religious terms or not, that begin as folk understandings of the world but can be highly elaborated. These narratives are developed, Barrett says, by filling in gaps, which may differ from one setting to another and that lead to various forms of cultural wisdom. Such ideas, he argues, can be developed by "cultural scaffolding" into scientific knowledge or highly developed theology. Theology then belongs to this highly developed "cultural scaffolding" that makes use of anchor ideas, "peculiar features of the cultural environment that support building ideas and practices far removed from the sure foundation of natural cognition."[38]

Barrett's argument leads me to ask: what if the particular impulses of fullness and reform, understood in the general way I have described them, provide particular "anchor ideas" for many people today? Granted the possibility of our typical distortions, what if the inclination to a broader concern for human welfare, for systemic changes in the direction of equality and fairness, and a greater concern for environmental renewal, have become for many "anchor ideas" that are a part of their normal cognitive functioning?[39] Whatever one's assessment of current cultural trends the question still presses: if "anchor ideas" truly reflecting Christian virtues could exist in a given cultural situation, what might this mean for doing theology? How might theology provide an appropriate "cultural scaffolding" for anchor ideas formed under the specific influence of Christianity?

Consider next advances made possible by *medical science* as further evidence for the presence of Christian values, something that is visible recently in research to find a vaccine and treatment for COVID-19, and other

---

in *Warranted Christian Beliefs*.

38. Barrett, *Cognitive Science*, 137–40, quote at 141.

39. This would account for the fact that writers sympathetic with the "Great Awokening" insist that there are some issues—like racism, or fairness, or justice—in which there are not "two sides."

diseases. Much of the advice offered by medical professionals is a remarkable commentary on the humanistic goals of modern medicine that work to protect, for example, those most vulnerable to the coronavirus—both the old and infirm and the front line medical workers. Reading a recent study of scientific advances impresses one with the universal concern to develop practices that balance progress with a deep empathy for those who suffer. Siddhartha Mukherjee's marvelous history of the gene, for example, offers a glimpse into the world of medical research and practice.[40] At one point Mukherjee, both a doctor and researcher, becomes acquainted with Erika, a fifteen-year-old who suffers from a rare form of muscular degeneration. He comes to admire Erika's courage but also her creativity in living with her condition. It is now possible to sequence the genes of unborn children and discover the presence of such abnormalities. But what, Mukherjee wonders, should be done with this knowledge? We could eliminate this from the human gene pool, but then we would eliminate Erika as well. To refuse to acknowledge her suffering, Mukherjee writes, is a "failure in our empathy," but to take steps to eliminate Erika would be a "failure in our humanity." Such sensitivities, though widely expressed in the medical community, are deeply Christian. And when we hear, for example, of Michael Blaese wondering: "What if we . . . took the T cells from the blood of ADA [deficient] patients and put the virus into the cells," so they might make the needed ADA protein to correct the deficiency, we are watching the creative impulse of the image of God at work. One cannot read such studies without coming away deeply impressed with the progress being made toward finding cures and giving hope of a better future, by a vast network of people advancing our common cultural wisdom. At their best—something that was on vivid display during the 2020 pandemic—this community of medical professionals often exhibited a self-sacrificing service that recalls the social pattern of Christ's life and teaching. It perhaps did not consciously or directly model this, but it often became a kind of grace that blessed many.

Something similar could be said about *economics*, which often comes in for probing criticism. Leading voices include people like Thomas Piketty, whose commitment to reducing inequality and restoring the balance in the direction of low-wage workers is well known, or Jean Tirole, the Noble Prize-winning economist, who admits that economics as a normative science must encourage pro-social behavior which is necessary to a good society.[41] Or consider a recent work by Samuel Bowles promoting

---

40. Mukherjee, *The Gene*, quotes which follow at 452 and 425 respectively.
41. See Piketty, *Capital*, and Tirole, *Economics*.

what he calls the *Moral Economy*.[42] He proposes that the assumption that people are motivated only by self-interest may reflect the kind of society that our economics has produced (3). Proper incentives often crowd out the better motives—social preferences—necessary to produce the healthy civic culture that we want (106). Early forms of capitalism, Bowles notes, "sustained vibrant civic cultures characterized by widespread conformity to cooperative and generous social norms" (114). Since good government is an "emergent property of a well ordered society" (14), he proposes, what makes an economic system work is the underlaying social order that mixes altruism and reciprocity (145). It is virtue not incentives, he argues, that makes an economy work; rules are necessary only to induce wicked people to act ethically (215). Bowles's wisdom, which may reflect his earlier experience supporting Martin Luther King, is widely respected as a part of the current wisdom of economics.

Perhaps wisdom of this kind does something more: perhaps it gestures toward an alternative pattern for human social organization that we proposed Paul was modeling in 2 Corinthians. In the body of Christ, Paul implies, God has made possible what Kathryn Tanner terms a "community of mutual benefit."[43] God's identification in Christ with the poor means making the good things God has created their property too, thus alleviating their poverty. That theological exchange, which is expressed in the sharing among members of the Trinity, where each gives to the other without diminishment or loss, and where the possession of each becomes the property of the other, becomes the basis for imagining a new kind of community. Tanner concludes: "The result is the possession and enjoyment of the very same goods in common: what we have for our own good is also the property of others from which they too can benefit." Bowles probably does not have this economic arrangement in mind, but he is pointing us in this direction; the replacing of shareholder capitalism with stakeholder capitalism, with its concern for the environmental, social, and governance issues, does not signal the arrival of the kingdom, but it does suggest a new direction in economic wisdom.

What finally might it mean to develop practices and policies in our *earthkeeping* that reflect what we called earlier a resurrection imagination? Here one might find many illustrations from those addressing issues of resource depletion in the context of climate change. Some time ago, one of

---

42. Bowles, *The Moral Economy*; pages in the text are to this source.

43. Tanner, *Economy of Grace*, 75–80, quote at 79–80. She contrasts this view with that of John Locke, who argues that one has a property right to his/her own life, liberty, and the pursuit of happiness. Unlike Locke, "we are our own and have for our own only as what we are and have remain God's own" (81).

the pioneers in these things, John Jeavons, developed the notion of what he calls "bio-intensive" farming. This proposed what he termed a nonviolent relationship with the earth. He argued, in language that reflects Genesis 2:15, that our tilling of the soil should be a blessing and not a curse. Unlike most agriculture, which disrupts the biotic structure of the soil, bio-intensive farming seeks to preserve and enhance the biotic community.[44] Everything grown in this process is either eaten or composted, that is returned to the soil. Food produced in this way is healthier, both in that plants are grown organically, but also in that vitamins and trace minerals are preserved and the soil at the end of the process is actually more fertile than it was at the beginning. From the perspective of the Christian story, this regeneration can become not simply a metaphor, but an actual anticipation of the renewed earth that God will bring about.

Others, working in this same spirit, have sought building and manufacturing processes that use only biodegradable materials, glues, and packaging. Like bio-intensive farming, this initiative insists that all manufactured products should not only contribute to a social good, but they should eventually enhance the earth itself. Architecture and manufacturing processes that respect the created order and preserve the natural environment has been the goal of William McDonough, one of the founders of green architecture.[45] He began a headquarters for the Gap in California by asking: what would birds flying over like to see when they look down? In manufacturing processes, he has proposed using only elements that can be returned to the soil in a way that enriches it. This process, which is sometimes referred to as "upcycling"—which means returning materials to the organic process with improved rather than degraded quality—preserves all the nutrients so that nothing is lost and much is gained. Such practices display the reality of a world where resurrection is not only a future hope but a present possibility, one that we all share together, and modeling a community that reflects the mind of Christ who came not to be served but to be a servant of creation.

Living out the new creation invites us to imagine a world in which our gardening and culture making enhance the created order. But why not apply this imagination to the growing service sector of our economy? Why not consider the way service industries like tourism and hospitality might be thought of as regenerative processes—socially and environmentally? In fact a new movement in tourism, growing out of previous developments in ecotourism, called regenerative tourism, has been proposed in a recent

---

44. Jeavons has written a number of books; see for example *How to Grow*.
45. McDonough, "A Field of Dreams."

global tourism conference in 2019 in Madrid.[46] As with the possible changes in economic practices, those proposing such practices argue that the impact of new ways of thinking about creation can result in public goods that everyone can share and enjoy and that enhance the environment. This is a new wisdom that is not the possession of Christians or churches, but has become a new kind of wisdom that is publicly available.

Alongside these indications in philosophy, psychology, medicine and economics, and ecology, *mainstream cultural and academic life* in recent years has experienced what some have called a "Great Awokening," that represents a set of metaphysical and moral commitments focusing on liberation of marginalized and oppressed populations that would have been inconceivable a generation ago. Adherents of these views refer to themselves as "woke" to the dangers of sexism and above all the many forms of racism. Zach Goldberg, a researcher of this movement, has presented evidence that this growing sector of the population, those "woken," show the most outgroup bias (that is more openness to groups different from themselves), a broader scope of empathy for suffering in these groups, with an emphasis on care, avoiding harm and violence (with a broad notion of harm), and promoting fairness.[47] Goldberg admits that this often leads to a strident and ideological triumphalism that is often exacerbated by social media, exposing the ambiguous character of any possible wisdom.

John McWhorter, professor at Columbia University, in an article on "Atonement as Activism,"[48] proposes that vast numbers of white young college students flock to lectures and books by Ta-Nehisi Coates in search of what he calls atonement for the racism they lament and in which they feel implicated. McWhorter in fact argues this population sees this as the new "original sin" they have inherited—present at birth and ineradicable. McWhorter highlights the religious language that accompanies the testimonies of complicity in the systematic racism in which they live. (Though he acknowledges this "recreational pessimism" is sometimes more about helping white people find "grace" or "atonement" than actually doing something about Blacks.) Be this as it may, as I write this, such sensitivities are sending crowds of people of all ages into the streets to protest the killing of George Floyd. And bookstores are reporting record sales of books by people like Coates and Michelle Alexander or Marie Gottschalk. Though playing out in

---

46. W. D. Roberts, Jr. and Grace Roberts Dyrness, "El reto del turismo"; and Josette M. Plaut and Emily Amedee, *Becoming a Regenerative Practitioner*.

47. Goldberg, "America's White Saviors." I owe this reference to Professor Ben Lima. *Woke* is a term originating in Black culture, and surely influenced by the Black church.

48. McWhorter, "Atonement as Activism."

multiple forms, the available evidence suggests that the modern imaginary of fullness, benevolence, and reform is alive and well.

Mutual service, forgiveness, bio-intensive gardening, and upcycling represent constructive and nonviolent interventions—all these suggest we need not be satisfied with death and violence, either toward each other or toward the created order, that we can imagine and work toward another order. And, I argue, they all express in various ways the goodness that God has placed in creation and, beyond that, the pattern expressed in Christ's teaching and embodied in his death and resurrection. They all make it possible for us to wonder: "What if the world were like that"? The desire for such a world reflects the longing that is placed in all of us, and can issue in an attitude toward culture that is generative and hopeful.

But even if I am right about this claim, and in our current cultural situation this benevolent influence of the gospel has become a component of the accepted cultural wisdom, these facts do not suggest the imminent arrival of God's kingdom. They may simply be celebrated as a human achievement, or even, for various reasons, opposed and subverted. Or they may reflect simply a cultural memory of a story heard long ago but whose contours and details have been lost. Though the facts on the ground cannot be ignored, and they provide the starting point of any cultural project, they carry the special risks I have highlighted throughout this book: They are sometimes wrong, or they are misconstrued, or worse, over time forgotten altogether. Walter Benjamin points out another problem with such facts: they too often become simply inert information—the banal images and cliches with which we are daily besieged. What is lost in information, Benjamin argues, is the story. And for this he suggests we miss storytellers. For most of history, he notes, people have lived by the stories sages told—what we are calling cultural wisdom. Sages mine the depths of human experience to awaken people to life. Here is how Benjamin describes their function: "The storyteller takes what he tells from experience—his own or that reported by others. And he in turn makes it the experience of those who are listening to his tale."[49] This practical orientation with its transformative potential, that characterized classical epics, or, we might add, Jesus' parables, has been lost. Or perhaps we should say it has been misplaced, existing in the fragments of a cultural memory. If Benjamin is right what must be recovered is the Story that lies behind what is worthy in our facts and information: that a loving God created a world that still produces its bounty, that this God made a surprise

---

49. Benjamin, "The Storyteller," quote at 87. Benjamin thinks the novel has not been able to accommodate the timeless role of storytelling, but it has been kept alive in the work of Nikolai Leskov, whose stories are deeply embedded in his Russian Orthodox imagination.

visit to restore a broken order, and promises to come back and finish the work of making all things new. However valuable and inescapable our facts on the ground, in themselves, they cannot by themselves tell this story. For that story we still need theology.

A Contemporary Rereading of Paul

Reflecting on this story and connecting it with the facts on the ground is the work of what we call theology. Our argument, however, is that the texture and beauty of this story must always emerge in the terms set out by the reigning cultural wisdom—elucidating, challenging, correcting and sometimes even celebrating them, but always pointing beyond what they can say. And to consider this part of our current situation we turn to a previous storyteller, the Apostle Paul and the story he tells to the believers in Rome.

Paul begins in Romans chapter one by claiming that everyone is able to know something about God from the created order, "his eternal power and divine nature," which can be "seen through the things he has made," even though this truth is often suppressed (1:20). As in his address on Mars Hill in Acts 17, the creation itself provides opportunity to know about and even seek God, something Paul supports there by quoting two Greek poets—the accepted wisdom of his day (Acts 17:27-28). In chapter two of Romans, Paul echoes Jesus by urging his readers—who were both Jewish and gentile believers—not to be too quick to judge others because they all will face God who will "repay according to each one's deeds" (2:6). He goes on: "To those who by patiently doing good seek for glory and honor and immortality, he will give eternal life," while those who are self-seeking will see God's wrath (2: 7-8). So, he tells his Jewish readers, don't think because you have the law you are somehow special. He goes on:

> For it is not the hearers of the law who are righteous in God's sight, but the doers of the law who will be justified. When Gentiles, who do not possess the law, do instinctively what the law requires, these, though not having the law, are a law to themselves. They show that what the law requires is written on their hearts, to which their own conscience also bears witness. (2:14-15)

Thus one might conclude from these chapters, that humans have, as Justin Barrett has argued, a natural awareness of God, one that is known externally by creation (Rom 1) and internally by conscience (Rom 2). But their problem, as we noted earlier, is that all of us, Jews and gentiles alike, seek self-mastery on our own terms. In this respect Paul says we are all alike; we are all guilty before God.

The gift of the law, like wisdom itself, Paul writes, though it is a great blessing, is no guarantee of salvation; possession of the law does not guarantee its obedience. And Scriptures are clear on this score: all alike, Jews and Greeks, fall short of this standard, as Paul reminds them (in 3:9), just before citing the FT (i.e. Jewish) sources on the universality of sin. Following this reminder, Paul reiterates the great affirmation of the gospel that will be the theme of the book: "But now, apart from the law, the righteousness of God has been disclosed . . . through faith in Jesus Christ" (3:21).

Paul's proposal here is a version of the gospel, the saving intervention of God in Jesus Christ. Our cultural wisdom may offer pointers to that story, but the full experience of that saving work is a work of God's spirit. Our contemporaries need first to encounter God, and realize that God is behind the impulse to equality and the call to a good life, and that the Christ story has opened the way to this. This is a new kind of wisdom, that comes from above—it is what we call theology. Though it helps explain much of what our contemporaries are feeling and what they long to be and do, this "good news" eventuates in something that goes beyond these pointers, what, Paul says, "no eye has seen, nor ear heard, nor the human heart conceived" (1 Cor 2:9, referring to Isa 64:4). Paul speaks here in 1 Corinthians 2 of what God has prepared for those who love God, indicating the wisdom from above that the apostle had introduced in the previous chapter—the trajectory of life that opens onto a whole new world. In the first chapter I questioned the "antitheses" that proponents of common grace are wont to insist on. Now however we can see that they are not wrong about this, but only mistaken to place it at the outset of our shared cultural world, rather than at the end toward which this is leading. The antithesis will be seen, revealed, but we do not yet have eyes to discern it around us. Our own vision is limited—we "see in a mirror dimly" Paul will remind readers later in this letter (1 Cor 13:12). Like our secular neighbors, we too struggle with a nature prone to prejudice and self-seeking. And they, for their part, often succeed in seeing what is right and working in that direction; while the church all too often fails to demonstrate this new order. We all jointly share and live from our common cultural wisdom even as we all struggle with our sinful nature. But what God is preparing will go beyond what any of us can imagine. Though we are grateful for vaccines and treatment that make use of gene therapy, what this progress points to, we believe, is resurrection; though we are grateful for economists who seek fair distribution of goods and services, what that gestures toward is a new kind of community, one that together will share the marriage supper of the Lamb. We long to see the earth healed, but that will only happen at the renewal of all things. The best of our cultural wisdom strains to see through all our celebrations to that final one, because in truth, they—we all—long to look on the face of God, which Paul says, alone, will heal our limited vision (1 Cor 13:12). That is, finally, a gift of grace, the wisdom from above.

8. Epilogue

When things are "unveiled," we stop taking things for granted. That's what major events like the COVID-19 pandemic do for us. They reframe reality in a radical way and offer us an invitation to greater depth and breadth. If we trust the universal pattern, the wisdom of all times and all places, including the creation and evolution of the cosmos itself, we know that an ending is also the place for a new beginning. Death is followed by a new kind of life.—Richard Rohr[1]

WISDOM, I HAVE ARGUED, expresses the natural capacities of people, always working from the order and potential of our beautiful and broken world, but reaching out for a new world that calls out to us. Wisdom, I have claimed, is structured by poetics and practice, breathing in and breathing out, what medieval monks called the *vita contemplativa* and the *vita activa*. The one fueled by desire for fullness, the other by a vision of something better.

The results of this, what we mortals make of the kaleidoscopic wonder of creation, always takes some particular cultural shape, locally typical but broadly recognizable. These facts on the ground, however cheerful or grim, cannot be ignored because they are the starting point for any possible future, and, I argue, they offer the texture—the look and feel—of any eventual theological statement. For this is the most surprising discovery we have made on this journey. We set out to discover how we might better understand the terrain called "common grace," what I argue might be better framed as cultural "wisdom." Though we have framed this as a common human project, we have also seen God's hand at every turn. And we have been startled to discover a (new) way of thinking about God's work in the world. A deep probe of wisdom, it turns out, runs directly into God's presence and grace, that is into revelation. In fact the very search scrambles received categories—wisdom, grace, general and special revelation. This suggests that

---

1. Rohr, "When Things are Unveiled."

we may have segregated these overlapping spheres too sharply. Wisdom is human work, human discourse; revelation is God's voice, God's work. Well, yes, but if we listen closely to the former, we sometimes end up hearing the latter. As Avery Dulles puts this: "Revelation should not be understood as an insertion of fully formulated divine truths into the continuum of human knowledge, but rather as the process by which God, working within human history and human tradition, enables his spiritual creatures to discern more profoundly the true meaning of their existence."[2]

Wisdom, recall, reflects the order and structure of creation and what the creative impulse—that central element of the divine image, is able to make of this order and its potential. But the argument of this book implies that we celebrate these gifts not only as human achievements but also as gifts of the Spirit of God. As John Calvin argued, in astronomy, philosophy, and medicine, "we see, at the present time, that the excellent gifts of the Spirit are diffused through the whole human race."[3] God still takes pleasure in watching the goodness of the world being celebrated, and even stakes a claim on its creation-sourced goodness.

And rereading the New Testament, it seems that Paul understood this trajectory. He tells the Ephesian believers how much he thanks God for them, for their faith and "love toward all the saints," but then he tells them he is praying "that the God of our Lord Jesus Christ, the Father of glory may give you a spirit of wisdom (*sophia*) and revelation (*apokalypsieu*) as you come to know him" (Eph 1:15–17). Perhaps a spirit of wisdom is preparation, perhaps even a precondition, for revelation. Though the sages didn't always realize it, the natural tendency of growth in wisdom is toward knowing God, the ultimate source of all wisdom. The one embodies the best of our life in God's good creation—its morning stillness, its flowered colors and scents—the other provides a space in which, in Augustine's words, "we find our rest." The end that is our beginning.

Here I pause a bit to reflect on our particular place, our embodied life in the world. Though its toil and trouble often make us yearn for some other world, the story that Christ has left for us says our goal is not world flight but resurrection. The intervention of Christ was to the end of a new creation; this represented a disturbing remaking but not an unmaking of this world. So we start with what we have—our few loaves and fishes that seem so inadequate. But our argument in the final chapter was that there are signs, both in our history and in our present, in what we call the

---

2. Dulles, "Revelation and Discovery," 21. Dulles acknowledges his dependence on Karl Rahner on this point.

3. Calvin, *Commentary on Genesis*, Gen 4:20 in loc.

Western world, that the gospel story does not seem so strange as it once appeared. Even resurrection may not be as unbelievable as it was to the sages on Mars Hill. There are even rumors, believe it or not, of a possible "Great Awokening" that grows from gospel seeds in the Black church. This particular situation, its history and trajectory, whatever its fragility and inconsistencies, must be the stuff from which we shape our particular version of the gospel story—our particular theology.

But let me be clear: nothing I say about the influence of Christian virtues on the modern imaginary suggests the continuing presence, or revival, of Christendom—the ecclesial domination of culture. In fact the larger culture is often rightly suspicious of Christians, evangelicals in particular, who seek to impose their values on everyone else. That was the mistake of Christendom. Christendom too often perverted the teachings of the Jesus enthroned in the churches. The power brokers of Christendom honored patience, nonviolence, and love of enemies with their lips, but their hearts (and actions) were far from this. The account I have given suggests that, in the history of the various relationships between the wisdom of culture and the story of Jesus, the balance has shifted, the integration of wisdom and the saving work of God seen in Jesus Christ, may be more believable today than it has been in a long time.

Perhaps this shows that forces of modernization may have succeeded in diminishing the influence of the institutional church while, ironically, enhancing the influence of the story Jesus actually told—even the suspicions of our secular neighbors are deployed by Christian-sourced values of tolerance and benevolence. The critical consciousness of professional football players standing up for social justice may not herald the arrival of the kingdom, but it is a sign that Christians would be foolish to ignore.

Though we did not follow in detail the narrative in which Charles Taylor develops his understanding of fullness and reform, it is instructive to note where he ends up in his "Epilogue." There he challenges his fellow Christian critics—he names specifically Radical Orthodoxy, but I would add many of my evangelical colleagues—who believe the contemporary situation is best understood in terms of its intellectual deviation from orthodoxy. While as a Roman Catholic Taylor understands these critics, he thinks the Reform Master Narrative better accounts for our modern social imaginary. Whatever the weaknesses of modernism, they cannot simply be fixed by correcting the intellectual deviations. "History cannot be separated from the situation it has brought about," he writes.[4] And, however

---

4. Taylor, *A Secular Age*, 776.

their source or orthodoxy is evaluated, it is these facts on the ground that call for our response.

But in addition to a careful assessment of our current facts, we have also seen the importance of a careful historical scrutiny of our deep past in order to see how we got to this place. This historical work, always carried on in the light of our current perspective, helps us see what we are glad to have left behind, and what we might have lost in the process. We might celebrate the demise of "paganism" or "polytheism," but their loss might also spur useful reflection. We saw, for example, a particular kind of wisdom lay behind Augustine's theological construction that has had powerful impact, for good or ill, on subsequent theological reflection. His impressive reflections on memory and time in the *Confessions* continue to amaze and puzzle contemporary students of human psychology, and they have given theologians materials with which to reread Paul and construct biblical notions of the will and freedom. But they have done something else that mostly passes unnoticed: Augustine's introspection has also opened a trajectory of understanding faith and, in the Protestant reading of this, the Christian life itself, as something that goes on largely in our heads—or what we more biblically call the heart.[5] But is this really consistent with Jesus' story? Perhaps the revival of pagan rituals, or the Gaia hypothesis, hint at embodied practices and sensitivities that some versions of Christianity have lost.[6] All this is to say that wisdom, even when it is wrong, has something to teach us about the way the world works.

But, to be truly wise, we need to look not only to the past, but to the future. Remember a core element of God's image in humans is the impulse to imagine a future and work toward it. Of course even this divine capacity fails to imagine what God will do with creation. When we hear the prophet Isaiah telling us that God is about to create new heavens and a new earth, a new Jerusalem, "as a joy and its people as a delight," a new social order, and a creation at peace (Isa 65:17–25), we are at a loss for words. We realize this newness, as Walter Brueggemann says, "does not emerge from within present public processes or through effective human agency."[7] And when the Apostle John sees this future on Patmos, he sees

---

5. Krister Stendahl may have been the first to point this out, more than fifty years ago. Augustine, Stendahl wrote, was the first "modern man," his "*Confessions* are first great document in the history of the introspective conscience." "The Apostle Paul and the Introspective Conscience of the West," 205.

6. See Taylor's discussion of these possibilities in *A Secular Age*, 771–72. He even proposes that the polytheism which we are proud to have left behind might have honored the diversity of life's demands in such a way as to avoid the totalitarian dangers of "outside the church there is no salvation."

7. Brueggemann, *Theology of the Old Testament*, 172. This he notes describes it apocalyptic character.

an entirely revised economic order in which gold and precious stones are not the prized possessions of the rich but public goods—paved streets and eternal foundations—to be enjoyed by all (Rev 21:19–21). This vision should stimulate our imaginations for what is coming—what God will do. But it will also suggest patience and a fresh perspective on our own streets. Things don't have to be this way; and one day they will be different. So we work and we wait in patience and hope. Here we need to recall our distinction between our human projects and God's work of bringing new creation. However valuable the social gifts of new creation may be for motivating our work, we need to remember that humans do not build the new Jerusalem—that is God's work. As Richard Mouw writes, we work with a vision of transformation—that is the best we can do; we do not actually transform the world. "We take on the present challenges of Christian discipleship with a *vision* of the ultimate transformation of things in Jesus Christ. We *await* the day when all things will be made new."[8]

Still, this vision of renewal should make us grateful for any advance toward that day. We need to keep in mind the fact of historical changes—sometimes radical—over time. We once understood the earth as the center of the universe; we now have a vastly enlarged view of the glorious solar system. We once viewed human slavery as a necessary part of the social structure; we now accept there can be no justification on any grounds for chattel slavery. Similarly attitudes toward women, care of the earth, economic inequality, and many other matters have changed over time. All these changes involve in critical ways new perspectives on how God intends the world to work.

And the way the world works, so I argue, must be seen in its intrinsic connection to revelation. This is seen perhaps with the greatest clarity in our poetics. As we listen carefully to contemporary longings, in a deep Spirit-led conversation with Scripture, we may hear the voice of God. Wisdom, we recall, like prayer, begins with perception, careful listening, paying attention, considering the lilies. Today this posture of wisdom resonates with the widespread popularity of meditation and mindfulness. The increasing complexity and sheer volume of modern life has led many to a deep desire to disconnect—something gratefully encouraged by the 2020 coronavirus lockdown. Sarah Coakley has used the contemporary fascination with gender, sexual desire, and contemplation as a possible window into God's presence in this culture. She notes that certain bodily and spiritual practices are the "precondition for trinitarian thinking of a deep sort."[9] If one is not engaged in such practices of contemplation, and, eventually, prayer and worship, this deeper presence is simply unavailable to one. The patient

---

8. Mouw, *All That God Cares About,* loc.1357. Emphasis original.
9. Coakley, *God, Sexuality, and the Self,* 16; see 6–36. Quote that follows at 10.

posture of wisdom is a necessary starting point, even if the eventual movement to prayer and worship will critique, expand, transform, and even at points reject this common wisdom. It is to this deeper knowledge of the trinitarian God that common wisdom is meant to lead us. Writing even before the outbreak of #MeToo, Coakley argues that sexual desire, even when it is perverted and addictive, remains "the precious clue that ever tugs at the heart, reminding the human soul—however dimly—of its created source." Sex reminds us that desire is fundamental to human life, and it ultimately refers us to God. For God's own desire infuses creation with the call of Lady Wisdom, which is ultimately an invitation, Coakley thinks, to share in God's own Trinitarian fullness. So the urgent focus on meditation, desire, and gender may not be a distraction but a possible pathway to open us to God. It is "the very threeness of God," Coakley argues, "transformatively met in the Spirit, which gives the key to a view of gender that is appropriately funded in bodily practices of prayer." God is not indifferent to these desires, Coakley thinks; in fact God stirs them up but then chastens and purges them, "forges them by stages of sometimes painful growth into the likeness of his Son." This growth recalls Jesus' teaching on patience, forgiveness, and trust. Contemporary interest in contemplation and related aesthetic experience, from this perspective, opens onto spiritual practice: "The very act of contemplation—repeated, lived, embodied, suffered—is an act that, by grace, and over time, inculcates mental patterns of 'unmastery'" and love.[10] Theology then turns out to enhance and give life to a growing natural interest in paying attention to one's life. In this sense, the call to look carefully, say, at a work of art is dangerous, because, George Steiner says, "it queries of the last privacies of our existence"; it can easily slip into prayer: let me change my life.[11] This possibility recalls Paul's extended prayer for the Ephesians: that they may have a spirit of "wisdom and revelation as you come to know [God]," so that "with the eyes of your heart enlightened, you may know the hope in which he has called you, what are the riches of his glorious inheritance among the saints" (Eph 1:18). The human wisdom (Gr. *Sophia*) he wanted for them provided an opening to revelation "as you come to know God," but this in turn offered a deeply enhanced wisdom from above. Where the one leaves off and the other begins one cannot always tell. It's a conversation going on all the time; you just have to listen for it.

---

10. Coakley, *God, Sexuality, and the Self,* 43, quotes at 34 and 6 respectively.
11. Steiner, *Real Presences,* 142. And see Frederick Buechner, *Listening to Your Life.*

Bibliography

Abraham, William J. "Revelation." In *Cambridge Dictionary of Christian Theology*, edited by Ian A. McFarland, 445–47. Cambridge: Cambridge University Press, 2011.

Alter, Robert. *The Art of Biblical Poetry.* New York: Basic, 1985.

Archer, Margaret. *Being Human: The Problem of Agency.* Cambridge: Cambridge University Press, 2000.

Armstrong, Karen. *Fields of Blood: Religion and the History of Violence.* New York: Alfred Knopf, 2014.

Ashford, Bruce Riley, and Craig Bartholomew. *The Doctrine of Creation: A Constructive Kuyperian Approach.* Downers Grove, IL: InterVarsity, 2020.

Augustine of Hippo. *City of God.* Translated by Henry Bettenson. New York: Penguin, 2003[1972].

———. *Confessions.* Translated by Henry Chadwick. New York: Oxford University Press, 1991.

———. *Contra Faustum Manichaeum.* In *Nicene and Post Nicene Fathers,* vol. 4, book 22, edited by Philip Schaff. New York: 1887–1902. https://www.ccel.org/ccel/s/schaff/npnf104.pdf.

———. *Eighty-Three Different Questions.* Translated by David Mosher. Washington, DC: Catholic University Press, 1977.

———. *On Christian Teaching.* Translated by R. P. H. Green. New York: Oxford University Press, 1999.

———. *Patience.* Translated by H. Browne. Newadvent.org/fathers/1315.

———. *Retractions.* Translated by Sister M. Inez Bogan. The Fathers of the Church, vol. 60. Washington, DC: Catholic University of America Press, 1999 [1968].

Baptist, Edward E. *The Half Has Never Been Told: Slavery and the Making of American Capitalism.* New York: Basic, 2014.

Barclay, John M. G. "Crucifixion as Wisdom: Exploring the Ideology of a Disreputable Movement." In *The Wisdom and Foolishness of God*, edited by C. Chalamet et al., 1–20. Minneapolis: Augsburg/Fortress, 2015.

Barrett, Justin. *Born Believers: The Science of Children's Religious Beliefs.* New York: Free, 2012.

———. *Cognitive Science of Religion and Theology: From Human Minds to Divine Minds.* West Conschocken, PA: Templeton, 2011.

Barrett, Nicholas. "Reading Every Square Inch of Creation: Towards a Neo-Calvinist Theology of Literature." Paper presented at Calvin College, April 2019.

Barth, Karl. *Church Dogmatics* II/1.1. Edited by G. W. Bromiley and T. F. Torrance. Edinburgh: T&T Clark, 1958.

———. *Church Dogmatics* III/1. Translated by J. W. Edwards, O. Bussey, and Harold Knight. Edinburgh: T&T Clark, 1958.

Bartholomew, Craig. *Contours of the Kuyperian Tradition*. Kindle ed. Downers Grove, IL: InterVarsity, 2018.

Bartholomew, Craig, and Ryan O'Dowd. *Old Testament Wisdom Literature: A Theological Interpretation*. Downers Grove, IL: InterVarsity, 2011.

Barton, Stephen C. "Gospel Wisdom." In *Where Shall Wisdom Be Found?*, edited by Stephen C. Barton, 93–110. Edinburgh: T & T Clark, 1999.

Barton, Stephen C., ed. *Where Shall Wisdom Be Found? Wisdom in the Bible, the Church, and the Contemporary World*. Edinburgh: T & T Clark, 1999.

Basso, Keith H. *Wisdom Sits in Places: Landscape and Language among the Western Apache*. Albuquerque, NM: University of New Mexico Press, 1996.

Bavinck, Herman. "Herman Bavinck's 'Common Grace.'" Translated and introduced by R. C. Van Leeuwen, *Calvin Theological Journal* 24 (1989) 35–65.

———. *Essays on Religion, Science, and, Society*. Translated and edited by John Bolt. Grand Rapids: Eerdmans, 2008.

Bazzell, Pascal Daniel. "Toward a Creational Perspective on Poverty, Genesis 1:26–28: The Image of God and its Missiological Implications." In *Genesis and Christian Theology*, edited by Nathan Macdonald et al., 228–41. Grand Rapids: Eerdmans, 2012.

Benjamin, Walter. "The Storyteller: Reflections on the Works of Nikolai Leskov." In *Illuminations: Essays and Reflections*, translated by Harry Zohn and edited by Hannah Arendt, 83–109. New York: Schocken, 1968.

Berends, William. *The Evaluation of Culture in Missiology*. PhD diss., Australian College of Theology, 1990.

Birch, Bruce C. *Let Justice Roll Down: The Old Testament, Ethics, and the Christian Life*. Louisville, KY: John Knox, 2007.

Blenkinsopp, Joseph. *Wisdom and Law in the Old Testament: The Ordering of Life in Israel and Early Judaism*. New York: Oxford University Press, 1995.

Bowles, Samuel. *The Moral Economy: Why Good Incentives Are No Substitute for Good Citizens*. New Haven, CT: Yale University Press, 2017.

Bonhoeffer, Dietrich. *Creation and Fall; Temptation: Two Biblical Studies*. Translated by John C. Fletcher. New York: Macmillan, 1959.

Bretherton, Luke. *Christ and the Common Life: Political Theology and the Case for Democracy*. Grand Rapids: Eerdmans, 2019.

Brown, Peter. *Augustine of Hippo: A Biography*. Berkeley, CA: University of California Press, 2000 [1969].

Brueggemann, Walter. *In Man We Trust: The Neglected Side of Biblical Faith*. Atlanta: John Knox, 1972.

———. *Theology of the Old Testament: Testimony, Dispute, Advocacy*. Minneapolis: Fortress, 1997.

Buechner, Frederick. *Listening to Your Life*. San Francisco: Harper, 1992.

Cahill, Lisa. *Blessed Are the Peacemakers: Pacifism, Just War, and Peacebuilding*. Minneapolis: Augsburg/Fortress, 2019.

Calvin, John. *Commentaries on the First Book of Moses, Genesis*. Translated by John King et al. Grand Rapids: Eerdmans, 1948 [1844–1856].

———. *Institutes of the Christian Religion*. Translated by F. L. Battles, edited by John T. McNeil. Philadelphia: Westminster, 1960.

Charlesworth, James H. "The Odes of Solomon." In *The Old Testament Pseudepigrapha*, 729–52. Garden City, NJ: Doubleday, 1985.

Clark, Andy, and David Chalmers. "The Extended Mind." *Analysis*, 58, vol. 1 (1998) 7–19.

Clements, Ronald. "Wisdom and Old Testament Theology." In *Wisdom in Ancient Israel: Essays in Honor of J. A. Emerton*, edited by John Day, Robert P. Gordon, and H. G. M. Williamson, 275–85. Cambridge: Cambridge University Press, 1995.

———. *Wisdom in Theology*. Grand Rapids: Eerdmans, 1992.

Clifford, Richard J. "The Hebrew Scriptures and the Theology of Creation" *Theological Studies* 46 (1985) 507–23.

Coakley, Sarah. *God, Sexuality, and the Self: An Essay "On the Trinity."* Cambridge: Cambridge University Press, 2013.

———. "Sin and Desire in Analytic Theology—A Return to Genesis 3." *The Analytic Theology Lecture*. American Academy of Religion, San Antonio, TX, November 20, 2016.

Craft, Jennifer Allen. *Placemaking and the Arts: Cultivating the Christian Life*. Downers Grove, IL: IVP Academic, 2018.

Crehan, Kate. *Gramsci's Common Sense: Inequality and its Narratives*. Durham, NC: Duke University Press, 2014.

Crenshaw, James J. *Old Testament Wisdom: An Introduction*. Atlanta: John Knox, 1981.

Croasmun, Matthew. *The Emergence of Sin: The Cosmic Tyrant in Romans*. New York: Oxford University Press, 2017.

Cyprian. "The Good of Patience." In *Saint Cyprian: Treatises*, translated by Sister George Edward Conway, 257–87. New York: Fathers of the Church, Vol. 36, 1958.

Davis, Ellen. *Scripture, Culture, and Agriculture: An Agrarian Reading of the Bible*. Cambridge: Cambridge University Press, 2009.

Dreyfus, Hubert, and Charles Taylor. *Retrieving Realism*. Cambridge, MA: Harvard University Press, 2015.

Dreher, Rod. *The Benedict Option: A Strategy for Christians in a Post-Christian World*. New York: Sentinel, 2017.

Driver, John. *How Christians Made Peace with War*. Scottsdale, PA: Herald, 1988.

Dulles, Avery. "Revelation and Discovery." In *Theology and Discovery: Essays in honor of Karl Rahner, S.J.*, edited by William Kelly, 1–29. Milwaukee, WI: Marquette University Press, 1980.

Dunn, James. "Jesus: Teacher of Wisdom or Wisdom Incarnate?" In *Where Shall Wisdom Be Found?*, edited by Stephen Barton, 75–92. Edinburgh: T & T Clark, 1999.

Dussel, Enrique. *The History of the Church in Latin America: An Interpretation*. San Antonio, TX: Latin American Cultural Center, 1974

Dyrness, William. "God's Play: Calvin, Theatre, and the Rise of the Book." In *Calvin and the Book*, edited by Karen Spierling, 123–36. Göttingen: Vandenhoeck & Ruprecht, 2015.

———. *Insider Jesus: Theological Reflections on New Christian Movements*. Downers Grove, IL: InterVarsity, 2016.

———. "Listening for Fresh Voices in the History of the Church." In *Teaching Global Theologies: Power and Praxis*, edited by Pui Lan Kwok et al., 29–43. Waco, TX: Baylor University Press, 2015.

———. *The Origin of Protestant Aesthetics in Early Modern Europe: Calvin's Reformation Poetics.* Cambridge: Cambridge University Press, 2019.

———. *Poetic Theology: God and the Poetics of Everyday Life.* Grand Rapids: Eerdmans, 2011.

———. "Poised Between Life and Death: The *Imago Dei* After Eden." In *The Image of God in an Image Driven Age: Explorations in Theological Anthropology*, edited by B. F. Jones and J. W. Barbeau, 47–65. Downers Grove, IL: InterVarsity, 2016.

———. *Senses of Devotion: Interfaith Aesthetics in Buddhist and Moslem Communities.* Eugene, OR: Cascade, 2013.

———. *Visual Faith: Art, Theology, and Worship in Dialogue.* Grand Rapids: Baker Academic, 2001.

Edwards, Michael. *Towards a Christian Poetics.* Grand Rapids: Eerdmans, 1984.

Eliot, T. S. "The Hollow Men (1925)." In *T. S. Eliot: The Collected Poems: 1909–1962*, 79–82. New York: Harcourt, 1962.

———. "The Journey of the Magi (1927)." In *T. S. Eliot: The Collected Poems: 1909–1962*, 99. New York: Harcourt, 1963.

Epps, Valerie. "Civilian Casualties in Modern Warfare: The Death of the Collateral Damage Rule." *Georgia Journal of International and Comparative Law*, August 2013. https://digitalcommons.law.uga.edu/cgi/viewcontent.cgi?article=1036&context=gjicl.

Erdozain, Dominic. *The Soul of Doubt: The Religious Roots of Unbelief from Luther to Marx.* New York: Oxford University Press, 2016.

Farrow, Douglas. "St Irenaeus of Lyon: The Church and the World." *Pro Ecclesia* 4, vol. 3 (1995) 333–55.

Ferguson, Everett. *The Early Church at Work and Worship: Catechesis, Baptism, Eschatology, and Martyrdom.* Vol. 2. Eugene, OR: Cascade, 2014.

Fergusson, David. "Interpreting the Story of Creation: A Case Study in the Dialogue between Theology and Science." In *Genesis and Christian Theology*, edited by N. McDonald, M. W. Elliott, and G. Macaskill, 155–74. Grand Rapids: Eerdmans, 2012.

Fiddes, Paul. *Freedom and Limit: A Dialogue between Literature and Christian Doctrine.* New York: St. Martin's, 1993.

———. *Seeing the World and Knowing God: Hebrew Wisdom and Christian Doctrine in a Late-Modern Context.* New York: Oxford University Press, 2013.

Fleck, Ludwik. *Genesis and Development of Scientific Fact.* Translated by Fred Bradley and C. J. Trenn. Chicago: University of Chicago Press, 1979.

Ford, David. *Christian Wisdom: Desiring God and Learning to Love.* Cambridge: Cambridge University Press, 2007.

Fretheim, Terrence. *God and World: A Relational Theology of Creation.* Nashville: Abingdon, 2005.

Galloway, Steven. *The Cellist of Sarajevo.* New York: Riverhead, 2008.

Gill, Robin. *Society Shaped by Theology: Sociological Theory.* Burlington, VT: Ashgate, 2013.

Gillespie, Michael. *The Theological Origins of Modernity.* Chicago: University of Chicago Press, 2008.

Goizueta, Roberto. *Caminemos con Jesus: Toward a Theology of Accompaniment.* Maryknoll, NY: Orbis, 1995.

Goldberg, Zach. "America's White Saviors." *The Tablet*, June 5, 2019. https://www.tabletmag.com/sections/news/articles/americas-white-saviors.

Goldingay, John. *Old Testament Theology: Israel's Gospel*. Vol. 1. Downers Grove, IL: InterVarsity, 2003.

Gordis, Robert. *Poets, Prophets, and Sages*. Bloomington, IN: University of Indiana Press, 1971.

Grant, Robert M. "Irenaeus and Hellenistic Culture." *Harvard Theological Review* 42 (1949) 41–51.

———. *Irenaeus of Lyon*. London: Routledge, 1997.

Green, Joel. *The Gospel of Luke*. Grand Rapids: Eerdmans, 1997.

Gregory, Brad S. *The Unintended Reformation: How a Religious Revolution Secularized Society*. Cambridge, MA: Harvard University Press, 2012.

Gunton, Colin E. "Christ the wisdom of God; A study of divine and human action." In *Where Shall Wisdom Be Found?*, edited by Stephen Barton, 249–61. Edinburgh: T & T Clark, 1999.

———. *The Triune Creator: A Historical and Systematic Study*. Grand Rapids: Eerdmans, 1998.

Haag, James W., Terrence W. Deacon, and Jay Ogilvy. "The Emergence of the Self." In *In Search of Self: Interdisciplinary Perspectives on the Person*, edited by J. Wentzel van Huyssteen and Erik P. Wiebe, 319–37. Grand Rapids: Eerdmans, 2012.

Hadot, Pierre. *Philosophy as a Way of Life*. Translated by Arnold I. Davidson. Oxford: Blackwell, 1995.

Harrison, Peter. *The Territories of Science and Religion*. Chicago: University of Chicago Press, 2015.

Hays, Richard. "Wisdom according to Paul." In *Where Shall Wisdom Be Found? Wisdom in the Bible, the Church, and the Contemporary World*, edited by Stephen Barton, 111–23. Edinburgh: T & T Clark, 1999.

Hayward, C. T. R. "Sirach and Wisdom's Dwelling Place." In *Where Shall Wisdom Be Found?*, edited by Stephen Barton, 38–39. Edinburgh: T & T Clark, 1999.

Helleman, Adrian. "A Non-Violent Revolution." In *To Be in History*, edited by Melba Maggay, 157–67. Manila: ISACC/Langham, 2019.

Henry, Andre. "Is Non-violence a Viable Choice?" Posted April 6, 2019. http://andrehenry.co/thoughts/2019/4/6/is-nonviolence-a-viable-choice?fbclid=IwAR2iwfeP2pfjfu9IbrCK4hEDXpDGohCLJoIFCR27V5dfO76wE3hUeVP1B10.

Hodgson, Peter. "Providence." In *Abingdon Dictionary of Theology*, edited by Donald W. Musser and Joseph L. Price, in loc. Nashville, TN: Abingdon, 1997.

Horowitz, Jason. "Italians find 'a moment of joy.'" *New York Times*, March 14, 2020 (updated March 16). https://www.nytimes.com/2020/03/14/world/europe/italians-find-a-moment-of-joy-in-this-moment-of-anxiety.html?_referringSource=articleShare.

Hutcheson, Francis. *An Inquiry into the Original Ideas of Beauty and Virtue in Two Treatises*. Translated and edited by Wolfgang Leiphold. Indianapolis: Liberty Fund, 2004 [1725].

Israel, Jonathan I. *Radical Enlightenment: Philosophy and the Making of Modernity 1650–1750*. New York: Oxford University Press, 2001.

Jeavons, John. *How to Grow More Vegetables*. Willits, CA: Ecology Action, 1978.

Jennings, Willie James. *Acts*. Louisville, KY: Westminster John Knox, 2017.

———. *The Christian Imagination: Theology and the Origins of Race*. New Haven, CT: Yale University Press, 2010.
Johnson, Mark. *The Body in the Mind*. Chicago: University of Chicago Press, 1992 [1987].
Johnston, Robert. *God's Wider Presence*. Grand Rapids: Baker Academic, 2014.
Jones, E. Stanley. *Christ of the Indian Road*. New York: Abingdon, 1925.
Julian of Norwich. *Revelations of Divine Love*. Translated by M. L. del Mastro. Garden City, NJ: Image/Doubleday, 1977.
Keck, Leander. *A Future for the Historical Jesus: The Place of Jesus in Preaching and Theology*. Nashville, TN: Abingdon, 1971.
Keel, Othmar. *The Symbolism of the Biblical World: Ancient Near Eastern Iconography and the Book of Psalms*. Translated by Timothy Hallett. New York: Seabury, 1987.
Kelly, J. N. D. *Early Christian Doctrines*. 5th ed. New York: Harper, 1978.
Kelsey, David. *Eccentric Existence: A Theological Anthropology*. Vol 1. Louisville, KY: Westminster John Knox, 2009.
Kline, Meredith. *Images of the Spirit*. Grand Rapids: Baker, 1980.
Kreider, Alan. "Military Service in the Church Orders." *Journal of Religious Ethics* 31, vol. 3 (2013) 415–42.
———. *The Patient Ferment of the Early Church: The Improbable Rise of Christianity in the Roman Empire*. Grand Rapids: Baker Academic, 2015.
Kuyper, Abraham. *Abraham Kuyper: A Centennial Reader*. Translated and edited by James Bratt. Grand Rapids: Eerdmans, 1998.
———. *Common Grace: God's Gifts for a Fallen World, The Historical Section*. Vol. 1. Translated by N. D. Kloosterman and E. M. van der Maas. Bellingham, WA: Lexham, 2015.
———. *Common Grace, The Doctrinal Section*. Vol. 2. Translated by Nelson Kloosterman and Ed M. van der Maas. Bellingham, WA: Lexham, 2015.
———. *Lectures on Calvinism*. Grand Rapids: Eerdmans, 1931.
———. *Principles of Sacred Theology*. Translated by J. Hendrik de Vries. Grand Rapids: Eerdmans, 1968.
———. *Wisdom and Wonder*. Translated by Nelson Kloosterman. Grand Rapids: Christian Library, 2011.
Kwok, Pui-Lan, et al., eds. *Teaching Global Theologies: Power and Praxis*. Waco, TX: Baylor University Press, 2015.
Kynes, Will. *An Obituary for "Wisdom Literature": The Birth, Death, and Intertextual Reintegration of a Biblical Corpus*. New York: Oxford University Press, 2019.
Lambert, W. G. "Some new Babylonian wisdom literature." In *Wisdom in Ancient Israel: Essays in Honor of J. A. Emerton*, edited by John Day, Robert P. Gordon, and H. G. M. Williamson, 26–40. Cambridge: Cambridge University Press, 1995.
Leclercq, Jean. *The Love of Learning and the Desire for God: A Study of Monastic Culture*. Translated by Catharine Misrahi. New York: Fordham University Press, 1982.
Lohfink, Gerhard. *Jesus and Community: The Social Dimensions of the Christian Faith*. Translated by John P. Gavin. Minneapolis: Fortress, 1984.
Luther, Martin. "Sermon on the Nativity." In *Martin Luther's Christmas Book*, edited by Roland Bainton, 27–33. Minneapolis: Augsburg, 1997.
Lynch, William. *Christ and Prometheus*. Notre Dame, IN: University of Notre Dame Press, 1970.

MacIntyre, Alasdair. *After Virtue*. Notre Dame, IN: University of Notre Dame Press, 2007 [1981].
Maggay, Melba Padilla, ed. *To Be in History: Dark Days of Authoritarianism*. Manila: ISACC/Langham, 2019.
Mathews, Thomas. *The Clash of Gods: A Reinterpretation of Early Christian Art*. Princeton, NJ: Princeton University Press, 1993.
McDonough, William. "A Field of Dreams: Green Roofs, Ecological Design and the Future of Urbanism." 2003. Green Architecture & Urbanism|William McDonough. https://mcdonough.com/writings/a-field-of-dreams/.
McLaren, Brian D. *We Make the Road by Walking: A Yearlong Quest for Spiritual Formation, Reorientation and Activation*. New York: Jericho, 2015.
McWhorter, John. "Atonement as Activism." https://www.the-american-interest.com/2018/05/24/atonement-as-activism/.
Meye Thompson, Marianne. *John: A Commentary*. Louisville, KY: Westminster John Knox, 2015.
Miller, Donald E., and Lorna Miller. *Becoming Human Again: An Oral History of the Rwanda Genocide against the Tutsi*. Berkeley, CA: University of California Press, 2020.
Morgan, David. *The Embodied Eye: Religious Visual Culture and the Social Life of Feeling*. Berkeley, CA: University of California Press, 2017.
Mouw, Richard J. *All That God Cares About: Common Grace and Divine Delight*. Kindle ed. Grand Rapids: Brazos, 2020.
Mouw, Richard J., and S. Griffoen. *Pluralism and Horizons: An Essay in Christian Public Philosophy*. Grand Rapids: Eerdmans, 1993.
Mukherjee, Siddhartha. *The Gene: An Intimate History*. New York: Scribner, 2016.
Murphy, Roland. "Israel's Wisdom: Dialogue between the Sages." In *Light in a Spotless Mirror: Reflections on the Wisdom Tradition in Judaism and Early Christianity*, edited by James H. Charlesworth and Michael A. Daise, 7–25. Harrisburg, PA: Trinity, 2003.
———. "The Personification of Wisdom." In *Wisdom in Ancient Israel: Essays in Honor of J. A. Emerton,* edited by John Day, Robert P. Gordon and H. G. M. Williamson, 225–35. Cambridge: Cambridge University Press, 1995.
———. *The Tree of Life*. Grand Rapids: Eerdmans,1996 [1990].
Oberman, Heiko A. *Luther: Man between God and the Devil*. Translated by E. Walliser-Roland. New York: Image, 1992.
O'Connor, Flannery. *Mystery and Manners: Occasional Prose*. Edited by Sally and Robert Fitzgerald. New York: Farrar, Straus and Giroux, 1961.
O'Donovan, Oliver. *The Desire of Nations: Rediscovering the Roots of Political Theology*. Cambridge: Cambridge University Press, 1996.
Oduyoye, Mercy. *Hearing and Knowing: Theological Reflections on Christianity in Africa*. Maryknoll, NY: Orbis, 1986.
Penchansky, David. *Understanding Wisdom Literature: Conflict and Dissonance in the Hebrew Text*. Grand Rapids: Eerdmans, 2012.
Penn, Michael Philip. *Envisioning Islam: Syriac Christians and the Early Muslim World*. Philadelphia: University of Pennsylvania Press, 2015.
Piketty, Thomas. *Capital in the Twenty-First Century*. Translated by Arthur Goldhammer. Cambridge, MA: Belknap Press of Harvard University Press, 2014
Plantinga, Alvin. *Warranted Christian Beliefs*. New York: Oxford University Press, 2000.

Plantinga, Cornelius. *Not the Way It's Supposed to Be: A Breviary of Sin.* Grand Rapids: Eerdmans, 1995.

Plaut, Josette M., and Emily Amedee. *Becoming a Regenerative Practitioner: A Field Guide.* Institute for the Built Environment. Fort Collins, CO: Colorado State University, 2018.

Ray, J. D. "Egyptian Wisdom Literature—the Ancient Near Eastern Setting." In *Wisdom in Ancient Israel: Essays in Honor of J. A. Emerton,* edited by John Day, Robert P. Gordon, and H. G. M. Williamson, 2–25. Cambridge: Cambridge University Press, 1995.

Roberts, W. D., Jr., and Grace Roberts Dyrness. "El reto del turismo para superar lo sostenible y lograr lo regenerative." Unpublished paper, San Jose, Costa Rica. March 2019.

Robinson, Marilynne. "Which Way to the City on a Hill?" *New York Review of Books,* July 18, 2019, 43–46.

Rohr, Richard. "When Things are Unveiled." https://cac.org/when-things-are-unveiled-2021-01-08/.

Sanders, James. "First Testament and Second." *Biblical Theology Bulletin* 17 (1987) 47–49.

Schafer, Peter. "Wisdom Finds a Home: Torah as Wisdom." In *Light in a Spotless Mirror: Reflections on Wisdom Tradition in Judaism and Early Christianity,* edited by James Charlesworth and Michael Daise, 26–44. Harrisburg, PA: Trinity, 2003.

Schilder, Klaas. *Christ and Culture.* Trans. A. H. Oosternoff, William Helder. Hamilton, ON: Lucerna, 2016 [1953].

Schnitker, Sarah A., Benjamin Houltberg, William Dyrness, and Nanyamka Radmond. "The Virtue of Patience, Spirituality and Suffering: Integrating Lessons from Positive Psychology, Psychology of Religion, and Christian Theology." *Psychology of Religion and Spirituality* 9, vol. 3 (2017) 264–75.

Shuster, Marguerite. *The Fall and Sin.* Grand Rapids: Eerdmans, 2004.

Sinclair, John. *Un esocés con alma Latina.* Mexico City: Cambridge University Press, 1990.

Smith, Christian. *To Flourish or Destruct: A Personalist Theory of Human Goods, Motivations, Failure, and Evil.* Chicago: University of Chicago Press, 2015.

Smith, James K. A. *Awaiting the King: Reforming Public Theology.* Grand Rapids: Baker Academic, 2017.

———. *Desiring the Kingdom: Worship, Worldview, and Cultural Formation.* Grand Rapids: Baker Academic, 2009.

———. *Imagining the Kingdom: How Worship Works.* Grand Rapids: Baker Academic, 2013.

———. *You Are What You Love: The Spiritual Power of Habit.* Grand Rapids: Brazos, 2016.

Stackhouse, Max. *Globalization and Grace.* Vol. 4 of God and Globalization. New York: Continuum, 2007.

Stassen, Glen. "The Fourteen Triads of the Sermon on the Mount (Matt. 5:21–7:12)." *Journal of Biblical Literature* 122, vol. 2 (2003) 267–308.

———. *Just Peacemaking: Ten Practices for Abolishing War.* Cleveland, OH: Pilgrim, 1998.

———. *Just Peacemaking: The New Paradigm for the Ethics of Peace and War.* Cleveland, OH: Pilgrim, 2008.

———. *A Thicker Jesus: Incarnational Discipleship in a Secular Age*, Louisville, KY: Westminster John Knox, 2012.
Stassen, Glen, and David Gushee. *Kingdom Ethics: Following Jesus in Contemporary Context*. Downers Grove, IL: InterVarsity, 2003.
Steiner, George. *Real Presences*. Chicago: University of Chicago Press, 1989.
Stendahl, Krister. "The Apostle Paul and the Introspective Conscience of the West." *Harvard Theological Review* 56, vol. 3 (1963) 199–215.
Sternberg, Meir. *The Poetics of Biblical Narratives: Ideological Literature and the Drama of Reading*. Bloomington, IN: University of Indiana Press, 1985.
Stowes, S. K. *A Rereading of Romans: Justice, Jews and Gentiles*. New Haven: Yale University Press, 1994.
Tanner, Kathryn. *Economy of Grace*. Minneapolis: Augsburg/Fortress, 2005.
———. *Theories of Culture*. Minneapolis: Fortress, 1997.
Taylor, Charles. *A Secular Age*. Cambridge, MA: Harvard University Press, 2009.
———. *The Sources of the Self: The Making of Modern Identity*. Cambridge, MA: Harvard University Press, 1989.
Terrien, Samuel. "Wisdom in the Psalter." In *In Search of Wisdom: Essays in Memory of John Gammie*, edited by B. Scott, and W. J. Wiseman, 51–72. Louisville, KY: Westminster John Knox, 1993.
Tertullian. "Patience." In *Tertullian: Disciplinary, Moral and Ascetical Works*, translated by Sister Emily Joseph Daly, 193–222. New York: Fathers of the Church, Vol. 40, 1959.
Thiselton, Anthony. *First Epistle to the Corinthians: Commentary on the Greek Text*. Grand Rapids: Eerdmans, 2000.
Thomas, D. Winton. *Documents from Old Testament Times*. New York: Harper, 1958.
Tirole, Jean. *Economics for the Common Good*. Translated by Steven Rendall. Princeton, NJ: Princeton University Press, 2017.
Towner, P. H. "Households and Household Codes." In *Dictionary of Paul and His Letters*, edited by Daniel Reid, 417–419. Downers Grove, IL: InterVarsity, 1993.
Tsevat, Matitiahu. "The Meaning of the Book of Job". *Hebrew Union College Annual* 37 (1966) 73–106.
Tyerman, Christopher. *God's War: A New History of the Crusades*. Cambridge, MA: Belknap Press of Harvard University Press, 2006.
Van Leeuwen, Raymond. "Theology: Creation, Wisdom, and Covenant." Unpublished article, 2018, 1–29. Available on Academic.edu.
Volf, Miroslav. *Exclusion and Embrace: A Theological Exploration of Identity, Otherness, and Reconciliation*. Nashville: Abingdon, 1996.
Von Rad, Gerhard. *Wisdom in Israel*. Translated by James D. Martin. London: SCM, 1972.
Ware, Timothy. *The Orthodox Church*. New York: Penguin, 1963.
Weeks, Stuart. "Wisdom in the Old Testament." In *Where Shall Wisdom Be Found?*, edited by Stephen Barton, 19–30. Edinburgh: T & T Clark, 1999.
Williams, Rowan. *On the Edge of Words: God and the Habits of Language*. London: Bloomsbury, 2014.
Wilson, Peter. *The Heart of Europe: A History of the Holy Roman Empire*. Cambridge, MA: Belknap Press of Harvard University Press, 2016.
Winthrop, John. "Model of Christian Charity." https://www.americanyawp.com/reader/colliding-cultures/john-winthrop-dreams-of-a-city-on-a-hill-1630/.

Winton, Alan. *The Proverbs of Jesus: Issues of History and Rhetoric.* Sheffield: JSOT, 1990.

Wirzba, Norman. *From Nature to Creation: A Christian Vision for Understanding and Loving Our World.* Grand Rapids: Baker Academic, 2015.

Witherington, Ben. *Jesus the Sage: The Pilgrimage of Wisdom.* Minneapolis: Fortress, 1994.

Wohlleben, Peter. *The Hidden Life of Trees: What they Feel, How They Communicate—Discoveries from a Secret World.* Translated by Jane Billinghurst. Vancouver, BC: Greystone, 2016.

Wolterstorff, Nicholas. *Justice: Rights and Wrongs.* Princeton, NJ: Princeton University Press, 2008.

Woodberry, Robert. "The Missionary Roots of Liberal Democracy." *American Political Science Review* 106, vol. 2 (2012) 244–74.

Wuthnow, Robert. *All in Sync: How Music and Art Are Revitalizing American Religion.* Berkeley, CA: University of California Press, 2003.

Young, Frances, and David Ford. *Meaning and Truth in 2 Corinthians.* Grand Rapid: Eerdmans, 1987.

Zimmerli, Walter. "The Place and Limit of the Wisdom framework of the Old Testament Theology." *Scottish Journal of Theology* 17, vol. 2 (1964) 146–58.

Zuckerman, Phil. *Society without God: What the Least Religious Nations Can Tell Us about Contentment.* New York: New York University Press, 2008.

Index

Abraham, William, 4
academic life, contemporary, 184–85
Adam and Eve, 64–71
    disobedience of, 71
aesthetics, 38, 44, 95, 175
    aesthetic practices, in lockdown, 171–72
    Christian aesthetic of life through death, 124
    and non-violence, 175
    in Romanticism, 169
    see also beauty, art, poetics
Against Heresies: On the Detection and Refutation of the Knowledge so-called (Irenaeus), 142–44
agape (unconditional love), in the New Testament, 172
Albinoni, Adagio in G Minor, 170–71
Alter, Robert, 95, 96
Ambrose of Milan, 160
Ancient Near East, 44
    creation accounts in, 58
    wisdom in, 84–88
antithesis, 19, 187
    of life worlds (Kuyper), 21
Apache, wisdom of, 44
Apartheid, 24
Apocryphal books, 6, 163
Apologists, 140
Apostolic Fathers, 140
Arendt, Hannah, 25
Aristotle, 153, 160, 169
art, and poetics, 38–39
    from darkness to light, 124
    in the Early Church, 150–51
    in Romantic period, 169

    in times of suffering as wisdom, 171
    see also aesthetics, poetics
Artius, 140
atonement, work of Christ, 105
Augustine of Hippo, Saint, 6, 36, 138, 152–61, 167, 168, 192
    contextual nature of his theology, 161
    conversion of, 152
    desire in, 153–56
    view of God, 156
    medieval synthesis of, 162–63
    patience in, 156–57
    and violence, 158–60

Babylon, exiles in, 42
    wisdom of, 86–88
Barclay, John, 120
Barrett, Justin, 179–80, 186
Barth, Karl, 55, 60, 61, 73
Bartholomew, Craig, 24, 81, 96–97
Barton, Stephen, 109
Basso, Keith, 44
Bavinck, Herman, 17, 27
beauty, 15, 40, 169–72
    calls observers to praise, 123
    of creation, 110, 57, 34
    and God in Augustine, 156
    see also aesthetics, art, poetics,
Benjamin, Walter, 185
Berbers of North Africa, 146, 159
    see also Donatist Church
bio-intensive farming (Jeavons), 183
Birch, Bruce C., 83
Black Church, 191
Black Lives Matter, 1, 16

Blaese, Michael, 181
Bocelli, Andrea, 171
Bonhoeffer, Dietrich, 63, 65, 71, 72
Bowles, Samuel, 181–82
Bretherton, Craig, 2–3, 41–42
Brown, Peter, 153
Brueggemann, Walter, 57, 78–79, 92, 192

Cahill, Lisa, on peacebuilding, 175
catechesis, in the Early Church, 141, 160
Calvin, John, 18, 23, 33–34, 123–24, 164, 190
Charlesworth, James H., 145
Christ, eschatological frame of his teaching, 108
    as wisdom incarnate, 106, 107
    teacher of wisdom, 105
    see also Jesus
Christendom, 163, 191
Christian Wisdom (Ford), 6, 139
Cicero, 150, 152, 160
City of God (Augustine), 158
Clark, Andy, 65
Clements, Ronald, 78, 102
Clifford, Richard, 76
Coakley, Sarah, 70, 193–94
Coates, Ta-Nehisi, 184
common grace, 4, 135, 189
    and creation, 17–20
    as wisdom theology, 26–28
common sense, 25–26
community, 1, 11, 128, 132, 150, 187
    of mutual benefit (Tanner), 182
    of mutual service in Christ's teaching, 126
concurrence, 5, 45–51
Confessions (Augustine), 152, 156, 192
Constantine, emperor, 149, 150
contemplation, contemplative tradition, 153, 194
    vita contemplative, medieval, 189
covenant with Israel, 97
    covenant story of deliverance, 122
Covid-19, 180
Craft, Jennifer, 39
creation, bounty of, 41, 60–63, 113
    communicative structure of, 65, 84

goodness, beauty of, 56–57, 106, 143
    limits built into, 65, 76
    moral structure of, 81
    original good of, 56, 66
    self-organizing processes of, 58
    as source of wealth, 43, 76
    two accounts of, as wisdom stories, 56
    voice of God in, 83
creativity, 14, 63, 65
    as reaching out for a new world, 68
Crenshaw, James, 79
cross and resurrection, as parable events, 122
    as wisdom events, 48, 121–23
    cross as cultural pattern, 125
crusades, 163
cultivation, of creation, 42, 48, 63, 183
cultural indebtedness, 13–15
cultural wisdom, 4, 30
Cyprian, 142, 147–48

Dante Alighieri, 163
Darwin, Charles, 19, 58
Davis, Ellen, 58, 63–64
Deism, 51
delegation, 4, 29–30, 50, 61
Descartes, Rene, 178
determinism, 3, 51
Didache in Syriac Church, 142
discernment, of wisdom, 16, 45, 94
Divine Institutes (Lactantius), 150
Divine Comedy (Dante), 163
Donatist Church (Berbers), 159, 160
Dreyfus, Hubert, 36, 178
Driver, John, 149
Dulles, Avery, 121, 190
Dunn, James, 109
Durkheim, Emile, 21

earthkeeping, 182–84
    see also ecology
Ecclesiastes, book of, 78, 86
ecology, care for the earth, 2
    earthkeeping and a resurrection imagination, 182–84
    encouraged by Christ and gifts of the Spirit, 105

regeneration of the earth in NT, 130–32
upcycling, 183
economics, as community of mutual sharing, 128, 132
    contemporary, 181–82
    of grace, 127–29
Eden, as delight, 67
    described, 62
Edict of Milan (312), 150
Edwards, Jonathan, 155
Edwards, Michael 97, 124
Egypt, wisdom of, 84–86
Eliot, T. S., 69–70, 124–25
Enlightenment, 19, 155, 165, 169, 178
    Scottish Enlightenment, 172
eschatology, bound up with creation 32
    as frame of Jesus' teaching, 109
eudaimonism, 154
    see also Stoics, stoicism
Evangelical Christians, 191
    during Pandemic, 2–3
    macro and micro ethics among, 11

facts on the ground, 2, 6, 13, 135, 138, 161, 168, 185
    defined, 2
    significance of, 7, 13–14, 135
fall, 17, 27, 30, 45, 55
    see also sin
Farrow, Douglas, 73, 106, 117, 144
Ferguson, Everett, 160
Fergusson, David, 58
Fiddes, Paul, 72
Fleck, Ludwig, 22
Floyd, George, 1, 184
fool, folly, 42, 46, 78, 83, 85, 98
Ford, David 6, 118, 128–29, 139
forgiveness, and mutual service, 120
Fretheim, Terrence, 55, 57, 59, 89, 92, 93–94, 101, 103
fullness, Taylor on, 168–70
    as call of Lady Wisdom, 168

Ghandi, 132, 173, 174
Gilgamesh epic, 87
Gill, Robin, 165–66
Gnostic, Gnosticism, 142–44

God, commitment to creation, 73
    and creation, 58–66
    and creation of Israel, 76
    as deliverer, 100
    and evil, 28
    and human responsibility, 11, 46–47
    as impassible, ineffable (in Augustine), 156
    permission of creation, 58
    presence in wisdom, 50, 189
    and salvation, 49
    taking credit for wisdom, 92
    transcendence and immanence in creation, 58
    watching, enjoying creation, 58, 64, 70
    and wisdom in creation, 31–32
Goizueta, Roberto, 38, 44–45
Goldberg, Zach, 184
Goldingay, John, 66, 68
"The Good of Patience" (Cyprian), 147
Good Samaritan, 111, 172–73
gospel, contribution to wisdom, 136–37
    gospel themes, 137
    in western cultures, 164–65
    gospel wisdom, 141
Grabar, Andre, 151
grace, 28, 167
    of the earth, in indigenous traditions, 26
    economics of, 128
    as gift in 2 Corinthians, 129
Gramsci, Antonio, 25–26
Grant, Robert, 143
Great Awokening, "Woke", 184–85, 191
Greco-Roman culture, 106, 118–20, 136–40, 143, 152
Green, Joel, 115
Gunton, Colin, 73, 74, 106, 107, 109, 156, 158
Gushee, David, 37, 110, 113

Hadot, Pierre, 153
Harrison, Peter, 153
Hays, Richard, 118
Heidegger, Martin, 36
Helleman, Adrian, 175
Hodgson, Peter, 3

Holy Spirit, 3, 116, 121
    enables creation to be temporal, spatial, 158
    poured out on all flesh, 6, 37, 115–16
    see also Pentecost event
Hopkins, Gerard Manley, 168, 170
household codes, 94, 119, 136
human responsibility
    for culture, 76–77
    for creation, 33–34, 48, 61, 64, 72–73
    and God's work, 46–49
    as spectator of creation, 33, 57, 123, 164
    in wisdom, 27, 93–95, 101
humanism and wisdom, 91–92
Hutcheson, Francis, 172

imago Dei (Image of God), 59–61, 192
    Christ as true image, 117
Institutes of the Christian Religion (Calvin), 33, 123
Irenaeus of Lyon, 73, 117, 142–44
Isaiah, prophecy of, 97, 192

James, the Apostle, 49, 74
Jeavons, John, 183
Jennings, Willie James, 16, 82, 113, 116
Jeremiah, prophet, 42
Jesus, as image of God, 76
    as Jewish prophetic sage, 109
    ministry to Jewish people, 111
    teaching of, as call of wisdom, 3, 107
    offers a new way of seeing, 109
    teaching of, in the Early Church, 142
Job, book of, 78, 86, 99
Johnson, Mark, 81
Jones, Earle Stanley, 174
Joseph as wisdom story, 98
"Journey of the Magi" (Eliot), 124–25
Julian of Norwich, 126
Just Peacemaking movement, 174
just war, 150, 160–61, 173
justice, as wisdom, 45
justification by faith alone, 3

Keck, Leander, 122
Keel, Othmar, 95–96
King, Martin Luther, 132, 173, 182
Kitzinger, Ernst, 151
Kreider, Alan, 141, 146, 158
Kuyper, Abraham, 4, 17–24, 26, 28–30, 50
Kynes, Will, 78, 80

Lactantius, Lucius, 150
lady wisdom, 42–43, 81, 101, 157, 168, 194
    Christ and, 107–8
    in Proverbs 8, 88–90
    as voice of the Spirit, 116
Lambert, W. G., 86
law, in the First Testament, see Torah
LeClercq, Jean, 135
Lohfink, Gerhard, 111
Luther, Martin, 37, 121

MacIntyre, Alasdair, 24
MacLaren, Brian D., 162
Manichaeans, 152, 155, 159
Marchino, Maurizio, 171
Marcos, Ferdinand, 157
Mars Hill, 136, 186, 191
Marx, Karl, 19
Mathews, Thomas, 151
Matthew, book of, 110–15
McDonough, William, 183
McWhorter, John, 184
medical science, 180–81
medieval synthesis of theology, 162
MeToo movement (#MeToo), 16, 194,
Meye Thompson, Marianne, 136
Milton, John, 68
Milvian Bridge, battle of (312), 150
modern culture and the gospel, 164–66
Mongolia, 103
Montanists, 147
morality, public and private, 12
    moral sense, in Hutcheson, 172
    see also virtue
Morgan, David, 35–36
Mouw, Richard, 28, 193
Mukherjee, Siddhartha, 181

Mughal civilization, 103
Murphy, Roland, 46–47, 88, 89, 98–99

natural covenant in creation, 13, 16, 26, 57, 76
Neo-Platonism, 152,155
new creation, 55, 97, 166–67, 183, 190
    in the New Testament, 117, 130–32
    see also re-creation
Nietzsche, Friedrich, 19
non-violence, 39–41, 132
    and benevolence, 172–73
    in the Early Church, 149–50
    in the First Testament, 90–91
    in Jesus' teaching 90, 114–15

O'Connor, Flannery, 6
Octavian (Augustus), Roman emperor, 119, 125
"Odes of Solomon" (Syriac Church), 145–46
O'Donovan, Oliver, 163, 165
O'Dowd, Ryan, 96–97
On Christian Teaching (Augustine), 154
Origen, 140, 149
Orthodoxy, Eastern, 65–66, 106, 142, 155

pandemic, 1, 181
    see also Covid-19
parables (*mashalim*), 107–8
Pater, Walter, 169
patience, 39–41
    in the early Church, 140–42, 146–48
    in Jesus' teaching, 114
    in the New Testament, 40, 123
    and wisdom, 39–40
"Patience" (Augustine), 156–57
"Patience" (Tertullian), 146–47
Patterson, Dudley, 44
Paul, Apostle, 26, 71, 94, 116–18, 130, 136, 190
    contemporary rereading of, 186–88
peacemaking, peace building, 174, 175
Penchansky, David, 47, 76, 98, 100
Pentecost event, 6, 115–16
perception, see seeing, sight

Peter, Apostle, 114, 116
Philippines, EDSA revolution, 175–76
philosophy, contemporary, 178–79
Piketty, Thomas, 181
Plato, 137, 155
Platonists, 152–53
    Christian Platonists, 153, 155
    see also Neo-Platonism
play, recreation, 38, 58
Plotinus, 137, 153, 154
poetics, and creation, 33
    of fullness, 168–70
    and wisdom, 33–35
poetry, 39, 44,
    in the First Testament, 95–97
    and wisdom, 95–96
poverty, poor, 2, 40, 83, 90, 111, 129, 182
practice(s), 41–43
    of reform, 177–78
    as *vita active*, 189
prayer, and wisdom, 40, 79, 149, 176, 193, 194
Prinsterer, Groen van, 19
Prometheus, 71, 125
Proverbs (book of), 40–43, 78, 98
Providence, 3–4, 17–18
Psalms, 41, 77, 90
psychology, cognitive, 179–80

racism, 184
Rad, Gerhard von, 79, 81, 84
Radical Orthodoxy, 155, 191
Ray, J. D., 84
re-creation, Christ and, 55
    see also new creation
redemption, for the sake of creation, 7, 55
Reform Master Narrative (Taylor), 191–92
reform, practices of, 177–79
Reformation, and justification by faith, 3
    and the modern world, 164–66
    and creation, 33
    and reform of society, 177–78
Reformed theology, 4
restorative justice, 176

resurrection of Christ, and new creation, 31, 190
  and regeneration of the earth, 131
  resurrection imagination, 183–84
revelation, continuing to present, 104
  and discovery, 121, 190
  general, 4, 17, 102–3
  relation of general and special, 103
  and reason, 163
  and wisdom, 190, 194
Revelation of John, book of, 7, 41, 55, 62, 192–93
Rohr, Richard, 189
Roman Empire, 135, 141, 150, 158–59, 163
Romans, book of, 186–87
Romanticism, Romantic period, 169–70

sabbath, 61
salvation, human role in, 49
sanctification, 3
Sarajevo, Siege of, 170
Satan and demons, 68
Schafer, Peter, 80
Schilder, Klaas, 17, 18
Schwab, Zoltan, 78
science, 64
Second Temple Judaism, 79, 106, 108, 136
secular, secularism, 164
A Secular Age (Taylor), 167, 168, 177
seeing, sight, in Jesus' teaching, 109–110
  oriented to the created order, 37, 64
  poetics of, 35–37
Sermon on the Mount, 108, 110–15, 141, 161
  as a new wisdom, 112
serpent, in Genesis 3, 68–69
sin, 12, 55–56
  as disruption, 71–73
  as misdirection of desire, 70
  original sin, 71
Sirach, book of, 80, 108
slavery, 163, 193
  cross as slave punishment, 120
Smailovic, Vedran 170
Smith, Christian, 22
Smith, James K. A., 27, 36

social relations, in Christ's teaching
  as mutual sharing, 128–30
  as non-violent service, 125–27
social transformation, 3
Sources of the Self (Taylor), 172
sower, parable of, 93
spectator of creation, humans as, 33, 57
  see also seeing, sight
Spengler, Oswald, 19
sphere sovereignty, 23–24
spirit, in the First Testament, 102
spirit of the age (Kuyper), 18–19
Stassen, Glen, 37, 106, 110, 112–15
  and a thicker Jesus, 106
  and Just Peacemaking movement, 174
Steiner, George, 194
stewardship, 61
  see also delegation, cultivation
Stoics, stoicism, 136, 140, 154, 155, 169
story, narrative, gives meaning to facts, 185, 121–22
  as basic to theology, 186
Stowes, S. K., 119
Synod of Arles (314), 149
Syriac Church, 142, 145

Tanner, Kathryn, 21, 128, 182
  community of mutual benefit in, 182
Taylor, Charles, 6, 20, 25, 35, 37, 178, 191
  and benevolence, 172–73
  and the search for fullness, 167–70
  and the quest for reform, 177–78
  and Reform Master Narrative, 191–92
Tertullian, 142, 146–47
theology, emerging in the Early Church, 135–36
  shaped in light of a particular cultural wisdom, 139
  Greco-Roman wisdom and, 152–55
  as story, 185–86
Thiselton, Anthony, 118
Tirole, Jean 181
Torah, law in the First Testament, 6, 57, 64, 80
  as cultural wisdom, 77

tourism, regenerative, 183–84
trajectories, of life and death, 45, 66–72
  reversed in life of Christ, 123
  wisdom and, 83
transforming initiatives, in Jesus'
  teaching, 112
  enabled by the resurrection of Jesus, 123
Trinity, 145–46, 194
Tsevat, Matitiahu, 99
Tyerman, Christopher, 161

Unbelief and Revolution, 19
upcycling, 183

Valentinus, 142–43
Van Leeuwen, Raymond, 79
violence, Augustine and, 158–60
  in the First Testament, 89–90
  in the French Revolution, 173
virtue, moral sense, 172
  expressive of wisdom, 132
Vischer, Wilhelm, 60
Visogoths, sack of Rome (410), 158
Volf, Miroslav, 38

war, and civilian casualties, 173–74
  see also non-violence, violence
Ware, Timothy, 67
Weber, Max, 165
Weeks, Stuart, 78
western cultures, and the gospel, 164
White Helmets, 173

Williams, Rowan, 82
Winthrop, John, 50
Wirzba, Norman, 61, 64, 67
wisdom, in Babylon, 86–88
  biblical, 5–6, 38–43
  Christ as, 6, 81, 107–8
  contemporary, multiple forms of, 178–80
  and creation, 56–57, 77–79
  cumulative character of, 137
  as deeds-consequence, 78
  defined, 31, 78–79
  early Christian, 138–40
  in Egypt, 84–86
  from above (James), 6, 74, 188
  as human work, 47, 138
  Jewish wisdom in Early Church, 140
  and language, 81–82
  limits of, 98–99
  new wisdom in Jesus' teaching, 6, 107
  wisdom literature, 78–79
Wisdom of Amenemope, 85
Wisdom of Solomon, book of, 80, 108
Witherington, Ben, 93, 107, 118
Wolterstorff, Nicholas, 154–55
wonder, beginning of wisdom, 33
word (*logos*), creation by, 136

Young, Frances, 128–29

Zimmerli, Walter, 101

www.ingramcontent.com/pod-product-compliance
Lightning Source LLC
Chambersburg PA
CBHW031358230426
43670CB00006B/584